COMMODORE VANDERBILT.

THE VANDERBILTS

AND

THE STORY OF THEIR FORTUNE

BY

W. A. CROFFUT

AUTHOR OF "A HELPING HAND," "A MIDSUMMER LARK," "THE
BOURBON BALLADS," "HISTORY OF CONNECTICUT," ETC.

———————

LONDON
GRIFFITH, FARRAN, OKEDEN & WELSH
ST. PAUL'S CHURCH YARD

PREFACE.

THIS is a history of the Vanderbilt family, with a record of their vicissitudes, and a chronicle of the method by which their wealth has been acquired. It is confidently put forth as a work which should fall into the hands of boys and young men—of all who aspire to become Captains of Industry or leaders of their fellows in the sharp and wholesome competitions of life.

In preparing these pages, the author has had an ambition, not merely to give a biographical picture of sire, son, and grandsons and descendants, but to consider their relation to society, to measure the significance and the influence of their fortune, to ascertain where their money came from, to inquire whether others are poorer because they are rich, whether they are hindering or promoting civilization, whether they and such as they are impediments to the welfare of the human race. A correct answer to these questions will solve half of the problems which most eagerly beset this generation.

This story is an analogue of the story of all American successes. When Commodore Vanderbilt visited Europe in 1853 at the head of his family, he seemed to defy classification. He was apparently neither lord nor commoner. He was too democratic for a grandee; too self-

poised for a plebeian. He was untitled, but his yacht
surpassed in size and splendor the ocean vehicles of
monarchs. No expense was too great to be indulged,
no luxury too choice to be provided, but he moved modestly and without ostentation, with the serene composure of a prince among his equals. There were wealthy
English citizens who could have afforded a similar out-
lay, but they would have been sneered at and charged
with pretentiousness and vanity, with aping customs
rightly monopolized by the nobility. They would have
been rated as snobs, cads, upstarts, and would have been
twitted with their humble origin, as if an improvement
of one's condition were a reproach instead of an honor.

But the cruising Commodore came from a land where
prevalent conditions and not antecedents are considered ;
where a coat-of-arms is properly regarded as a foolish
affectation ; where a family's " descent " is of no importance, and its ascent of all importance ; where the wheel
of fortune runs rapidly around and every man is not
only permitted but required to stand for what he is.

So when William H. Vanderbilt erected for himself
a palace, and enriched it with an art collection more
valuable than any private gallery in Great Britain, the
English found it impossible to think of him as he was—a
quiet citizen, despising parade and display—and the London *Spectator* said when he was dead: " He occasionally
flaunted his wealth in a manner a Roman noble could
not have exceeded. He gave an entertainment, it is
said, one day last year at which his guests ate off gold
laid upon fine lace, the wines cost thousands, and flowers
were brought from the Southern States at an expense of
£4,000." And the editorial inventor went on to an-

nounce that the host on this occasion " was accused of giving each journalist among his guests a thousand-dollar note tied up in his napkin, in order that his magnificence might be reported in detail." This from one of the most cautious and conservative journals in England ! The British mind apparently cannot conceive of a man who has made a hundred million dollars and yet is not a pompous vulgarian filled with " the pride that apes humility."

America is the land of the self-made man—the empire of the parvenu. Here it is felt that the accident of birth is of trifling consequence ; here there is no " blood " that is to be coveted save the red blood which every masterful man distills in his own arteries ; and here the name of parvenu is the only and all-sufficient title of nobility. So here, if nowhere else in the world, should such a dominant man without hesitation or apology assume the place to which he is entitled, in commerce or the industrial arts, in professional life or society.

A wealthy man is as much in the public eye and as much an object of popular interest as a successful general, a famous inventor, a great poet, or a distinguished statesman, and an opulent family is the focus of much legitimate and respectful curiosity. Neither Stephen Girard, John Jacob Astor, nor Alexander T. Stewart is a familiar personage to this generation, because there is no complete narrative of their lives, thoughts, and methods, telling how they acquired their money, and to what purpose they lived. Traditions there are, in abundance, and rumors and myths, largely discreditable ; but the real men are not known, and probably never will be. Yet a rich man, if only because he possesses the rare gift of money-getting and money-keeping, and the skill and wisdom that are a part of it, is necessarily one of the most interesting figures of his generation. In this is a sufficient justification for the preparation of this work.

Acknowledgment is gratefully made to Chauncey M. Depew, Isaac P. Chambers, Dr. Jared Linsly, Thomas C. Purdy, Robert Bonner, E. H. Carmick, Dr. Fuller-Walker, and Rev. Dr. Deems, for valuable information, and to Mrs. Frank Leslie and Harper & Brothers for illustrations.

CONTENTS.

CONTENTS.

THE VANDERBILTS.

CHAPTER I.

ANCESTORS.

The Dutch Emigrants—Men Self-made or not Made at all—Distinguished Examples—Aris on Long Island—Jacob goes to Staten Island—The Moravians—Jacob's Son and Grandson—Thrifty but Unambitious—The Fruit of the Family Tree.

A GENERATION or two after the Hudson River was discovered and the bold explorer who gave his name to it had perished in the Arctic seas, the Vanderbilts came with the early Knickerbockers to the Western World. They settled on New York Bay because it seemed like their home in the Low Countries—the same wash of the aggressive wave, the same stretch of indented shore, different only in its peaceful aspect. Holland is always besieged by an alert and sleepless foe. Inheriting the savage conflict from generation to generation, the garrison has thrown up huge fortifications a thousand miles long, stronger than Gibraltar or the dykes which wall in the great harbors of France; for many centuries they have slept on the battle-field, weapon in hand and armor on, never relaxing vigilance, never beguiled by a treacherous flag of truce. The incessant combat has made them a robust, patient, abstemious and obstinate people. More than five hundred years ago the weary fight began; it will continue, undiminished in ferocity, five hundred years hence. The foe is the sea; his allies, the rivers and the lakes.

Manhattan Island had won the alluvial battle centuries before and was at peace. The army of observation had ceased to countermarch along the parapet, and had exchanged its weapons for implements of husbandry; so the fugitives from the Holland conflict found it a grateful and restful camping-ground.

The founder of the wealth of the Vanderbilts, known to New Yorkers for half a century as "the Commodore," was, like almost all men of unusual vigor and personal power, a rustic of humble origin. Few boys born in homes of luxury ever greatly increase their wealth or attain a leading position among men. The dominating and over-mastering qualities are nurtured in poverty and grown in hardy soil. Nine-tenths of all the citizens of the metropolis who have acquired conspicuous influence in manufactures, commerce, literature, or professional life, have been born and reared afar in farming districts, and have been thrown upon their own resources from their very earliest years. In this country men are either self-made or not made at all. Parental nursing and coddling seem to be enfeebling in their effect on boys: they make the muscles flabby and the energies inert. "Young man!" said Henry Ward Beecher, the greatest preacher of our days, "if you are poor, thank God, and take courage; for he has given you a chance to be somebody!" The young learn the value of money only from needing it and earning it by hard work. Abstinence is the mother of competence; self-denial the cradle of wealth.

Peter Cooper wandered hither from Peekskill, and worked joyously and faithfully for $25 a year and his board. Cyrus W. Field descended from the sterile hills of Berkshire, and served A. T. Stewart as office-boy, at $2 a week. Horace Greeley migrated from the wilds of New Hampshire. The founders of the house of Harper were Long Island farm-boys, and they came to the city and paid $20 a year apiece for the privilege of working. William E. Dodge and P. T. Barnum emerged from Connecticut, and began at the lowest round of the ladder; so did George Law, for he was a hod-carrier in Troy. Russell Sage escaped from an Oneida County grocery-store. Daniel Drew was a Putnam County plow-boy. John H. Starin came from an obscure family in the middle of the State. John Kelly, John Roach, Robert Bonner, and A. T. Stewart were penniless Irish boys, and they acquired their trades as they could, in spite of every impediment. John G. Moore rebelled against the fate of a Maine skipper, to which he seemed destined. Thurlow Weed was a printer's "devil." Thomas A. Edison was a Michigan news-boy, and Rufus T. Bush was a Michigan school-teacher. Roswell P. Flower was a chore-boy on a wretched farm in Jefferson County. F. B. Thurber had a similar matriculation in Delaware County, and when this large-hearted merchant-millionaire, then a hardy boy, was hoeing potatoes in Delhi, Jay Gould was still bellows-blower and clerk for a Roxbury blacksmith, at $2 a week, only five miles over the hill.

Scratch a New York millionaire and you will gener-

ally find a farm-boy underneath—a youth with a strong
back and resolute will, with the umber of toil on his
hands, and in his heart the determination to conquer.
If Commodore Vanderbilt had been born to a valen-
ciennes christening-robe and a heritage of plenty—had
grown to be a child with a nursery full of toys, and
afterward a youth with a pocket full of money, there
is little chance that he would ever have been heard of
beyond the shadow of the Moravian church. Nature
seems to begrudge her highest favors to all except those
who walk through the thorny lane of penury, and become familiar with her in her capricious and hostile
moods.

The early arrangement of the family name was Van
Der Bilt, and they were farmers for generations. Just
when the first immigrant came from Holland is uncer-
tain, but he settled on Long Island near Brooklyn. We
hear of Art Jansen Van Der Bilt who settled in Flat-
bush, and was the grantee of a considerable part of the
territory of that town under the Dongan patent of 1685.
Twenty-one years earlier the English had taken possession of Manhattan Island, and sixty years earlier the
Dutch had bought it for $24, and founded New Am-
sterdam. Contemporary with Art Jansen—perhaps his
brother—was Aris, who, with his wife Hilitje, dwelt in the
same town. They worked hard to get a living and give
bread to a large and growing brood. The family seems
to have been of some social consequence, for one of them
was an elder in the church, and another presented to the
religious edifice " a fine bell imported from Holland."

Among the children of Aris was Jacob Van Der Bilt,
born January 25, 1692. In 1715 Jacob was accepted

in marriage by Eleanor* and to set him up in life his father "sold" him a large tract of land "at Staaten Island," probably obtained by him from the Indians, for this was then a frontier settlement. The consideration given by Jacob is not stated, but thither he and his young wife repaired and founded the Staten Island branch of the Vanderbilt family. During the next thirty years eleven children were born to them.†

About this time some of the persecuted followers of John Huss, called Moravians, fled to this country, and a few of them settled at New Dorp. This destination was most natural. Already the beautiful and lonely island had become the refuge of bands of Huguenots, Waldenses, and Walloons, who had clustered here and there in detached communities. So thither the exiled Protestants from Bohemia flocked and told their story of outrage. The Van Der Bilts became converts.

In 1741 Count Zinzendorf, the founder and patron of this martyr-sect, having been banished from Saxony, came to America, and visited, among others, the little community on Staten Island. It is related that the primal wilderness was then so untamed and New Dorp so difficult of access, that he had a long search for the place on the wandering Indian trails and cowpaths. The visit of the illustrious exile fired the half-dozen Moravians with uncommon zeal, and the feeble church, of

---

* Called, in Dutch, Neilje.

† Aris, born February 2, 1716 ; Dennys, born September 5, 1716 ; Hilitje, born March 22, 1720 ; *Jacob*, born January 6, 1723 ; Magdelena, born December 1, 1725 ; John, born November 15, 1728 ; Cornelius, born September 22, 1731 ; Anna, born February 11, 1734 ; Phebe, born April 27, 1737 ; Anthea, born January 31, 1739 ; Eleanor, born September 13, 1742.

which Jacob Van Der Bilt and his wife and children were chief pillars, resolved to build a ship to assist the immigration of the United Brethren from Germany. This missionary vessel was launched May 29, 1748, and was in the service of the builders nine years. She crossed from New York to Amsterdam and back twelve times, bringing each time a freight of refugees. In 1757 she was captured by a French privateer and driven to wreck off Cape Breton. In the records of the United Brethren at that time, Jacob Van Der Bilt of New Dorp is mentioned as the most active and persevering member.

The religious services of the Moravians were held first in a private residence, and then in a school-house at New Dorp, but in 1762, the Cornelius Van Der Bilt whose birth has been recorded, joined his neighbors in an application to the authorities of the church in Beth- lehem, Pa., for the construction of a Moravian meeting- house and society on Staten Island. On July 7, 1763, the corner-stone of the edifice was laid, and it was con- secrated just before the year closed, only to be burned to the ground by the British soldiery fourteen years later.

Of the liberal brood of Jacob Van Der Bilt, above mentioned, Jacob, jr., who first saw the light in 1723, is the only one in whose personal fortunes this history is interested, as he appears " in the line of promotion." He married in due time Mary Sprague who bore him seven children,* and these, during their life-time, learned

---

* Eleanor, born ———— 1747 ; Jacob, born January 6, 1750 ; John, born May 9, 1752 ; Dorothy, born July 29, 1754 ; Oliver, born June 10, 1757 ; Joseph, born September 6, 1761 ; *Cornelius*, born August 23, 1764.

to economize by uniting the first two syllables of the
family name and writing it "Vander Bilt."

The last of these, Cornelius, born 1764, married Phebe
Hand, and they, in time, had nine children * born to
their humble house. A hard time they seem to have
had supporting life respectably and keeping the family
together.

About this time it was that the Rose-and-Crown
cottage was kept at Stapleton by one of the Vander
Bilts, and it is known in Revolutionary story as having
been much frequented by British officers and made
prosperous by British guineas.

During this century and a half, from the coming of
Aris to the birth of the sturdy "Commodore," Cornelius, the hundred male members of the family and
its collateral wings had all been solid and stolid tillers
of the earth. They had carted on the manure and
carted off the rocks. They had rendered arable the
stony and fruitful the sterile land. They had pastured
the cows and milked them. They had planted and
hoed, ploughed and sowed, drudged and delved, died
and been buried in the town where they were born.
The average workman in the employ of the New York
Central Railroad to-day lives better and gets far more
of the real comforts of life than any of the Vanderbilts

* Mary, born December 21, 1787, and died August 10, 1845 ; Jacob,
born August 28, 1789, and died October 3, 1805 ; Charlotte, born
December 29, 1791, married Captain John De Forest, died January
5, 1877 ; *Cornelius*, born May 27, 1794, died January 4, 1877 ; Phebe,
born February 19, 1798, died young ; Jane, born August 1, 1800, and
became wife of Colonel Samuel Barton ; Eleanor, born January 4,
1804, died April 21, 1833; Jacob Hand, born September 2, 1807 ;
Phebe, born February 9, 1810, died April 23, 1885.

of the last century. They were not unhappy, for they had that contented mind which, the philosopher tells us, is a continual feast. But the standard of their existence was simple.

In the very mode of life they had adopted, they were preparing for a colossal output. They were practising an untiring industry and an economy that knew no bounds. They were wrestling with all the indescribable difficulties of a new settlement. They had attached themselves to a persecuted church, and were learning self-denial for the sake of sympathy and deep religious feeling. They were delving in an inhospitable soil, and facing hostile elements, and inuring themselves to hardship and exposure, and thus getting the muscles of steel, the unflinching pluck, and the unconquerable will that move and mould the world. Unconsciously, nerve by nerve, and fibre by fibre, they were building up the man who was to illustrate their name.

There was, indeed, a cousin, John Vanderbilt, who became a member of the Assembly from Long Island. But he did not win fame. His principal mission as a legislator doubtless was, to move to adjourn when the appointed hour came around; as the local records show that he was chosen to the office, not for his probity and ability, though he was probably both talented and honest, but "because it was his turne." The case is too ambiguous to disprove the rule of mediocrity.

Generation after generation, the Vanderbilts had fed their stock and tilled their tough acres and asked no more. They had stood, successively, father and son, on the same green hill-side and looked down the bay through that open gateway, the Narrows, to the sea beyond, without desiring to occupy it. They had glanced languidly up the bay to the shining city in the distance without burning to get a mortgage on it. They had gazed joyously round upon the opulent earth without resolving to own it. Indeed, during all these years, the members of this family do not seem to have cherished any ambition of any kind, except to pay their taxes promptly, go to church regularly, and get to Heaven at last. With this they were satisfied.

The fruit of the family tree was not yet ripe, but it was ripening. The man had not yet come who, filled with divine greed, would go forth on a magnificent crusade of conquest; who, inspired by personal avarice, would enter into the commercial emulations of his time with beneficent results; who, determined to be master, would become pre-eminently the servant of his countrymen; who, aiming only to push forward his own interests, would mysteriously advance the interests of all, promoting traffic and transit, increasing the general wealth and thrift, and augmenting the universal comfort beyond the dreams of philanthropy. Such a man, at the end of the fourth generation, made his appearance in the person of Cornelius Vanderbilt.

CHAPTER II.

BOYHOOD AND POVERTY.

His Father and Mother—The Humble Home—Avoiding School—Fun
and Hard Work—Wants to be a Sailor—Earns a Periauger—
Ready for Business at Sixteen.

OF the father of Cornelius we know little. He had
no start in life, as he did not inherit even the meagre
patrimony; for his father and mother died when he
was a child, and the property that existed was dissipated
by incapable or faithless trustees. As he grew to manhood he got a living as he could, assisting the farmers
at their work, and sailing a boat up to New York with
produce. It is alleged that he was the first boatman
who established the habit of leaving his wharf near
the Quarantine ground at a regular time every morning, and quitting New York for home at a uniform hour
in the afternoon. Thus he became, to a certain extent,
the founder of the Staten Island Ferry that now carries
twenty thousand passengers a day.

He had just succeeded in getting a few acres together,
when he made his fortune by meeting and marrying
Phebe Hand, a woman of rare qualities. She was born
over in Rahway, and both of her grandfathers were
farmers. Her uncle, Colonel Hand, fought at the battle
of Long Island. A competence was left her by her

THE COMMODORE'S MOTHER.

maternal grandfather, but the family patriotism invested it in "Continental bonds" and it was almost wholly lost, so she was compelled, as she emerged into womanhood, to rely upon her own labor for support. When she first became acquainted with Mr. Vanderbilt, she was residing in the family of a clergyman at Port Richmond, on the north side of the island, and there they married and set up housekeeping.

He seems to have been an industrious plodder, but he was not very thrifty or forehanded. In fact, he was inclined to be improvident and to indulge in speculations that did not terminate profitably. They lived in a small house at Port Richmond.* More than once Mrs. Vanderbilt saved the little family from want, and it is known that on one occasion, when her husband was in a dire strait, she drew from an old clock $3,000, the careful hoardings of years, and rescued the place from his creditors. Her energy, forethought, and self-reliance served as an admirable counterpoise to the visionary projects and scheming propensities of her husband. The scanty family record shows that she was possessed of a high and strong character, and to this fact her favorite son always bore unstinted testimony.

The family lived for some years at Port Richmond, on the Kill Von Kull, and then moved to Stapleton, the residence being on the eastern face of Staten Island, on a gently sloping lawn that was washed by the tides of the Narrows. It stood ten rods or so back from the beach, and was not lifted more than six or eight feet above high water. It was shingled all over, was of one story, with a loft above under a steep roof lighted by

* Still standing, and the property of Dr. Harrison.

dormer windows, and there could not have been more
than five rooms in the whole house. This made rather
cramped quarters for the father, mother, and nine lively
children. Even the great chimney seems to have felt
the need of elbow-room, for it went outside and stood
up like a grenadier at the gable end of the cabin. Cornelius and the older children were born at Port Richmond. They had opened their eyes on the light of the
sky in a much smaller and humbler residence, and the
father moved to Stapleton because it had become im-
peratively necessary to "have more room." Taking
possession of the fine five-roomed house on the beach
was, in the Vanderbilt hive, analogous to swarming.*

Cornelius Vanderbilt,† born May 27, 1794, was the
second son, but when he was eleven years old his elder
brother died, leaving him heir-apparent. The dauphin
had not a very brilliant prospect before him. His
great-grandfather had brought up eleven children, his
grandfather seven, and his father nine, and this severe
service had quite exhausted the few acres on which the
thrifty Aris had planted the family tree eighty years
before. They had sailed a little, fished a little, and
delved in the soil a good deal, and had managed to survive in the humble fashion of those days.

Cornelius attracted much attention by his personal

---

* For description, see Appendix A.

† He always wrote his name "Van Derbilt," as in the autograph
upon the cover of this book; but he directed everybody else to
write the name as one word. His oldest son, during his youth, compromised between his father's custom and his command by leaving
a space after the first syllable, thus "Van derbilt." On the old family
tomb, built by the Commodore, the name stands "Vander Bilt," but
on the new mausoleum it appears as "Vanderbilt."

resoluteness and his love of out-door sports. That is to say, in the direct language of that uncircuitous age, " he was obstinate and disobedient, and hated to go to school." Indeed, he would not go to school if he could help it. When given his choice, limited to the two things, he even preferred to work. But play suited him best of all. He was hearty, hardy, tall, and strong of his age, bold, quick as a cat, sinewy, a good oarsman, an expert swimmer, an unsurpassed climber, a wrestler whom few could lay upon his back. In fact he seems to have had a remarkably vigorous mind, as well as body ; he early learned how to sail a boat and he learned the use of all accessible tools,—he could learn anything but his lessons. His mother used to tell of his riding an impromptu horse-race, bare-back of course, before he was six years old. His antagonist was a slave-boy two years his senior, and both of them went at full speed. The black contestant lived to be a Methodist minister.*

Books and school Cornelius shunned. Multiplication was vexation, and Division was still worse, while he never heard of the Rule-of-Three. He often lamented his illiteracy in after days. The Bible and spelling-book were the only books he remembered ever having used in school. But even orthography was a profound mystery to him, and all his life he insisted on " spelling according to common-sense "—a system which the English language cannot tolerate.

If young Cornelius avoided school, he loved the water. He seems to have been the first of his line who felt entirely at home upon the surface of the bay, and who

* They met again at the Commodore's house, in Washington Place, after a separation of seventy-five years.

looked down through the Narrows with an acquisitive eye. Whole summer afternoons, when he should have been, or at any rate, might have been, studying, he lay upon the lawn or sat in a tree-top near the house and watched the incoming and outgoing craft. It was a superb outlook, for the bay of New York is unequalled in the world for its generous expanse, its pleasant embrace of fertile shores, its ever-changing beauty and its panorama of picturesque activity. Opposite was the forest of Bay Ridge; further off were the vacant slopes where now rise the white spires of Greenwood. Up the harbor were the first roofs of infant Brooklyn, and in the background, beyond, the greater city was dimly visible against the sky.

The boy was observing and had a retentive memory along the line of his predilections. He soon distinguished the difference between a schooner and a ship, a brig and a barkentine; and it is alleged that it was not long before he knew by sight every ship belonging to the port, and learned the rig and outline of every fishing-smack or coaster that trafficked on the rivers.

Like the other farmers along the shore, his father at last came to own a clumsy sail-boat of primitive pattern, with which to carry his produce to the city market. It had two masts and no deck, and its name had been Americanized from mellifluous Spanish into "periauger." * On this rude water-vehicle young Cornelius made himself useful, and thus escaped torment at the dreaded school. He got, at an early age, so that he

* It was the predecessor of the cat-boat of the present day, and its name was probably carried to the Netherlands by the terrible Alva.

could be trusted to sail and steer the "periauger" as well as anybody, for there were yet no steamers to run him down.

A story is told at this time which indicates that the family thrift was already brewing in his father's arteries. The boy, as a reward for special hard work, hoeing potatoes, had been promised a holiday "next Tuesday," during which he and a neighboring crony, Owen, could "go up to New York and have a good time." The morning came, and the father said: "Now Cornele, there's the periauger for you; I've pitched on more than half of the hay, you and Owen can just pitch on the rest, and take it up and unload it at the wharf as usual, and you can play on the way—both ways, going up and coming back! Here's sixpence for you, my boy." The Commodore, in telling the story in after years, used to add, "A boy can get fun out of 'most anything, and we got some fun out of that; but I remember we were just as tired that night as if we had been working."

Before Cornelius had finished his eleventh year, his father had come to trust him to oversee and manage jobs requiring the prudence and thoughtfulness of a man, sometimes sending him many miles away from home with teams and men to assist in the unloading of stranded vessels. He always proved himself equal to such emergencies.

When he was twelve years old, his father took a contract for getting the cargo out of a vessel stranded near Sandy Hook, and transporting it to New York in lighters. It was necessary to carry the cargo in wagons across a sandy spit. Cornelius, with a little fleet of lighters, three wagons, their horses and drivers, started from home solely charged with the management of this difficult affair. After loading the lighters and starting them for the city, he had to conduct his wagons home by land—a long distance over Jersey sands. Leaving the beach with only six dollars, he reached South Amboy penniless, with six horses and three men all hungry, still far from home, and separated from Staten Island by an arm of the sea half a mile wide, that could be crossed only by paying the ferryman six dollars. This was a puzzling predicament for a boy of twelve, and he pondered long how he could get out of it. At length he went boldly to the only innkeeper of the place, and addressed him thus:

"I have here three teams that I want to get over to Staten Island. If you will put us across, I'll leave with you one of my horses in pawn, and if I don't send you back the six dollars within forty-eight hours you may sell the horse."

The innkeeper looked into the bright, honest eyes of the boy for a moment, and said:

"I'll do it."

And he did it. The horse in pawn was left with the ferryman on the island, and was redeemed in time.

At last came the inevitable hour. The seductive vision of moving sails had done its work on the boy's imagination. The wizard sea had wrought its spell. He slyly announced to his mother that he was going to be a sailor and should ship before the mast. He was sixteen years old, stalwart, tough, and hardy. Of course, he would have to run away, for the youth of those days had not the freedom they have at present—every boy's labor belonged to his father absolutely until he was twenty-one, and the law held him bound to render that service.

His mother pleaded with him to give up his crazy fancy, and set before him its exposures, hardships, and dangers. He listened to her. She was not only the family oracle, but she was the oracle of the neighborhood, whose advice was sought in all sorts of dilemmas, and whose judgment had weight. But he loved the sea and hated the farm, and he would be one of those

" Who reap, but sow not, on the rolling fields."

A compromise was possible. If he could not ship as a sailor, might he buy a boat? If he only had $100 with which to buy a boat! The mother's love directed her to a solution of the problem. After thinking of the matter over night she promised the boy * that if he would earn the hundred dollars he should have it. There was on the farm an eight-acre lot, so hard, rough, and stony that it had never been ploughed. The bargain was that if he would plough and harrow that eight acres and plant it with corn before the 27th of the month, the day when he would be sixteen, he should have the $100. He closed the contract and he executed it—partly by hard work, partly by stratagem. He interested some of the neighboring boys in his scheme. He confided to them the fact that he was to have " a new periauger" of his own as soon as he got the patch planted, and he added casually that anybody who helped him finish the job right up in a hurry would be permitted to sail in the wonderful craft, and perhaps

* On May 1, 1810.

to some extent assist in managing her. The remark bore fruit. Recruits flocked to his standard. And the field was all ploughed, harrowed, and planted complete the day before his birthday.*

He claimed his reward—it was reluctantly given—produced, no doubt, from his mother's inexhaustible clock. She had not much faith in his venture. He had long had his eye on a new and beautiful " periauger " over at Port Richmond, which the owner wanted to sell, and now he rushed off and secured it. It would carry twenty passengers. He used to say, in later days, when in a reminiscent mood, " I didn't feel as much real satisfaction when I made two million in that Harlem corner as I did on that bright May morning sixty years before when I stepped into my own periauger, hoisted my own sail, and put my hand on my own tiller." It will be noticed that, up to this time, the boy had not been " a favorite of Fortune," as the envious called him in after years ; he had been helped by no special "good luck ; " every step had been won by hard work.

Next morning he had his anchor up bright and early, and announced that he was ready to carry freight and passengers to New York. Those who came down the beach to look at the craft found a capable-looking youth of sixteen standing in the stern—tall, vigorous, firmly-knotted, broad of shoulder, bright of eye, deft of hand, with a complexion of white and pink, and a reassuring and agreeable smile. He could back a wild colt and subdue it, and sail a boat on the maddest sea, but he could scarcely write his name.

* He had evidently been reading about the decorative exploits of "Tom Sawyer."

CHAPTER III.

YOUTH AND AMBITION.

Sails his Boat on the Bay—Fare, Eighteen Cents—Makes $1,000 a
Year—Sturdy, Abrupt, and Honest—In War Times—Beats Van
Duzen—Marries at Nineteen.

In those days New York City was a cluster of houses
and stores below Fulton Street; Broadway came up to
where the City Hall was rising, and disappeared in the
cornfields to the north. The Bowery was a country lane,
leading to the cow-pastures above Fourteenth Street.
Canal Street was a brook running to the Hudson through
huckleberry-fields. Centre Street was a lake covering
ten acres, and a great marsh-bordered pond spread over
the area which is now spanned by the approaches to the
Brooklyn Bridge. New York had overtaken and passed
Boston and Philadelphia, and it was growing. Most
of the business was done in Hanover Square and Pearl
Street; there was no Water Street or South Street
or Front Street or West Street, and " up-town " was in-
habited only by farmers.

This was the place to and from which " Young Cornele," as he was called, began his first trips of transportation. A single fare was eighteen cents. He worked
about sixteen hours out of every twenty-four. He car-

ried by daylight the casual freight or incidental passenger, and at night he bore across the Bay, whenever he
could get a load, parties of the young of both sexes who
went to enjoy the revel of promenading on the Battery
in the moonlight, behind the rows of old cannon which
still lingered there, and winding up the wild festivity
by partaking of walnuts and flip in the fashionable
tavern of Bowling Green. The lad made money. At
the end of the first year he gave $100 to his mother for
the "periauger," and $1,000 besides. At the end of
the second he gave her another $1,000, and in the mean-
time had bought a fractional interest in two or three
more "periaugers."

Just at this time there came an extraordinary demand
for boats. On account of the joyful manner in which we
heard of and commented on the triumphant march of
Napoleon in Europe the relations of this country with
Great Britain were becoming strained, and war was
menaced. So our seaports were immediately strengthened. The forts now flanking the entrance to the
Sound and the Narrows were hastily begun, and all
available boatmen were kept busy bringing materials for
their construction. Cornelius got his full share of the
business. Often he skipped his dinner, and always
went to bed late and was out with the dawn.

The young boatman was not blessed with popular
manners. He was not conciliatory, and never seemed to
care what people thought or said of him. He lacked
the affability and suavity which are born of a love of
approbation—the desire to please. He was not choice of
his language. He was sometimes harsh, abrupt, uncere-
monious, and even uncivil—like Julius Cæsar, Napoleon

Bonaparte, Wellington, Von Moltke, Belmont, and a good many others who have never attained either wealth or fame.

But he was honest. He charged fair prices. He allowed nobody to underbid him. He believed in the competitive system of labor, which all sluggards who are beaten in the competition denounce as barbarous. He believed in "the survival of the fittest," a law of nature that is never liked by the weaklings or by those who are unable to cope with their fellows on equal terms. He was thoroughly capable and willing. So he soon came to be the first person called on when anything difficult or dangerous was to be done. When the winds were fierce, and the eyes were blinded with driving sleet, and the waves raged and howled for a victim, then the youth was in demand if anybody needed to go upon the bay.

In this instance, as ever, the boy was father of the man. The traits he showed as a boatman on the bay were the very same that distinguished him fifty years later—the power of doing what he set out to do in spite of all obstacles. This was the key to the achievements of his life.

When the British fleet tried to force its way past Sandy Hook, "to lay New York in ashes," as the Admiral gayly observed, the ill-equipped forts beat it off. The batteries had an important ally in a fearful storm that was raging at the time, but this made it all the more difficult to inform the commanding officer in the city of the attack and the repulse, and to obtain instant reinforcements. A messenger was sent to Staten Island for its most expert boatman. Cornelius was found and

summoned.   Arriving at Sandy Hook, a staff officer
asked him if a boat would live in such a sea.

" Yes, if properly handled," was the answer.

" Will you take us to the Battery ? "

" Yes ; but I shall carry you part way under water."

" All right, young man ; we can stand that."

They started, and after several hours of terrible exposure to cold and wet he landed them safely at the
stairs at Whitehall.   They were like drowned rats, and
one of them declared that he did not draw one full
breath throughout the stormy journey.   But there they
were, and the fort at Sandy Hook was reinforced next
morning.

He allowed nobody to beat him at the business he
followed.   One day, when the wind was off, and he was
pulling his boat-load of passengers up through Butter-
milk Channel, between Governor's Island and Brooklyn,
he suddenly found his boat neck-and-neck with the boat
of his tall rival, Jake Van Duzen.   Beaten he must
never be, and by the most powerful exertions he sent
his boat swiftly forward to its destination.   But he held
the pole against his breast, and he put forth such efforts
that it bored through the flesh to the bone, and made
there a scar which he carried to his grave.

One day during the war an advertisement appeared
in the papers which stirred up some emulation.   When
the boatmen were anxiously considering what they
should do to escape the draft and thus keep at their
profitable work, a card was issued from the office of the
Commissary-General, Matthew L. Davis, inviting bids
from the boatmen for the contract of conveying provisions to the posts in the vicinity of New York, during

the three months—the contractor to be exempt from
military duty.   The boatmen caught at this, as a drown-
ing man catches at a straw, and put in bids at rates
preposterously low—all except Cornelius Vanderbilt.

"Why don't you send in a bid?" asked his father.

"Of what use would it be?" replied the son.   "They
are offering to do the work at half price.   It can't be
done at such rates."

"Well," added the father, "it can do no harm to try
for it."

So, to please his father, but without the slightest ex-
pectation of getting the contract, he sent in an application, offering to transport the provisions at a price which
would enable him to do it with the requisite certainty
and promptitude.   His offer was simply fair to both
parties.

On the day named for awarding the contract all the
boatmen excepting him assembled at the commissary's
office.   He stayed at the boat-stand, not considering
that he had any interest in the award.   When they all,
one after another, returned without the prize, he strolled
over to the office, and asked the commissary if the contract had been given.

"Oh, yes," said Davis; "that business is settled.
Cornelius Vanderbilt is the man."

He was thunderstruck.

"What!" said the commissary, observing his astonishment, "is it you?"

"My name is Cornelius Vanderbilt."

"Well," said Davis, "don't you know why we have
given the contract to you?"

"No."

" Why, it is because we want this business *done*, and
we know you'll do it."

When he was nineteen years old he fell in love with
Sophia Johnson, an attractive and capable young woman,
and the daughter of his father's sister Eleanor. His
mother objected to the match on the ground of con-
sanguinity, and his father on the ground that so useful
and profitable a member of the household could not be
spared ; but he overcame both impediments and married her.*

There are on the lips of the old people of Staten Island
and New York many picturesque traditions of the prow-
ess of young Vanderbilt about these days. One tells how,
when injustice was attempted against him, he attacked
with his fists an armed officer in the midst of a battalion
of soldiers, and compelled him to succumb. Another
narrates how, when riding up Broadway at the head
of a cavalcade of eight hundred Staten Islanders, in a
procession, he was insulted by " Yankee Sullivan,"
whereupon he calmly dismounted and beat that re-
nowned pugilist " till he couldn't stand." These stories
have an internal resemblance to the myths wherewith
popular prodigies and heroes are always glorified, and
the details need not be recounted here.

War was raging around, and business was brisk. The
young husband had obtained the contract to carry provisions to the six forts around New York, and this immediately entailed extraordinary labors. To supply each
of the six forts took one day, and each needed provi-
sioning once a week. His boat was busy on the Staten
Island route during the day, so he did the additional

* December 19, 1813.

work at night, loading up at the Battery every evening after the day's ferriage was over. Sunday furnished the only day or night of unbroken rest.

The profits were large, and he was now enabled to build a beautiful little schooner for the coasting-trade, which he called the Dread, and which he sent under a captain up and down the Sound or ocean-shore, wherever a paying cargo could be found. From his several ventures he was earning a good deal of money, and the following year he built a very large schooner named after his sister Charlotte, and put it on the line between New York and Charleston, commanded by her husband, Captain De Forest.

In one of his cruisings up the river he stopped with a community of Shakers. After he had remained with them a day and a night they refused to take any pay for the hospitality. The circumstance made a deep impression on his mind, and he never forgot it.*

He did coasting or river business indifferently, transporting or peddling, as the case might be. He was above no honest toil that brought in money. Now he would carry boat-loads of shad up and down the shore looking for a purchaser. Now he would collect tons of melons in Delaware, and boat them up to Albany, selling them out, wholesale and retail, at the little towns on the way.

When the war closed and he had passed his twenty-first birthday, he began earnestly to plan methods of improving the shape and build of ships. He allowed

---

* Many years afterward, when president of the Harlem, he granted to them an important and unusual concession, much to the surprise of his associates.

himself to be hampered by no precedents, and he introduced such innovations and modifications as attracted
the attention of ship-builders, and made " Vanderbilt
models" and " Vanderbilt methods" discussed even
among the experienced and practical men of his craft.
He soon built another vessel, a still greater departure
from the usual patterns, and worked on.   Between ship-
building and ship-owning, when he was twenty-three
he balanced his books* and found that he was worth
$9,000 in cash, besides his interest in various stanch
sailing-vessels.   But a new candidate had come to contest with Boreas the supremacy of the sea, and Cornelius
Vanderbilt sat down on New Year's Day and thought it
over.

* December 31, 1817.

CHAPTER IV.

STEAMBOAT AND TAVERN.

Abandons Sails for Steam—New York to New Brunswick—Fight
    with a Monopoly—Dodging the Sheriff—Making his Point—
    Large Profits—Pluck and Enterprise.

THE new-comer was Steam. Two years after Cornelius Vanderbilt was born, John Fitch, of Connecticut,
had launched a steam-yawl, propelled by a stern-screw,
on Collect Pond, a body of fresh water sixty feet deep,
where the Tombs now stands, and though he had but a
twelve-gallon pot for a boiler, he ran his nondescript
around the pond with great rapidity.* The achievement was almost forgotten when Robert Fulton, eleven
years later, launched the Clermont on the Hudson and
steamed toward Albany against wind and tide at the
rate of five miles an hour. John Stevens simultaneously launched the Phœnix on the Delaware.

These events caused a sensation, and were heard of
and talked of even in Staten Island. The State of New
York hastened to grant exclusive patents to Fulton and
Livingston for the running of steamboats on all the

* Fitch had been before his invention a penniless adventurer, captured and bartered for tobacco by the Indians of Ohio ; and, after
his failure to attract attention by his steam vessels on Collect Pond
and the Delaware, he returned to the West, disgusted with the
world's stupidity, and died of drink in the wilderness of Kentucky,
while Fulton and Livingston were reaping his harvest.

waters within its jurisdiction, and the patentees proceeded to profit by it. Better boats than the Clermont were built, a higher speed was attained, and in some places they even drove off the sloops and schooners and took their place. By 1810 Fulton and Livingston had four regular steamboats plying on the Hudson, one on the Delaware and one on the St. Lawrence.*

Ship-owners, as a class, derided the steamboat as "a mere plaything," which might answer for Sunday-school picnics, but could never be used to carry freight to advantage, because the machinery took up so much room. Young Vanderbilt was a leader among this class, and participated in this sort of talk, but he did not allow it to blind his judgment as to probabilities. He went and carefully examined Fulton's craft, took passage to Albany and back, studied the engines and machinery, and reluctantly made up his mind that the future of navigation belonged to steamboats.

He saw that the usefulness of sailing-vessels was limited by various conditions, while the scope of steam was practically unbounded. To the astonishment of his friends, he suddenly turned his back on sails, gave up the coasting business, sold out his interest in half a dozen vessels, and looked vaguely around for a steamboat. He was eager to learn the business on any terms.

Fulton and Livingston had been granted by the Legislature a monopoly of the new motor in New York State, but the privilege was not uncontested. Thomas Gibbons, a man with money and spirit, had started a transportation line from New York to Philadelphia, by

* There was only one steamboat on the Mississippi at the time of the battle of New Orleans.

steamer from the Battery to New Brunswick, at the head of Raritan River, thence by stage to Trenton, and by steamer again from Trenton to the point of destination. Livingston fought him in the courts, got a decision against him, obtained an injunction to prevent the trip from the Battery to New Brunswick, and put in the hands of officers warrants for the arrest of Gibbons and his captain. Gibbons appealed to higher courts, but personally he stayed in New Jersey, and made reprisals as he could. In his defence, New Jersey passed a retaliatory law, threatening with State prison any officer of New York who should arrest any citizen of New Jersey for steamboating in New York waters. But the officers attempting to execute the Livingston writs were careful to keep on their own side of the bay and the river. It was a bitter contest, and prolonged from year to year.

Vanderbilt was naturally pugnacious. He always took sides in a fight, and generally with the weaker party. So now, he announced himself a Gibbonsonian, and was welcomed as an important recruit. A man of grit was needed to command the Mouse-of-the-Mountain, and though Vanderbilt had been clearing $3,000 a year by luffing and tacking, he now accepted $1,000 a year as captain of that diminutive steamboat. He at once introduced a new order of things. He improved the Mouse in various ways, made his trips on time, discharged all superfluous help, cut down running expenses, and at the end of six months, the line began for the first time to return a profit to Gibbons. In a year the Bellona, a larger steamer, was built under Vanderbilt's supervision, and substituted for the Mouse-of-the-Mountain.

The half-way-house at New Brunswick, where all passengers had to tarry over-night to take the morning stage, was dirty and badly-managed, and Vanderbilt's offer to "take it and run it," was promptly accepted. Thither he moved his wife with her babes from his father's little house at Stapleton, and put her in charge of the way-side tavern. This step was abundantly justified by the results. Like his mother, his wife proved to be a rare woman—strong, industrious, neat, frugal, skilful, courageous, and business-like. She turned the house wrong-side out and up-side down, cleaned it, renovated it, fumigated it, and made it fit for guests. The same energy, care, thrift, and economy which her husband exhibited for the next twelve years in command of the Bellona, she practised in command of Bellona Hall. The line at last was made to pay $40,000 a year to Gibbons, and Captain Vanderbilt's salary was raised to $2,000. Besides the salary, the house at the point of transfer was a constant source of revenue.*

During more than half of these twelve years of apprenticeship to steam, Vanderbilt's life was one incessant fight with the monopoly created by the Legislature. The Bellona violated the patent of Fulton and Livingston from the moment she entered New York Bay, and the captain was subjected to repeated arrests and constant annoyance. There was one period when for sixty successive days an attempt was every day made to arrest him, but the captain baffled each attempt. He fought

---

* Captain Vanderbilt is known to have expressed some socialistic notions about these days, such as that John Jacob Astor was a dangerous monopolist, and "no man ever ought to be worth more than $20,000."

the monopoly by every device he could think of, and, as in the fable of old, made the tail of the fox eke out the skin of the lion. When defiance failed to protect him, he resorted to stratagem and finesse. He took a young woman into the pilot-house and taught her to steer the boat, so that when the officers of the law boarded the trespassing vessel off Governor's Island, they were greeted only with a confusing vision of petticoats at the helm. They searched the lower decks on these occasions, but the crew had all been left in New Jersey, and the captain had retreated and hidden himself in a panel-closet which they could not find. This went on week after week, the writ of arrest being regularly returned with the indorsement, *non est inventus.*

In 1819 Captain Vanderbilt was caught on the wharf. In the custody of the exasperated and indignant sheriff he was taken to Albany on the next steamboat which the Stevenses sent up, and there was arraigned before the Chancellor, Livingston's successor, to answer for contempt of court. When the trial came off, it was found that the audacious captain had set a trap, and had gone ashore on purpose to be captured, having for that day only (Sunday) hired out to one Tompkins, who held a license under the Fulton-Livingston patents. He was released.

A little incident of these years he has sometimes related to his children. In the cold January of 1820, the ship Elizabeth—the first ship ever sent to Africa by the Colonization Society—lay at the foot of Rector Street, with the negroes all on board, frozen in. For many days her crew, aided by the crew of the frigate Siam, her convoy, had been cutting away at the ice; but as more ice formed at night than could be removed by day,

the prospect of getting to sea was unpromising. One afternoon Captain Vanderbilt joined the crowd of spectators.

"They are going the wrong way to work," he care-
lessly remarked, as he turned to go home. "I could
get her out in one day."

These words from a man who was known to mean all
he said made an impression on a bystander, who reported them to the anxious agent of the society. The
agent called upon him.

"What did you mean, captain, by saying that you
could get out the ship in one day?"

"Just what I said."

"What will you get her out for?"

"One hundred dollars."

"I'll give it. When will you do it?"

"Have a steamer to-morrow, at twelve o'clock, ready
to tow her out. I'll have her clear in time."

That same evening, at six, he was on the spot with
five men, three pine boards, and a small anchor. The
difficulty was that beyond the ship there were two hundred yards of ice too thin to bear a man. The captain
placed his anchor on one of his boards, and pushed it
out as far as he could reach; then placed another board
upon the ice, lay down upon it, and gave his anchor
another push. Then he put down his third board, and
used that as a means of propulsion. In this way he
worked forward to near the edge of the thin ice, where
the anchor broke through and sunk. With the line attached to it, he hauled a boat to the outer edge, and then
began cutting a passage for the ship. At eleven the
next morning she was clear. At twelve she was towed
into the stream.

Every effort was made by the rich North River alliance to induce this plucky young captain to desert to their side. They sent an emissary who offered him $5,000 a year to take charge of their largest boat. He declined. "No," he said, "I shall stick to Gibbons. He has always treated me square, and been as good as his word. Besides, I don't care half so much about making money as I do about *making my point, and coming out ahead*."

In 1824, when he had continued the battle against monopoly seven years, the cause of Gibbons *vs.* the successors of Livingston was decided in favor of Gibbons, in the Supreme Court of the United States. Daniel Webster made his great speech against the granting of such an exclusive privilege, and Chief Justice Marshall delivered the judgment of the Court, that it was unconstitutional. Thenceforth the boats were run in peace, and there was no longer before the captain's eyes the fear of a jail.

The following is an advertisement of those early days:

UNION LINE.

For Philadelphia and Baltimore.

Through

To Philadelphia in ONE DAY!

Twenty-five miles

of land carriage, by New Brunswick, Princeton, and Trenton!

The splendid new steamer, EMERALD, CAPTAIN C. VANDERBILT, leaves the wharf, north side of the Battery, at 12 o'clock noon every day, Sunday excepted. Travellers will lodge at Trenton and arrive at Philadelphia by steamboat at 10 o'clock next morning!

FARE ONLY THREE DOLLARS!

For seats, apply to York House, No. 5 Courtlandt Street.

New York, September 15, 1826.

Another boat left at a later hour, whose passengers stopped all night at Bellona Hall, New Brunswick.

During these years, too, Captain Vanderbilt had been making a profound study of the shape and equipment of steamboats; had been locating their weaknesses, and drawing crude designs to remedy them. Fulton and Livingston were long since dead, but their intro-duction of steam had been followed by tremendous growth in all directions. Captain Vanderbilt told his wife that he must take a hand in the spoils of this newly discovered realm, and to do so advantageously they must leave New Brunswick and return to New York Bay. Woman-like, she dreaded to give up her home to try experiments. "I love this place," she said. "Our children have been born here. We have friends about us. We have prospered and can now count up $30,000 of our own. Why should we tempt misfortune by changing now?"

She had a strong ally in Thomas Gibbons, who warmly remonstrated with the captain. "If you leave me, Vanderbilt, it will break up the line. I can't get along without you. I will double your pay. Stay and I will let you have half of the line at your own price, and you may pay for it out of the profits." But Van-derbilt's eye was fixed on the traffic of the Hudson and the Sound; his acute commercial brain showed him how these could be marvellously expanded and devel-oped, and how he could put in practice those new prin-ciples of construction that he had forged during his meditations.

So in 1829 he resigned and took his now numerous family back to New York City. In the spring of 1830

he made his appearance among the transportation
grandees who controlled the waters of the State. They
were richer than he, but they already knew him and
feared him. It was a case of superior sagacity against
long purses. He began to build boats with novel improvements and run them in opposition to the old established lines. His chief and most enterprising antagonist, Stevens of Hoboken, amazed at the dash of
his onset, and supposing that he was "backed by Gibbons," surrendered the fight and withdrew from the
river rather than waste a fortune in cutting rates; but
that doughty couple, Daniel Drew and Dean Richmond,
took his place in the battle. Vanderbilt constructed
magnificent boats, faster, better, and more commodious
than ever before seen, and he ran them at the lowest
paying fares. His foible was "opposition;" wherever
his keen eye detected a line that was making a very
large profit on its investment, he swooped down on it
and drove it to the wall by offering a better service and
lower rates.*

To understand what tremendous improvements were
introduced into steamboating by this trio of giant com-
manders, it is necessary only to travel on the shabby
English river-boats or the primitive Rhine steamers of
to-day, where the influence of these enterprising rivals
was never felt.

The Caroline, a little steamer which Vanderbilt constructed at this time, met with an unusual doom. She
was put on Lake Erie, and there was used by the in-
surgents during the Canadian "rebellion." She was

---

* After leaving Gibbons he made $30,000 a year for the first five
years, then doubled it in 1836.

captured by an excited band of loyalists, in the Niagara River, and then she was cut from her moorings, set on fire, turned down the rapids, sent, like some splendid sacrificial offering over the mighty Falls, and torn to pieces in the mad whirlpool below.

It is a fact worth noting that, although Vanderbilt, at one time or another, built or bought a hundred vessels, not one of them was ever wrecked, burned, or destroyed while in his possession. This must be assigned to the extreme care with which he selected his officers and men.

He never insured a vessel. He used to say, when spoken to on the subject: "Good vessels and good captains are the best sort of insurance. If corporations can make money out of insurance, I can."

Captain Vanderbilt came naturally by his early prejudices against railroads. In October, 1833, the first serious railroad accident in America occurred on the Amboy Railroad, in New Jersey. The Captain came near losing his life. He was pitched out, dragged along the track, and flung down a thirty-foot embankment. Several of his ribs were broken and pushed into the lungs, and the air escaped into the cellular tissue. His body was dangerously swollen, and he was subjected to heroic treatment at his house, 134 Madison Street,* by Dr. Jared Lindsey, then a young man. "I staid with him three weeks," says the doctor. "One night I bled him three times, and thus subdued the inflammation."

* See Appendix B.

CHAPTER V.

HOME AND CHILDREN.

His return to New York Harbor—Residence in the City—A New House on Staten Island—His Three Sons—Stern Management— William H.'s Exile to New Dorp.

WHEN he left New Brunswick, in 1829, with his wife and children,* he took them first to a quiet and humble tenement in Stone Street, near the Battery. The surroundings were narrow, unwholesome, and uncomfortable, especially for the children, who seriously felt the contrast with the open country to which they had been accustomed.† From here he soon sought a little more comfortable quarters in East Broadway, but this tenement was the reverse of spacious, and he shortly returned with his increasing family to the little house at Stapleton, where his mother still resided with some of her daughters.

This, of course, was far too cramped to be longer tolerable, and Captain Vanderbilt, already regarded as a man of means, built his first family mansion on Staten

---

* There were thirteen children in all, and ten of them were born in New Brunswick. One (Francis) died in infancy, and the story of the other three boys will be told. The nine girls all lived to marry and have families, but the captain and his wife were too busy to make a family record, and diligent inquiry fails to ascertain the dates of their children's birth.　　　　　† See Appendix B.

Island, in one corner of the ancestral farm. He had
his eye on this lot early in life, and years before he built
his permanent home there it was known among the
neighbors as "Corneel's lot." Its site was on the northeast corner of the farm, near the water, on a rise of land
overlooking the bay, midway between Stapleton and
Tompkinsville, and those passing down that road may
still see, surrounded by an iron fence, the residence of
the great railroad king. It is an imposing dwelling,
conspicuous for its high portico and tall Corinthian columns in front. Here he lived several years, during the
youth of his children.

It was not until 1846 that the family moved to New
York and made, at No. 10 Washington Place, a permanent residence. It was a little too far up-town, but
the tide was setting toward it. The "upper ten," as
they were called, had begun to abandon that choice
locality, St. John's Square, now occupied by the great
freight depot of the Hudson River Railway Company.
Bleecker Street, even, was ceasing to be the fashionable
thoroughfare, and Washington's Parade Ground, its
name modernized to Washington Square, had become
the aristocratic heart of the city. Trees had been
planted, greensward put down, the stream that ran
through it turned aside into the new sewer, and it had
become the most desirable centre of resort and residence. There the opulent West India merchants lived,
and the great real estate owners and bankers, the Rhine-
landers, Jays, Schuylers, Lispenards, Van Rensselaers,
and leaders of society.

Long before this time, Vanderbilt had attracted great
attention among the rich and pushing men of the city.

In a quaint list of such he is thus mentioned : " Cornelius Vanderbilt, $750,000, of an old Dutch root; has evinced more go-aheaditiveness than any other single Dutchman ever possessed. It takes our American hot suns to clear off the fogs and vapors of the Zuyder-Zee and wake up the phlegm of a descendant of old Holland." There were sixteen millionaires in the list, most of them now forgotten. Who remembers the millionaires Brandegee, Bowne, Barclay, Glover, Ward, Leggett and Parrish, who flourished only forty-five years ago ?

Captain Vanderbilt had striven to give all his children a fair education, and to prepare his three sons to follow in his footsteps and take care of the estate he was to leave behind him. Of these last, George, the youngest, was his favorite, though, when he was old enough, he sent him to West Point, thus apparently taking him out of the line of the commercial succession.

His oldest son, William H.,* was never in early days regarded with great favor by his father. He seemed to him dull and commonplace, and in his candid moments the elder Vanderbilt was accustomed to call him a fool to his face. He usually addressed him and spoke of him as " Billy; " sometimes, resentfully, as " Bill."

The second son, Cornelius Jeremiah, was antipathetic to his father in all things : he was physically weak, and an epileptic—moody, irascible, unstable, indolent, petulant, extravagant, and fond of the gaming-table.

The strong man had no toleration for this invalid ne'er-do-weel, and he early announced that no son of his should have any of his wealth until demonstrating his

---

* William Henry, named after his father's hero, General Harrison, who had won the battle of Tippecanoe ten years before.

capacity to support himself without any aid from him. Cornelius always wanted money, and one day, during the California excitement of '49, when his father, as usual, refused his demands, he ran away, and shipped before the mast for the land of gold. He went around Cape Horn, and the voyage tended to increase his physical debility. A short stay was enough, and he returned home again, only to be arrested on his arrival by his father and confined as a lunatic in the Bloomingdale Insane Asylum. The evidence offered to prove that he was crazy was that he had used his father's name to procure funds when suffering from want in Sacramento. The incarceration was short, and his father thenceforth made him a moderate annual allowance, increasing it considerably after his marriage in 1856. Thus Cornelius J. was early seen to be a failure, and the exacting father was not slow in assigning William to the same category.

The Captain was not only the incumbent of the throne, but the power behind it also. He ruled home, wife, and children with a rod of steel, and brooked no disobedience or contradiction. He manifested scant affection for his children, seldom sought their love or confidence, and treated them very nearly like anybody's else.

After William was born at New Brunswick, in 1821, his father noticed him only as much as he was compelled to. The boy went to the country school for four or five years, but he was not apt or ambitious in his studies, and when he was nine went with father and family to New York. Here he attended the Columbia Grammar School, and got some of the rudiments of youthful learning. At the age of seventeen he went into business in a small way as a ship-chandler; but when he was eighteen his father transferred him as a clerk to the large banking-house of Drew, Robinson & Co., in Wall Street, the senior partner being Daniel Drew.

The young bank clerk recalled the inverted compliments which his father had heaped upon him from time to time, and he resolved to disprove their applicability. He worked hard from morning to night. He was not very quick to comprehend or to learn, but by stubborn plodding he mastered the details of the business, and slowly but surely won the approval of his employers. His salary the first year was $150; the second year it was $300; and the third year it was made $1,000.

During his twentieth year his affections became entangled with those of Miss Maria Louisa Kissam, an educated young woman, and the daughter of a Brooklyn clergyman, and her he married—of course against the remonstrances of his father.

" What are you going to live on ? " inquired the latter.

" Nineteen dollars a week," replied the son, nothing daunted.

" Well, Billy, you *are* a fool, just as I always thought ! " and the great ship-owner went off disgusted.

The young bank clerk and his wife lived on the nineteen dollars a week in a cheap boarding-house in East Broadway. The Captain was worth a million dollars, but he had made up his mind that William was shiftless and reckless, and going to the dogs, and it was useless to spend money in trying to prevent the inevitable. Or perhaps he thought, If I give him money now he will never learn those important lessons which only Poverty teaches. The young clerk struggled on, and his young wife proved a blessing to him in every way. His home life, thence onward for forty-five years, showed a wholesome and agreeable contrast to that of his father, who was cold and suspicious, and whose imperious will compelled everybody about him to move as he directed. He imagined that the fact that " Billy " was his son was the cause of his advancement at the bank, and gave him little credit for it.

Suddenly William's health began to fail, and the physician notified his father that he would probably die if he were not taken from the confinement at the bank.

The Captain said, " Well, Billy, what next ? "

" I don't know," said the young husband, " but I can support us two at almost anything."

" You two ! " exclaimed his father ; " but there'll be more than two. I know the way of our family. You must go on a farm, where there'll be room."

He bought a little farm of seventy acres of unimproved land at New Dorp, Staten Island, between the old Moravian church and the sea ; and he no doubt remarked to himself, " I am the only one of all our breed that is fit for anything except digging in that dirt ! " The young couple accepted the gift without the blessing, and took possession of the lonely little homestead. It stood on the slope of the southeast shore of the ancestral island ; a third of the horizon was the billowy sea, and straight in front of the cottage, toward the summer sunrise, the nearest land was Spain.

CHAPTER VI.

FROM STEAMBOATS TO STEAMSHIPS.

Running Steamboats in all Directions—To California via the Isth-
mus—Worth Ten Million Dollars—A Yachting Cruise to Europe—
A Line Across the Atlantic—The Mails—Lending a Vessel to the
Government.

BEFORE he had reached the age of forty he was worth
half a million dollars. He had a score of vessels in commission, most of which he had built himself, and these
were of so superior a character and so rapidly increasing
in number that there was bestowed upon him by acclamation the title of "Commodore." This honorary
badge of distinction he wore all his life, and the designation, first applied facetiously, was at last universally employed as a serious recognition of his worth and power.

During the next fifteen years he launched out broadly
upon all the waters around New York. He ran boats
to Albany, sometimes at a loss, but generally at a profit,
till Robert L. Stevens & Son* bought him off. He
built boats of new models and of great power, and established lines to Bridgeport, Norwalk, Derby, New
Haven, Hartford, New London, Providence and New-

* The Commodore afterward said of the Stevenses, "They were
the greatest projectors of their day, with more faith than Fulton, or
Livingston, or any of us. They projected the New Jersey Railroad
and Canal, which nobody else thought would ever pay a dividend."

port, and even Boston. He reached in all directions for patronage, and the supply was equal to the demand. From 1840 to 1850 he made a great deal of money.

On the outbreak of the gold fever of California in 1849, the Commodore hastened to avail himself of the opportunity which it offered to the enterprising carrier. The Pacific Mail Steamship Company monopolized most of the transportation service, running steamers in connection with both shores at Panama. The price for the round trip was $600, and the service was very bad. " I can improve on that," said Vanderbilt; " I can make money at $300, crossing my passengers by Lake Nicaragua, a route six hundred miles shorter."

He built a fine large steamer, the Prometheus,* and steamed down to the Nicaragua crossing, three or four hundred miles this side of Panama, dragging a small, side-wheel steamboat, the Director, in tow.† This last was for transporting passengers across Lake Nicaragua, which is a hundred miles long and fifty broad, located among the tops of the Andes. How to get the boat up into the lake was the question. The San Juan River empties out of it, into the Caribbean Sea, near where the Prometheus was anchored, but no boat had ever tried to ascend it. Vanderbilt sent his engineers to explore it. They were gone a week, and reported that the stream was not navigable; that there were bars and rocks, fallen trees and rapids and cascades in great

* This was the first steamer ever owned by an individual.

† He was so secretive about this venture that he left home in 1850, it is alleged, without bidding good-by to his wife. She missed him and made inquiries, found that the steamer had gone, whither no one knew, and that he had been recently much seen studying a map of Central America. In three weeks he was heard from, via Panama.

numbers; but that they might drag the boat along by easy stages, and cut side canals around the places that were too steep to climb.

This report disgusted the Napoleon of navigation, who felt that he was losing $5,000 a day by the delay. He fired up the little Director, boarded her with thirty men, and announced to them that he was going up to the lake "without any more fooling." The engineers were appalled, but on he went. Sometimes he got over the rapids by putting on all steam; sometimes when this did not avail, he extended a heavy cable to great trees up stream and warped the boat over in that way. Every device was resorted to. On returning to New York the engineers reported that he "tied down the safety-valve and 'jumped' the obstructions, to the great terror of the whole party."

He finally got to the lake and established his through line. It was a good deal like the old Gibbons line—a boat at each end and a portage between. Then came an enormous rush of passengers, and the means of transportation were increased. Two steamers were placed on the river, the Clayton and Bulwer, and a large one, the Central America, on the lake. On the Atlantic side the Commodore put the Prometheus, which was his first ocean-built steamer, the Webster, the Star-of-the-West, and the Northern Light, and on the Pacific side five others. He started a boat from New York every fortnight, and soon had the bulk of the travel, making large sums and swelling his already immense fortune.

He made more than a million dollars a year in Nicaragua, besides the revenue from other enterprises at the same time. In the will contest, March 15, 1878, Jacob J. Van Pelt, who had known the Commodore for fifty years, said: "I remember when the Commodore went off with his family in the North Star. I asked him if he had everything fixed. He said yes, and added: 'Van, I have got eleven millions invested better than any other eleven millions in the United States. It is worth twenty-five per cent. a year without any risk.'"

In 1853, thinking he deserved a holiday, he sold out his Nicaragua route to the Transit Line, and celebrated his commercial success by going to Europe in the world-renowned North Star, the largest pleasure steam-yacht that had ever been constructed. It was a vessel of two thousand tons, palatial in capacity and equipment. Accompanying him were his wife, and eleven children.*

It was an exhibition to Europe of a notable specimen of republican institutions. The steamer was the largest that had ever been afloat at that time.† It was con-

---

* 1, Phebe Jane, wife of one of her father's steam-ship captains; 2, Ethelinda, wife of D. B. Allen, a retired merchant; 3, William H. ; 4, Emily, wife of W. K. Thorne ; 5, Eliza, Mrs. Osgood ; 6, Sophia, wife of Daniel Torrance, a Montreal merchant ; 7, Marie L., wife of Horace F. Clarke ; 8, Frances, who died at the age of forty ; 9, Maria Elecia, wife of N. La Bau ; 10, the wife of Captain Barker ; 11, George, the youngest.

† The steam-yacht North Star was built expressly for the pleasure excursion to Europe, by Commodore Vanderbilt. It was 260 feet long on the keel, 270 feet on the spar-deck, had a breadth of beam of 38 feet, and was 28 feet 6 inches deep. It was furnished with two lever-beam engines, and had four boilers, each 24 feet long. The main saloon was fitted up with satinwood with just sufficient rose-wood to relieve it. The furniture was of rosewood carved in the style of Louis XV., and upholstered with figured plush velvet, a green ground filled with flowers. The two sofas cost $350 each ; the

structed on American models, by American workmen, in an American ship-yard, and was commanded by the man who was at once the owner, captain, designer, and builder, himself the most remarkable of American products, for he had risen to his position without the aid of ancestry behind him or influential friends about him, and was travelling in an ocean palace, the centre of a flock of children equal to those of patriarchal times. His story, repeated from nation to nation, did much to stir the hopes and hearts of millions of peasants and turn their eyes across the western sea. Everywhere Vanderbilt and the North Star were received with honors. It was difficult to make the people of Europe believe that he was not a titled personage; for in no other

---

four couches $300 each; and the six arm-chairs $50 each. There were ten elegant state-rooms connecting with the saloon, each with a large glass door, the plate being 40 by 64 inches, and costing $100. The berths were furnished with silk lambrequins and lace curtains. Each room was in a different color, as green and gold, crimson and gold, orange, etc. Forward of the grand saloon was a magnificent dining-room. The walls were covered with a preparation of "ligneous marble," which was polished to a degree of mirror-like brightness that marble is incapable of receiving. The panels were of Naples granite, resembling jasper, and the surbase was of yellow Pyrenees marble. The ceiling was white, with a scroll-work of purple, light green, and gold surrounding medallion portraits of Webster, Clay, Washington, Franklin, and others. The china was of ruby and gold finish, and the silverware was the finest that could be had. With the exception of a chaplain and family physician with their wives, the passengers in the North Star were all members of the family of Captain Vanderbilt, twenty-three persons in all. The cost of this excursion was half a million of dollars. The party visited Southampton, London, Stockholm, up the Neva to St. Petersburg, then back to Gibraltar, and on to Naples, Malta, Athens, Constantinople and Alexandria. [For further, see Appendix C.]

way could they account for the magnificence and elegance in which he moved.

In Southampton he was honored with a ceremonious dinner at which two hundred sat down, many of them the best known publicists of England. At Boulogne, Marseilles, and Genoa he was received with deep and wide-spread interest, and saluted by the assembled shipping. At St. Petersburg the Grand Duke Constantine and the Admiral of the Russian Navy visited the ship and obtained permission to have drawings made of her model.

At Constantinople the officers of the Sultan were equally inquisitive, and tendered to the Commodore many compliments, doubtless in view of the existing difficulties with "the Bear of the North," and the need of American sympathy in the preparations being made for that Crimean War which broke out the next year.

At Leghorn, under the dominion of Austria, the North Star was regarded as a spy, and was even believed to be laden with munitions of war for the enemy at the Bosphorus. So it was placed under surveillance, frowned on by the guns of an Austrian man-of-war, and when the visitors walked abroad in Leghorn they were escorted by a military officer for fear of unpleasant accidents, with a crowd of the ununiformed *sbirri* hovering about them.

On the return of the party to New York, the Commodore rounded to in front of his old home at Stapleton, and gave a royal salute to his venerable mother, who lived in the little brown house upon the slope—the mother whose wisdom and frugality had supplied him with $100 to buy his first "periauger." Then he went

W. H. VANDERBILT.

off in a boat and paid her an affectionate visit before
proceeding on his way.   Within three months the old
lady died, expressing in her last words the pride and
pleasure she felt in the love of her rich and successful
son.   [See portrait.]

He now found himself in trouble with the Nicaragua
Transit Company, to which he had sold a controlling
interest in his short route for the transportation of Cali-
fornians.   The men to whom he sold had got rich, and
now refused to pay him according to the terms of the
contract.   To prosecute them under the forms of law
would be an international affair, and would involve great
expense and much time.   So the Commodore wrote them
a note, which for brevity and energy recalls those marvelous epistles of twenty words which Napoleon uttered
when he wrote to the King of Prussia, " The success of
my arms is not doubtful.   Your troops will be beaten."
The steamship general now wrote :

GENTLEMEN : You have undertaken to cheat me.   I won't sue
you, for law is too slow.   I will ruin you.
Yours truly,
CORNELIUS VAN DERBILT.

He kept his word.   He put on another fleet of
steamers, and in two years the opposition line was irretrievably bankrupt.   Vanderbilt remained in the California shipping business nine years more, making money
all the while, and accumulating not less than $10,000,000
in the business.   At this time a remarkable character
appeared on the Central American stage—the filibuster,
Walker.   Vanderbilt refused to transport his men or
munitions.   Needing some money to carry out his revo-

4

lutionary schemes, he seized upon the Vanderbilt franchise, and arbitrarily confiscated it and resold it to creatures of his own. Vanderbilt managed to save his steamers from capture, and as soon as possible he brought them again under the protection of the stars and stripes ; for he had another large venture on his hands which needed attention.

When he returned from Europe he found the Crimean war already broken out. The Cunard line of steamers had been withdrawn for service between England and the Black Sea. Collins was running a weekly line of very good American steamers, but this was only half the service required, and Vanderbilt offered to form a partnership with him and put on two more steamships. Collins declined ; he feared to let the terrible man get a foothold on his property.

"Very well," said the Commodore. He then went to Washington and offered to put on two Atlantic steamers, running once a fortnight, if Congress would pay him for carrying the mail the same that the English steamers had been getting—$16,000 a trip. The Collins line (American) was running, and receiving for the mail $33,000 a trip, and Mr. Collins now visited Vanderbilt to beg him not to bring down the price. "If you will charge $33,000," said Collins, "I will back your bill with my whole Congressional influence, and we can pass it."

"No," said the inexorable Commodore ; "my motive is a patriotic one. If an Englishman can carry the mails for $16,000, I can. I won't admit that a Britisher can beat us."

"It is not business, Commodore," said the man of

subsidy, "to take $16,000 when you can get twice that. I can't make it pay as it is."

"Then you are probably in a business that you don't understand," persisted the Commodore; "let me try it."

In response to Collins's urgency he substituted another proposition, which he called a "compromise," to carry the mails for $19,750 a round trip, and agree that he should not be paid anything if he failed to beat the Collins steamers *every trip*.

But he could not get even this measure through Congress. The Collins subsidy influence was too strong. Yet he was not embittered, and when the Arctic was lost he offered his rival the North Star for nothing, till he could replace her. Then he calmly went to work, built three Atlantic steamers, finer and faster than any in the world, and organized a new line from New York to Havre. These vessels were the Ariel, the Harvest Queen, and the never-to-be-forgotten Vanderbilt; and their accommodations were so palatial, and their speed so great, that they became the favorites of travellers.

The ocean races of this time were most exciting, and attracted world-wide attention. The racers of the Collins' line were the Arabia and Persia, and those of the Havre line the Vanderbilt and the Ariel. The Commodore's steamers made the quickest time nine trips out of ten.

Then he proclaimed his grand *coup*. He offered to carry the foreign mails for nothing. This struck terror to the heart of Collins. President Pierce vetoed his subsidy, and the "Collins Line" disappeared from the ocean.

Vanderbilt did not seize upon the Atlantic carrying

trade as it was expected he would do when he got such a firm hold of it. He was not a man of sentiment or of chimeras. There was nothing Quixotic about him. He carefully examined the business, and concluded that it "wouldn't pay to push it." So he sold some of his vessels, transferred some to other lines of travel, and gradually began to withdraw his money from shipping, where it must always suffer from European competition, and invest it in railroads which were protected from the rivalry of half-paid Italians and Scandinavians. When the Rebellion broke upon the country, a good many of his investments had already been transferred from the water to the land, so that his prosperity suffered no shock.*

He was now an old man; but his usefulness was not yet over. When the rebel ram, Merrimac, burst out of its hiding-place, and made such fearful havoc among

---

* In 1818 Mr. Vanderbilt attended to the building of the steamer Bellona, of which he was afterward Captain. He afterward built many other steamships, as follows: In 1820, the Caroline; 1821, the Fanny; 1822, the Thistle and Emerald; 1824, the Swan; 1826, the Citizen; 1827–28, the Cinderella, Bolivar, Clifton, Clayton, Union, Champion, New Champion, Nimrod, Hunchback, Livingston, Director, Cleopatra, Westchester, Sound Champion, Linnaes, North Carolina, Governor Dudley, Vanderbilt, and Gibraltar, the four last for the regular mail line between Washington and Charleston. Then followed the Gladiator, Kill von Kull, Central America, Sylph, Westfield, Augusta, Wilmington, Red Jacket, Traveller, Huguenot, Graysia, Hannah Burt, Eastern, C. Vanderbilt, and Commodore, the last two forming the great Boston line, via Stonington. He next placed on the route across the Isthmus eight steamships, and the five vessels that ran between Havana and Matanzas. He also built the Prometheus, Daniel Webster, Star of the West, Northern Light, and North Star. At this time he gave employment to more men than any other one man in the country.

our frigates in Hampton Roads, great was the consternation in Washington. Ericsson's little Monitor, arriving at Fortress Monroe in the nick of time, had driven the monster into his cave, but it was feared that he would emerge again presently and continue the devastation.

Thurlow Weed was at the Capital at the time, and he telegraphed to Commodore Vanderbilt, with whom he had already been associated in the work of sending soldiers to the front. The Commodore went at once. On his arrival, he was taken into the presence of the President, whom he found in great distress and alarm. His attention was called to the condition of affairs at Fortress Monroe, and Mr. Lincoln asked:

"How much will you take to stop that rebel ram and keep it away?"

"No money will hire me to do it," said the visitor. "I will not make money out of the sorrows of my country."

The President was perplexed and silent, but the Commodore presently said: "I have a ship that I believe will take care of that devil. If you will man it I will take the command, and go down there and do the business up myself. I ask only that I may be free from the bossing of the Navy Department."

Instant relief was felt and expressed. He returned to New York on the first train, and in thirty-six hours he was steaming past Fortress Monroe into the mouth of the James River, and the admiral in charge looked inquiringly and admiringly at the steamer whose shadow loomed over the water like a great cloud. The Commodore was then sixty-seven years old, and the ship was his sturdy namesake, the Vanderbilt. She was the pride of his heart, the concentrated result of all his matured knowledge of ship-building.

He showed his credentials. The officer in charge asked him what he proposed to do if the Merrimac should reappear. "Run her down," he said, "as a hound runs down a wolf; strike her amidships and sink her."

"How can I help you?"

"Only by keeping out of the way when I am hunting the cutter."

The Merrimac was seen no more. She kept her hiding-place. After the danger was over, the Commodore returned home, and was superseded by a naval officer. He wrote and offered the vessel to the government till the war should be over, and the offer was gladly accepted. When the Alabama commenced her ravages, the Vanderbilt, now equipped as a war-vessel, went after her and hunted her for twelve months.

At the close of the war, during which Vanderbilt had made great contributions, and had given the life of his favorite son, the government, instead of returning the borrowed vessel to her owner, had her mustered into the United States Navy, and formally returned thanks for the present!

The following are the resolutions of Congress:

"*Whereas*, Cornelius Vanderbilt, of New York, did, during the spring of 1862, make a free gift to his imperilled country of his new and stanch steamship Vanderbilt, of five thousand tons burden, built by him, with the greatest care, of the best material, at a cost of $800,000, which steamship has ever since been actively employed in the service of the republic against rebel devastations of her commerce, and

" *Whereas*, the said Cornelius Vanderbilt has in no manner sought any requital of this magnificent gift or any official recognition thereof ; therefore

" RESOLVED, *By the Senate and House of Representatives of the United States of America in Congress assembled*, That the thanks of Congress be presented to Cornelius Vanderbilt for his unique manifestation of a fervid and large-souled patriotism.

" RESOLVED, That the President of the United States be requested to cause a gold medal to be struck which shall fitly embody an attestation of the nation's gratitude for this gift, which medal shall be forwarded to Cornelius Vanderbilt ; and a copy of it shall be made and deposited for preservation in the Library of Congress."

An " appropriate " medal was struck of solid gold, weighing six ounces, and measuring three inches across. On the reverse is the likeness of the donor, or, rather, of the former owner of the vessel, and the legend " A grateful country to her generous son," and on the obverse, in *bas relief*, the figure of Columbia with Neptune laying his trident at her feet, and the motto, " *Bis dat qui tempori dat* " (he gives best who gives quickly), and in the back-ground a correct outline of the steamer Vanderbilt.

The Congressional Committee authorized to present him with the resolutions and the twenty-five-dollar medal had rather a stormy time of it. He rehearsed the particulars of the theft, and asked them if that was the way a great and noble nation ought to conduct itself. Some of them declared that they had misunderstood, and wanted to return the vessel. " No! devil take your impudence ! " shouted the Commodore, " keep her. I don't care about a little thing like that ! "

Commodore Vanderbilt was now one of the richest

men in New York. Nearly a hundred vessels answered
to his call. His keels fretted every sea. He never
speculated, but always bought property to improve it.
He was not content unless everything that he owned
prospered. The magnates of Wall Street began to look
at his great wealth with an inquiring eye, for when the
Rebellion broke out he was worth not less than twenty
millions of dollars.

CHAPTER VII.

TWENTY YEARS A FARMER.

William at New Dorp, Staten Island—The Farm—Energy and Economy—The Seat on the Fence—A Mortgage and Consequent Wrath—"Four Dollars a Load"—A Spurt on the Road—A New House—The Farm Pays.

WHEN, in 1842, William H. Vanderbilt went to his farm on the southeast shore of Staten Island, at the foot of the lane leading from the New Dorp church to the beach, he was no better off in this world's goods than his farming neighbors. Indeed, he was poorer than most of them. The house to which he took his young wife, and in which he lived till 1864, was a small, square, plain, two-story structure facing the sea, with a lean-to at one end for a kitchen. All told, it could hardly have contained more than five rooms—about as many as that in which, two generations before, his grandfather had reared his family at Stapleton, five miles north across the fields.

The little farm was a part of the neglected barrens of Staten Island, and needed abundant fertilizing and careful tillage to render it fruitful. Fortunately, it proved tolerably easy to cultivate. It was almost as level as a house-floor, without a stone or stump, and the soil a thin sandy loam. Then, as now, there were but few trees on the place, and these mostly clustered about the front of

the house, or fringed the lane leading up to the road.
Then, as now, all of these shore farms had a bit of
woodland back on the hills, sufficient to furnish fence-
rails and fuel for the winter's fires.

From the first, Mr. Vanderbilt determined to make a
success of farming. He was poor, but he meant to be
better off. The house was small, but he resolved that
it should be larger. The land was poor, but he planned
how to enrich it and make it profitable. He was un-
known and unnoticed, but he meant by-and-by to be on
a social and financial equality with his neighbors.

His method was novel in that region. He never
worked much with his own hands, following the plow
or hoeing corn, but he took care that those whom he
employed did a good day's work, and he was always
master of the situation. He was what is called "a gentleman farmer;" but he gave his undivided attention to
the business in hand, and got as much as it was possible
to get out of his narrow acres.

One of his old farm-hands says : "He was a hard master to work for. He would hire fresh hands in the
spring or during haying 'on trial,' and naturally they
would take care to produce a good impression with their
first day's work. At night Mr. Vanderbilt would count
the number of rows of corn they had hoed, or the
number of bales of hay they had pressed, and then require them to do the same amount of work every day."
He would tolerate no shirk on the place; and if a man
did not come up to his requirements, he was paid off
and discharged.

"Billy," said the Commodore, visiting him one day,
"I think you work your men too hard."

"They are willing to work hard if I have the money to pay them," was the reply, and the old millionaire was no doubt secretly pleased.

"He was a downright square man," says one who worked for him for twenty years, "sociable, reliable, honest, prompt to pay, quick to recognize merit. I don't want any better boss."

He looked sharply after his men, and allowed none to idle. His favorite occupation was to sit upon the top rail of the fence surrounding the field, and whittle a stick or read a newspaper while watching the men. All the neighbors laughed at this method of tilling the earth, and even the workmen had their quiet fun over it. One of these, still living, tells a story to the young farmer's disadvantage. He was directed one afternoon to repair the fence where they were planting corn, and he adjusted the top rails with their sharp edges up. Mr. Vanderbilt came out in the morning as the men went to work, and walked all round the field looking for a comfortable place to sit.

"How's this?" he shouted to the fence-builder. "What did you put all the rails on this way for—sharp edge up?"

"Because," answered the man, as his fellows began to titter, "so's folks won't be coming along and sitting on 'em and wearing 'em out."

He was already fond of horses, and at times he rode behind the mowing-machine; and every afternoon about four o'clock he went for a drive along the smooth roads of Staten Island. Society, finance, the great city, the world beyond the bay, seemed to have no attractions for him. He was essentially a domestic man, lived largely in the midst of his family, and spent all his evenings at home. On Sundays he took his wife and his growing children behind him, and had a spin up the island to the Episcopal church at Clifton, passing the little Moravian church of his ancestors on the way. The farming experiment was a success. He had in five years transformed the wastes of his little farm into a blooming garden. The seventy acres returned a fair income, and enabled him to support his family well, and to keep the best horses on the island. But he was ambitious to enlarge the field of his operations, and through a friend he applied to his millionaire father for a loan of $5,000.

"No!" was the answer. "It is just as I expected. He is a lazy spendthrift, and will never amount to anything."

William then borrowed $6,000 of a neighbor, gave a mortgage on his farm for it, and bought enough of the adjoining land to give him three hundred and fifty acres. He also enlarged his house. The neighbor of whom he borrowed the money was more talkative than discreet. In the grocery down at the village he took the large note from his pocket and exhibited it, casually remarking: "Some folks says that Cornele Vanderbilt is wuth two million dollars or more, and there's folks that believes it. Well, mebby he is; but you can't tell how much them New Yorkers is wuth—nor how little neither."

The old man heard of the speech, and the next Sunday he drove down to New Dorp and asked his agricultural son to go out riding with him. The invitation was accepted, and a conversation ensued, which was told of afterward by the unhappy son.

"Billy, have you borrowed money of that —— old fool?"

"Yes, father; I couldn't help it."

"You know what I think of such things?"

"Yes, father; but —— "

"Bill, you don't amount to a row of pins! You won't never be able to do anything but bring disgrace upon yourself, and your family, and everybody connected with you. There's nothing *to* you, and I've made up my mind to have nothing more to do with you!"

When he had a chance to speak the young farmer remarked that he had done nothing to be ashamed of; that the mortgage was a business operation, and he could and should pay it off when due; that he had always tried to please his father, and should need no money from him at any time.

The next morning the Commodore sent him a check for the $6,000, with the remark that he was "lending a little on real estate himself just now," and orders to his son to pay off the mortgage before he slept.

In farming William H. Vanderbilt gave his attention chiefly to hay, corn, potatoes, and oats. Sometimes he raised annually some 400 tons of timothy, 1,500 barrels of potatoes, 1,000 bushels of corn, and 10 acres of oats. Some years he had a good-sized patch of cabbages, the product of which he sold in Clifton. He was not a "truck-farmer," growing only enough vegetables for his own use, and keeping enough cows to supply his family wants.

At first he took his hay and corn up to New York on schooners, and sold them in open market; but when his father became interested in the horse-railway he had a sure market, at top prices, for all he could raise. During the war he made money rapidly, selling all of his hay to the Government at Camp Scott, on the island, where Sickles's Brigade was formed, and disposing of his potatoes at the rate of $6 a barrel.

In a bargain made about this time he got ahead of his father and turned toward himself, temporarily at least, some of that gentleman's admiration. His fertilizing material he obtained from the city, and one day he got some from the Fourth Avenue stables and carried it down on a scow. The next day he saw his father and asked him how much he would charge for ten loads.

"What'll you give?" asked the Commodore.

"It's worth $4 a load to me," said the farmer.

"Good enough, I'll let you have it for that," answered the railroad man, having a very decided impression that the price named was at least twice as much as the stuff was worth.

Next day he found his rustic son with another scow just loaded for home.

"How many loads have you got on that scow, Billy?" asked the Commodore, in excellent humor.

"How many?" repeated the son, feigning surprise, "one, of course."

"One! why there's at least thirty!" the old gentleman exclaimed, inspecting it curiously.

"No, father, I never put but one load on a scow—one scow-load! Cast off the lines, Pat!"

The senior Vanderbilt made no reply. He would let it go so, and Bill should have the rest of it. He was struck dumb with a mixture of chagrin and gratification. The workman who narrates the incident adds: "The Commodore wa'n't no gret hand to stan' around, and I never see him stan' still so long before as he stood that afternoon on the dock, looking at that scow goin' across the harbor." He was probably sizing up "Billy" anew, and wondering whether he might not make a railroad man after all.

At one time Mr. Vanderbilt was deeply interested in a gentleman's club, of which he was made president, and which had a trotting-course on his farm, near the beach. None but members were admitted, and these consisted of the well-to-do farmers of the island. Vanderbilt's horses were considered the best.

He had conformed to his father's taste in raising choice stock and good horses. He became very fond of horse-flesh, and had a pair that he felt sure nothing on the island could pass. He was not in the habit of taking anybody's dust. One day when he was out on the road exercising his favorite span, and passing everything upon the way, he suddenly became half conscious of rolling wheels behind him. The half consciousness of rolling wheels soon became full consciousness of approaching wheels. "Aha!" he said to himself, "somebody around here has got a new team. I'll show them!" And he drew tighter those leathern conductors which convey the purpose of a driver to an intelligent and spirited horse, and as his speed increased he resumed the conversation with his companion. In a minute he felt that the wheels were gaining on him, and he uttered to his team that sound of encouragement which the horse knows so well, " t—ck! t—ck!" following it with a "G'-long!" The buggy spun over the smooth road, and William complacently thought that the mysterious wheels had vanished. Not so. Their solid thump behind him grew painfully distinct, and he drew from the socket the whip and gave a couple of smart cuts to those astonished horses that had not been struck before in a year; and he remarked to his guest, "They are not feeling very well to-day." No use; the spinning vehicle buzzed nearer and nearer, the noses of the mysterious steeds were opposite his seat. He half turned and glanced at them out of a corner of his eye, then hauled up and exclaimed, "Why, father! It's you, is it? I wondered who on earth it could be!"

"Yes, it's me, Billy. Them's good horses of yours, but you must give 'em some more oats before you go out racing!"

Mr. Vanderbilt took no part in politics or public affairs, and is not known ever to have made a speech in his life. In 1855 he reconstructed the old farm-house of five rooms, and made large additions, more than doubling it in size; the whole forming a country villa in the Italian style, with tower, piazzas, bay-window, etc. He used to regard it as the finest house in the country, and expected and hoped to end his days there. Within these walls all of his children were born, and there he spent the happiest days of his life.

He was no longer a poor farmer. He had proved a success. Years before he was called by his father to engage in those vast affairs which finally crushed the life out of him, he had become an independent man—a farmer of ample means and plenty of money for all his wants, who afforded himself the luxury of a coachman, fine horses, and various sorts of equipages. Now and

[From Currier & Ives.]

W. H. VANDERBILT DRIVING MAUD S. AND ALDINE.

then a large entertainment was given at the farm-
house, with a city caterer; trees were hung full of Chi-
nese lanterns, and guests were present from all parts of
the island.

When he finally abandoned the farm to go to New
York, it was yielding him an income of $12,000 a year,
or $1,000 a month, or $34 a day, or $1.42 an hour
(in the impressive method of calculating revenues which
has of late come so much in vogue), contrary to the pre-
dictions and expectations of the exacting and skeptical
millionaire.

CHAPTER VIII.

WILLIAM'S APPRENTICESHIP.

The Staten Island Railroad—Its Ruin and Regeneration—Death of Captain George—An Obedient Son—New Schemes.

Four or five years before the war an event occurred having an important bearing on this history. Largely through the efforts of William H. Vanderbilt the Staten Island Railroad, thirteen miles long, was built, skirting the eastern shore of the island from Vanderbilt's Landing. It was a great public convenience, and was indispensable to the development of the island, but shortly it was well-nigh wrecked by the gross mismanagement of its officers and directors. It was overwhelmed with debts and embarrassments; and, as Mr. Vanderbilt was one of the most prominent of its projectors and stockholders, and his father was a large owner, it was unanimously decided to make him receiver of the bankrupt road. It is reported and understood that the proposition came from his father, who still had a lingering curiosity to know whether there was "anything in Billy." Without hesitation the farmer accepted the trust. He had had no experience as a railroad manager, but he possessed hard sense and business capacity, and there was general confidence in him.

He went at the work with much energy. He reduced expenses at once; practised rigid economy; stopped all leaks; discovered new sources of patronage; connected the road with New York by an independent line of ferry-boats, and began to pay off the claims. The little road was without money, without credit, without materials, without organization; but he introduced system, and in two years of the hardest times he had paid off the last dollar of indebtedness, and put the company on a secure and permanent financial basis. Then, by acclamation, he was made President of the road and continued successfully to administer its affairs.* It may well be believed, as is alleged, that his father looked on with astonishment. Chagrin may even have been mixed with his surprise, and a suspicion that he might have made an erroneous estimate of the qualities of his son. It was probably at this time that he began slowly to revise his old conclusions. "Is that the fool of the family?" he said to himself. "Or have I made a mistake?"

Another thing happened which seriously affected the Commodore. His youngest son, the West Point cadet, George, in whose high future he had great hopes, went to the war, rose to the rank of captain, and broke down from exposure in the field in front of Corinth. He had been one of the most athletic young men that ever graduated from our military college; he was tall, powerful, and on his twenty-second birthday lifted a dead weight of nine hundred pounds. But the hardships of the war were too much for the young captain, and he was now sent to Europe to save his imperiled life. He

* When he took hold of the road it was worth less than nothing, and in five years its stock sold at $175 a share.

lingered in the Riviera, but got worse rather than better. His father, now thoroughly alarmed, sent William to Europe to take care of him. The two brothers traveled together a year, to no good end, and the young soldier died at Paris.

Already there were numerous evidences that William H. would win his obdurate father's confidence at last. After his railroad Receivership, they saw more of each other, and the son was treated with somewhat less reserve. He was prudent and obedient, as he had always been. He stooped to conquer. From his boyhood he had given instant and willing submission to the despotic will of his father, and had made boundless sacrifices to please him. Most men would have burst defiantly away from the repressive control and imperious requirements; but he doubtless thought that for the chance of becoming heir to $100,000,000 he could afford to remain long in the passive attitude of a distrusted prince.

It was known to the Commodore's business associates at the office, that the way to please him was to agree with him. When his favorite watch was criticised by some visitor as being "too fast," the railroad-king is reported to have exclaimed, "Guess not; how is yours, R——?" calling to a clerk in the next room. "Same as yours, Commodore!" replied the sapient youth.

William H. was almost equally acquiescent. He tried in every possible way to please his father. It is related that when the famous trip to Europe was made in the North Star, the father and son were walking the deck one day, both smoking energetically, as usual.

"I wish you wouldn't smoke, Billy; it's a bad habit," said the father; "I'll give you $10,000 to stop it."

"Why, I didn't know as you objected to it, father," said the man of thirty. "You needn't hire me to give it up. Your wish is enough. I will never smoke again." And off the blue Canaries he flung his last cigar into the sea. But his father smoked till he died. Such a son was sure to make his way at last, through even an iron-plated distrust.

The Commodore was much afflicted by the death of George, and, though the proud man probably did not confess it to himself, his heart turned thenceforth more warmly toward the successful farmer of Staten Island.

About this time Harlem Railroad stood at three cents on a dollar, and there was no sale. Charles W. Sandford, its counsel, viewing with alarm its deplorable condition, sought an interview with the Commodore for the purpose of urging him to become a director, and to give the property the benefit of his great executive ability. Vanderbilt shook his head, and was with difficulty persuaded to embark in the enterprise. Finally, however, he consented to take a little interest if Daniel Drew would go in with him. "Uncle Dan'l" consented. They invested.

Seeing that more money would thereafter be made on the land than on the sea, the Commodore had sold all his ships to Allen & Garrison for three million dollars in cash, and had put it into railroad stock. He was now nearly seventy, the Psalmist's allotted age, and everybody said it was high time for him to retire, and live a quiet life during the evening of his days. He had accumulated, men said, not less than twenty millions of dollars. It was enough. He ought not to risk it in speculations, and it was not likely he would do such a mad thing. Some laughed and shook their heads, and said, " Like other old men, the Commodore fancies that he is as young as ever, and it would be just like him to rush into the railroad business, which he knows nothing about, merely because he has succeeded in steamboating, which was his trade ! "

There was sense in what was said. It was fair and reasonable to assume that a man who had proved himself so superior to all others in one important sphere of activity, and had practised it with rare success for more than half a century, could not, when past the allotted age of man, learn the methods and acquire all the difficult details of an entirely new business. But this was not an ordinary man, and he could not be judged by ordinary rules. As a matter of fact, this giant of achievement had just entered upon the most brilliant period of his life, and he doubled his wealth four times during the next fifteen years.

CHAPTER IX.

THE HARLEM CORNER.

THE Commodore was a novice in the railroad realm,
but he took a little turn in Wall Street in his sixty-ninth
year.* He went to buying stock in the Harlem Road.
He did not buy it to speculate by selling it again, but he
bought it to hold it.

Indeed, he was not a speculator. None of the Vanderbilts have ever been speculators in the Wall Street
sense, and neither the Commodore nor his son was a
member of the Stock Exchange, where gamblers and adventurers howl at each other and wildly play battledore
and shuttlecock with the table of values. The Commodore did not believe in buying or selling invisible
things. And he did not believe in selling the same
thing that he bought. He bought opportunities, and
sold achievements. He bought nest-eggs, and sold

---

* It is related of the Commodore that, being solicited to subscribe
to start the Harlem Road, in 1832, he abruptly declined, explaining :
" I'm a steamboat-man, a competitor of these steam contrivances that
you tell us will run on dry land. Go ahead. I wish you well ; but
I never shall have anything to do with 'em ! "

chickens. He bought roads that were thriftless and in
disorder, and he sold them when they had become
models of order and thrift ; or, oftener, he did not sell
them at all, because he could make them pay more than
anybody else could. During a stress of affairs once, a
reporter called on him at his office, No. 5 Bowling Green,
and a brief talk was had, as follows :

" Good morning, young man."

" What do you say about the panic, Commodore ? "

" I don't say anything about it."

" What do you think about it, then ? "

" I don't think about it at all."

" What would you say about it if you thought about
it, Commodore ? "

" How can I tell ? " said the interrogated magnate,
laughing. " See here, young man, you don't mean to
go away till I say something. Very well ; I'll say something. Don't you never buy anything you don't want,
nor sell anything you hain't got ! "

This was his settled principle. He skinned the wolves,
but not the " lambs." He played a strong game, but it
was not the game of the juggler. So now he went into
Harlem stock, in the winter of '62–'63, from an honest
conviction that it was a good thing to buy and own. This
was the first railroad built running out of New York
City in any direction, and during its earlier years it
went only up into Westchester County and stopped.
Even thus it was the wonder of that time. But it had
fallen into the hands of the incompetent and the dis-
honest ; it had been badly managed and looted ; its
credit was gone ; its roadbed was shaky ; and its stock,
which went at $3 a share in 1857, and was worth only

$6 a share in 1859, and $8 or $9 in 1860, sold not much higher when he began to buy heavily.

When he had advanced a considerable sum of money to the road, the stock doubled in value under the magic of his name, and before spring grass was green it sold at 30. This was more than it was worth, the "knowing ones" said; and when he went on buying right and left, they exchanged sympathetic nods and said, " His second childhood ! This dabbling in railroads springs from the morbid, irrepressible activity of old age, and will end in his ruin." The world had accepted him as the greatest steamboat manager that ever lived, and it could not comprehend that he was equally great at everything.

Along toward April a rumor was in the air that the Commodore had got some new franchise, or advantage, but nobody seemed to know exactly what it was. Stock crept up to 50. Suddenly, on the evening of April 21st, the Common Council of the City of New York passed an ordinance authorizing him to build a street railroad all the way down Broadway to the Battery ; and next day, when the brokers heard of it, up went Harlem to 75 at one jump, then crept along to par. The Commodore and his friends felt rich, and he was elected President of the road on May 19th ; but the game was not yet finished.

Late in June a curious phenomenon was noticed by close observers : the very Aldermen who had been so generous with their franchises began to sell Harlem short—that is, sell it for future delivery at a price lower than the price then prevailing. These men had made up their minds that they could all get rich by selling the

4

stock short, and then repealing the ordinance they had just passed giving the street-railroad franchise to the Commodore. They let their confidential friends into the secret, and they gave their confidential friends the "point," till there were a thousand men throwing Harlem upon the market.

To the uninitiated it may be well to explain this familiar trick of stock-gamblers: When stock in Harlem was selling at 100, they could get plenty of people to agree to take it in a month at 90; then they could repeal the ordinance that had sent it up, and, logically, it ought to drop to 50 or 60. By buying at these prices and delivering at 90, they could make the difference, $30 or $40 a share. This is what they attempted to do.

The Commodore heard of the perfidy, but he calmly went on buying, and got others to buy for him. He took all the "shorts" which Drew and the other "bears" had to offer; and, as the total amount of the stock was not large (one hundred and ten thousand shares), the greedy operators had, before they knew it, sold more than existed. Then the Council rescinded the ordinance, and Judge Brady simultaneously, in the Court of Common Pleas, enjoined the laying of rails in Broadway. Everything looked like disaster for Vanderbilt. The merry brokers kept selling short. The stock dropped to 72, rebounded, dropped, and rose and fell again with febrile symptoms.

At this juncture those who had sold short wanted to deliver, and went into the market to buy "cheap." Up went Harlem to 100, 115, 120, 130, 140, 150, 170! There was a panic and a howl of dismay. The shorts could not be covered, because the Commodore held all of the stock. Seeing that the assault had been made on him personally, he was inexorable. He and his partners in the bull movement took a million of dollars from the Council that week, and other millions from others, and compelled them to make their last settlements at $179 a share! The Common Council was ruined.

Stock soon settled again toward the former rate, Vanderbilt selling meantime and making a good deal of money. He strengthened his hold of the property by associating his son William H. with him as vice-president. The president did not often feel the need of consulting the vice-president as to projected ventures, but he left to him the management of details and the execution of the schemes he planned. William H. immediately put in practice here the same method which he had used with such brilliant results in the resurrection of the dead little road on Staten Island. It was found to be equally adapted to large roads and large results. They repaired the track, improved the speed, and managed the road as a great property ought to be managed to make money decently. Before long traffic and travel increased, and it became obvious that this was a good property to own. Everything combined to favor the Vanderbilt experiment; even the presence of desolating war increased the revenues.

Commodore Vanderbilt's methods in railroad management may be briefly summarized: 1, buy your railroad; 2, stop the stealing that went on under the other man; 3, improve it in every practicable way within a reasonable expenditure; 4, consolidate it with any other road that can be run with it economically; 5, water its stock; 6, make it pay a large dividend.

Having Harlem well in hand, in the fall of 1863 the
Commodore began to buy Hudson River Railroad stock.
It had been going at 25. The road had never paid, and
was a foot-ball in the street. He bought everything
in the open market without concealment. He did not
want to speculate; he wanted to make the road make
money. Nobody understood him. He was in his seven-
tieth year, but his faculties were very alert, and he
was physically almost as lively as when he proudly
stood in his own "periauger." Before many months he
had secured control of the road. He saw that the two
lines were rivals without any good result to either their
owners or the public, and he now made up his mind to
procure their consolidation.

With this purpose he caused a bill to be introduced
into the Legislature at Albany authorizing that act. It
was an enormous project, and its value was not under-
estimated by members of the Senate and Assembly.
The owners of the Central and directors of the Erie
fought him by every device, but the Commodore went
up and engineered his own bill with results that promised high success. He secured the pledge of a majority
of the members that they would pass the measure, and
of the governor that he would sign it. Stock immediately leaped up again to 75, and then to 100, 130, 150,
the Commodore buying all he could at reasonable prices.

After he left Albany, in February, 1864, treachery began to show itself among the members who had pledged
themselves to him. They concluded, as the Aldermen
had done a year before, that they could make a good
deal more money by selling Harlem for future delivery,
and then defeating the bill, than they could by passing

it. The gentlemen who had charge of the matter reported their perfidy to the Commodore, who, in anticipation of success, had been heavily buying stock. He was enraged at their trickery, but he went on buying as usual. They carried out their new programme—they defeated the bill. From 150 stock fell off fifty-nine points, and there it stuck, refusing to go below 90. A damage of millions had been inflicted on Vanderbilt and his friends. If the gamblers had been satisfied to deliver the stock then, they would have made a good deal of money. But this was not at all what they had looked for and bargained for. They expected the stock to go down to 50, giving them a clear profit of four or five million dollars. And this was worth waiting for. So they waited.

At this juncture the Commodore sent for John Tobin, who had formerly been a gate-keeper of the first ferry-house on Staten Island, but who was now worth two or three million dollars, a part of which was made in the Harlem corner with the Commodore during the previous summer. He, too, had been buying heavily of the stock, paying above par for a good deal of it. They talked the matter over.

"They stuck you, too, John. How do you feel about it?" asked the president of Harlem.

Tobin said he had held on to his stock; so he should meet no actual loss, unless he sold.

"Shall we let 'em bleed us?" continued the Commodore. "John, don't them fellows need dressing down?"

Tobin agreed that they did.

"Let's teach 'em never to go back on their word

again as long as they draw breath. Let's try the Harlem corner."

Tobin acquiesced, and said he could spare a million dollars for it, and the senior partner in this plot of retribution agreed to put in as much more as was needed. To buy at par all the rest of the stock that was out of their hands would require four or five millions of dollars. They began to buy secretly but rapidly.

Meantime, the treacherous members of the Legislature, having what they considered "a sure thing," not only sold Harlem short for all they were worth, but confidentially let their friends in, so that in a month millions of dollars' worth had been sold to be delivered during the summer at various prices below par, the coalition supposing and alleging to each other that in two months Harlem could "be bought for a song."

They were surprised that their treachery did not bring the president of Harlem to Albany to remonstrate with them. No; he stayed at home and bought stock. The bill for consolidation had been defeated, and the conspirators, rich in anticipation, waited, expecting to see Harlem drop to "where it ought to." To their astonishment it stood firm; and when they went into the market to buy for delivery, there was none to be had. They were caught as the Aldermen had been. Great were the chagrin, alarm, and distress of the too-cunning law-makers who had set the trap. They were at once compelled to buy at whatever price the holders chose to exact in order to deliver on "call." The Vanderbilt pool had bought twenty-seven thousand more shares, including contracts, than the entire stock of the road.

"Put it up to 1,000!" exclaimed the remorseless Commodore, "this panel-game is being tried too often!" It would have been easy to put up the stock to 1,000; but his allies, John Tobin and Leonard Jerome, urged prudence, for, as Jerome declared, "it would break every house on the street." The next day contracts for fifteen thousand shares matured, and the holders let it go at 285! Vanderbilt and his chief partner gained millions each. Many of the "bears" were absolutely ruined. There are men who were rich when they went into that "speculation," who have not yet recovered from the disaster, and never will. The Commodore, in telling the story used to say, "We busted the whole Legislature, and scores of the honorable members had to go home without paying their board-bills!" Drew was among the heaviest losers, but he pleaded that he did not understand what he was doing, and by a long suit forced a compromise, paying $1,000,000.

By this time a tacit understanding seems to have crept around among the frisky "boys" of Wall Street that the old man of three score and ten could take care of himself, and stood in no pressing need of their sympathy or protection.

An English writer in *Fraser's Magazine* said of Drew and Vanderbilt: "Between the two preference is decidedly to be given to Mr. Vanderbilt, who must be acknowledged to have his good traits, and to be in many respects superior to professional speculators, among whom he assumes the royal dignity and moral tone of a Gætulian lion among the hyenas and jackals of the desert."

Touching on the same comparison, Charles Francis

Adams said, in the *North American Review*, in one of that remarkable series of articles that began after the periodical had felt the strong touch of Thorndike Rice: "Vanderbilt must be allowed to be far the superior man. Drew is astute and full of resources, and at times a dangerous opponent; but Vanderbilt takes larger and more comprehensive views, and his mind has a vigorous grasp which that of Drew seems to want. In a wider field, the one might have made himself a great and successful despot, but the other would hardly have aspired to be more than the head of the jobbing department of some corrupt government. While Drew has sought only to carry to perfection the old system of pirating successfully from the confidential position of director, neither knowing anything nor caring anything for the railroad system except in its connection with the movements of the Stock Exchange, Vanderbilt has seen the full magnitude of the system, and through it has sought to make himself a dictator in modern civilization, moving forward with a sort of pitiless energy which has seemed to have in it an element of fatality."

A rigid system of reform meantime had been inaugurated and enforced in the Harlem road, under the immediate eye of William H. Vanderbilt. He had dismissed incompetent men; got rid of supernumeraries; completed the double-track; built new stations; increased the rolling-stock; checked extravagance and looked after small economies whose aggregate was large. Before anybody suspected it, the road was a paying investment.

Delighted and even convinced by this result, the Commodore placed his son by his side as vice-president of the Hudson River road, and to that they strenuously

CORNELIUS VANDERBILT.

applied the same remedies. " I tell Billy," he was fond
of saying, "that if these railroads can be weeded out
and cleaned up, and made ship-shape, they'll both pay
dividends." The old man was gifted with prophetic
vision. In a few months it was earning a net profit.
This was partly the result of the great prosperity which
overflowed the whole country at the close of the war ;
but a cause quite as potent as this was the thorough
renovation which the road received from its new owner.

The Commodore did not at once renew the attempt
to consolidate his two roads, but he plainly saw how he
was hampered and embarrassed by a short line, and how
necessary it was to have a trunk line to the lakes under
one management. He began to buy stock in the New
York Central; in fact he put into it two of the millions
he had made in the "Harlem pool."

In 1864 the Central was controlled by Dean Richmond and Peter Cagger, the remains of the old Albany
Regency. They looked with jealousy and apprehension on the appearance of several Vanderbilt directors
in their board, for they felt the approaching shadow of
the Commodore. In order to keep him away, they got
up a quarrel with him. Daniel Drew had control of the
Hudson River steamboats, and with him the Central
managers made a league, offensive and defensive, against
the ogre from the South who coveted the line in the
Mohawk Valley, and was the dreaded rival of the boats.
During the winter, when the boats were absent, armed
neutrality prevailed, for the roads were equally dependent on each other for an outlet ; but when the ice broke
up in the spring, the Central resumed its habit of cutting the acquaintance of the railroads and shipping its

4*

passengers and freight, as far as possible, *via* the river.
It sold through tickets by way of the river and made
connection with the boats, arranging as often as possible
to arrive at Albany after the last Hudson River train
had gone.

The Commodore endured being thus discriminated
against for one winter. He remonstrated, but his remonstrances were in vain. He proposed different forms
of compromise, but his overtures were declined. He
waited till the Hudson River froze up solid and the
boats were congealed at their wharves, then he sent out
the stern mandate, "Take no more freight from the
New York Central!"   .

It was a silent order, addressed to his officers only,
and he left them to execute it in their own way. The
next train that went north did not connect with the
Central at all, did not even cross the river, but stopped
half a mile east of the bridge that leads into Albany.
The passengers—some of them members of the State
Government protested and supplicated, but to no purpose. The train stopped there for the night; the fires
were banked; and the passengers had to walk the rest
of the way to the city, or get vehicles as they could.
No more trains went to Albany, and the perishable
freight hither-bound probably suffered.

Great was the excitement. No more through freight
came over the Central. Its stock went down fifteen per
cent. at a blow. The stock of the Hudson River Railroad kept mysteriously rising.

When the Legislature convened, it was felt to be
proper to "investigate" the arbitrary conduct of the
Commodore in refusing to come all the way to Albany,

and, if necessary, to do something to him in defence of the dignity of the State.

A committee summoned him to testify. He went. They asked him how he came to be guilty of such high-handed conduct. He showed them an old law which prohibited the road from running trains across the river, a law which had always before remained a dead letter, as it has since.

"But why did you not run the train *to* the river?"

"I was not there, gentlemen."

"What did you do when you heard of it?"

"I did not do anything."

"Why not? Where were you?"

"I was at home, gentlemen, playing a rubber at whist, and I never allow *anything* to interfere with me when I am playing that game. It requires, as you know, undivided attention."

It was apparent to everybody that a crisis had come in the affairs of the New York Central, and the result of it was, that the Commodore's grasp on the road was tightened rather than relaxed. He made a dash for the management in the fall of 1866, but missed it, and Henry Keep was chosen President, as a friend of all parties. It was only a temporary makeshift, and a year afterward Mr. Keep resigned, and the directors, representing a large majority of the stock, sat down and wrote to the all-conquering Commodore as follows:

NEW YORK, November 12, 1867.

C. VANDERBILT, Esq.

The undersigned, stockholders of the New York Central Railroad Company, are satisfied that a change in the administration of the Company, and a thorough reformation in the management of its affairs, would result in larger dividends to the stock-holders and greatly promote the interests of the public. They therefore request that you will receive their proxies for the coming election, and select such a board of directors as shall seem to you entitled to their confidence. They hope that such an organization will be effected as shall secure to the Company the aid of your great and acknowledged abilities.

Yours respectfully,

EDWARD CUNARD,
JOHN JACOB ASTOR, Jr.,
BERNARD V. HUTTON,
JOHN STEWARD and others,

representing over thirteen millions of stock.

He accepted the trust in the spirit in which it was given. An eyewitness of the election the next month thus describes the scene :

" The recent revolution in the Central Railroad sug-gests the changing nature of all earthly things. Only a short time ago the Pruyns, the Martins, the Pages, and other leading men of the road were to be seen in the directors' rooms, but they passed away like a dream. Even Erastus Corning, the beloved manager, whose fiat was law, is here no more, and another dynasty appears on the stage. The change was wrought by an agency of the most simple character, and one from which no such great end might have been expected. It was a slip of paper a few inches square and containing a few lines of written characters. The circumstances were these. On the eleventh day of December a half-dozen gentlemen marched into the rooms of the Company, rooms into which this was in some instances their first entrance. At 11.15 one of these gentlemen arose and dropped a piece of paper into the ballot-box, and presto, the change is wrought, an old empire passes away and a new empire is inaugurated.   The appearance of the gentleman referred to was striking and impressive.   He was of large size and finely proportioned, a splendid specimen of muscular and intellectual development, with an easy bluff air which suggested the quarter-deck, and with that peculiar at-home-ness which showed that he felt himself master of the situation.   Such was the style of the last election of the 'Central.'   At eleven o'clock the poll was opened, and remained open for five hours ; for five weary hours the inspectors stood guard over the ballot-box, and during that time one vote was received.   When the poll was closed the potency of the solitary ballot was discovered.   It bore the names of thirteen directors, and represented stock to the amount of $18,000,000.   Such was Commodore Vanderbilt's accession to the control of the Central.   He came, bringing his directors with him, elected those directors, and then received through them the management."   It was a signal triumph for a man seventy-three years of age.

Then he gave that road, too, what he vigorously called " an overhauling."   He gave it the same medicine that he had already applied through William H. to the Harlem and the Hudson River.   He administered even a more drastic dose.   He improved it enormously in its rolling-stock, its time-tables, and its service, ballasted anew the track, straightened out the kinks in it, and multiplied its connections.   The stock rose from the moment his mysterious talisman touched it.

CHAPTER X.

THE ERIE WAR.

The Commodore Covets Erie—Daniel Drew's Little Game—The Vanderbilt Party Buys—Drew and Gould Sell Short—Drew's Duplicity—Fisk Throws 100,000 Bogus Shares Upon the Market—Dodging the Sheriff—Flight to Jersey—Surrender and Restitution.

Now a battle of magnificent proportions took place between the Commodore and those whom, by his aggressiveness, he made his enemies. Having bought and regulated the great trunk lines to the north, he looked around to see where else he was "needed," as he called it. The Pennsylvania was out of the State and strongly buttressed; but there was the Erie.

In 1859 it had failed to meet the interest on its first, second, third, fourth and fifth mortgages, and had passed into the hands of a receiver. It emerged in a crippled condition, and Daniel Drew and other railroad wreckers went for the flotsam and jetsam. "Uncle Dan'l" was known by the dishonorable designation of the Speculating Director, because he used his official position in the Erie road to put its stock up or thrust it down, whichever would enable him to make money. He was a very devout man, and occupied as much time at prayer as Vanderbilt did at whist. He was a curious combination of simplicity and cunning, of boldness and cowardice, of

frankness and secretiveness, of honesty and unscrupu-
lousness, of superstition and faithlessness. An English
critic * says of him : "Daniel Drew had for a long time
regarded Erie as his own special preserve. It was set
all over with his spring-guns and man-traps in which he
daily caught throngs of unwary intruders, and never let
them go till they had emptied their pockets into his
private coffers." He cared nothing whatever for the
road except for what he could make by juggling with
its stock.

Drew was naturally destructive, not constructive. So
he was always a "bear," fond of depreciating values, of
tearing down, and disappointing the hopeful. While
Vanderbilt was fighting for his property, as narrated in
the preceding chapter, Drew was planning a deep game,
and was selling Erie short. To his great grief, the stock
kept going up. Promptly he developed his game.
Drew, in his official capacity of Treasurer of Erie borrowed $3,500,000 in cash of Drew in his private capa-
city as Individual Speculator, giving him as security
28,000 shares of capital stock hitherto unissued, and three
million dollars' worth of bonds alleged to be convertible
into stock. Then Drew the Treasurer obligingly converted the bonds into stock at the request of Drew the
Speculator, and when the latter had sold as much stock
at current prices for future delivery as he could induce
anybody to buy, he threw the 50,000 shares on the market. There was consternation, distress, and terror.
Stock went down in two days from $97 to $50, and
" Uncle Dan'l " pocketed the difference in millions of
dollars and presented a new Methodist Church to his

* In Fraser's Magazine.

Bishop. Charges of malfeasance in office were brought against him.

This man, who begged off from his indebtedness the previous year, was still treasurer of the Erie and virtually at its head. The road was acting as a guerilla, cutting rates very sharply and without system or reason, and Vanderbilt wanted to prevent that. It was owned by nobody, was a foot-ball in Wall Street, falling first into the hands of one set of speculators and then another; it made rates and broke rates, not in the interest of the public, or of the road, but only of the speculators of the hour, who effected heavy combinations when they wanted to put the stock up, and drove the corporation to the verge of a receivership when they wanted to force the stock down. Erie had been the barometer of the market, but it was the butt and derision of the street.

This recklessness seemed to be injurious to everybody, and the Commodore made up his mind that the only way to bring order out of chaos was to " absorb " the road and run it himself. This, he always alleged, was his motive, but he may have been somewhat influenced by a subsidiary purpose, always attributed to him, to corner Erie and take millions out of the "bears," as he had done in the " Harlem pool."

At any rate he went at it in the old way and obtained stock, beginning in the summer of 1867, his brokers buying large blocks of the coveted stock, and he electing some of the directors. Early the next year he formed an alliance with a knot of speculators who controlled the Boston, Hartford and Erie Railroad, and forced the cunning treasurer of Erie to come to terms. At the

next election Drew was left out of the Directory. That
night he went and made a personal appeal to Vanderbilt not to ruin him ; he shed tears at the picture which
he conjured up of the beggary about " staring him in
the face," and the Commodore yielded. A New Hampshire director immediately resigned at his request, and
the lachrymose millionaire was restored to his old position, he agreeing to represent Vanderbilt's interests and
give the market an upward tendency. His presence in
the Board was more full of perils than the admission
into the beleagured capital of that ancient animal which
neither of the schemers had ever heard of—the Trojan
horse. He had made a large fortune through his connection with the road. "Them air Erie shears," had
been alternately depressed and advanced by him, and
had been made to pay tribute to " Uncle Dan'l " whenever they passed through his hands. He had no idea
of allowing his giant rival to capture the goose that laid
his golden eggs. Drew was not a strong man. He was
parsimonious, ambitious, timid, emotional, and possessed
of a low cunning. By his retention on the Erie Board
Gould and Fisk came into power. They had little
money, but one had brains and the other a cheek of
brass.

The purchase of stock went on. Vanderbilt had a
majority of it, but he wanted it all, so that he could
put his own price on it. Then came rumors of Drew's
treachery and of an intention to issue more stock. This
was in obvious and wanton violation of law, and must
be prevented. Hostilities began in court. Judge Barnard enjoined the Erie Directors from issuing any more
stock, and ordered Mr. Drew to return to the treasury

one-fourth of that already out. Judge Balcom, of Binghamton, ordered a stay of these proceedings. A New York judge forbade any meeting of the Erie Directors unless Mr. Vanderbilt's representative was restored to his seat. Judge Barnard forbade the conversion of any Erie bonds into stock.

This was deemed a victory for Vanderbilt, and he continued to buy fast and much. The price rose with a bound to 50, 60, 70, and 80. When it reached 84 the Vanderbilt party had nearly two hundred thousand shares in their possession, and the stock was virtually cornered. Drew, Gould, Fisk, and their backers and allies, had been "bearing" the stock with all their might —selling short for future delivery—and when it persistently rose, it looked as if they were irretrievably ruined. But, still in charge of the machinery of the Company, they had an audacious trick in reserve which was quite beyond the Commodore's experience. As he had a large majority of the stock, getting control of the property seemed a result not very difficult to attain to a man who had wrought so many commercial miracles. He did not dream that the plot of Gould and Fisk and Drew rendered his project impossible of realization. But so it proved. He was dealing with no ordinary men.

One hundred thousand shares of new stock was signed in blank and deposited in Drew's safe. On March 10th the contracts for the delivery of stock generally culminated. The court had enjoined the Secretary from issuing any more stock, but early on the morning of the eventful day he directed an employé of the road to take the books of stock from the office in West Street to Pine Street. While on his way the messenger was robbed! James Fisk met him outside the door, wrenched the books away from him and ran away with them. They were taken in the bold conspirator's carriage to his office in Broad Street, and thrown on the market. Over ten million dollars' worth of the stuff, manufactured for the occasion in defiance of law and the Court's decree, were sold to all comers.

Vanderbilt went on buying till he was loaded up with the so-called "stock," which had no legal existence. He took it in million-dollar blocks. His allies and brokers were John Tobin, Frank Work, Rufus Hatch, William Heath, and Augustus and Richard Schell. "Over-issue of Erie!" was the rumor on the Street. When the Commodore wanted more money he sent that bold and reckless financier, "Dick" Schell, to negotiate with the banks.

"We can't lend on Erie," they said, "there is an illegal issue of stock, and Erie isn't worth anything."

"What will you lend on?" inquired Schell.

"Central—that's good," they answered.

Schell inquired, and found out that they all had Central.

"Very well, gentlemen!" said Schell, as if by authority; "if you don't lend the Commodore half a million on Erie at 50, and do it at once, he will put Central at 50 to-morrow and break half the houses on the Street! You know whether you will be among them."

Thereupon they made the loan, and the intrepid Commodore went on buying. It was like trying to dip out the ocean. The manufacturer gayly remarked to confidential friends, "If this printing-press don't break down, I'll be —— if I don't give the old hog all he wants of Erie." The printing-press was strong, and he succeeded. It is a wonder that even Vanderbilt, rich as he was, was not driven into bankruptcy by these desperate gamesters. When the exposure was first made his best friends supposed he was ruined past hope. Not quite so bad as that, the sequel proved, but he was behind six or seven millions of dollars. Tobin, ex-president of the Central, lost $2,500,000. Half of the buyers were absolutely driven to wreck. But the chief victim of the conspiracy had some money yet unexpended, and a great deal more pluck.

Drew, Fisk, and Gould had the assurance to go to their offices next morning, but they soon heard that warrants for their arrest were out, and then a strange sight was seen: "At ten o'clock on the morning of the eleventh, the astonished police saw a throng of panic-stricken railroad directors, looking more like a frightened gang of thieves disturbed in the division of their plunder, than like the wealthy representatives of a great corporation, rushing headlong from the doors of the Erie office and dashing off in the direction of the Jersey City Ferry. In their hands were packages and files of papers, and their pockets were crammed with assets and securities. One individual bore away with him in a hackney coach bales containing $6,000,000 in greenbacks! *

"The attempted 'corner' was a failure, and Drew was victorious—no doubt existed on that point. The question now was, could Vanderbilt sustain himself? In spite of all his wealth, must he not go down before his cunning opponent? When night put an end to the conflict Erie stood at 78, the shock of battle was over,

* Charles Francis Adams in North American Review, 1869.

and the astonished brokers drew breath as they waited
for the events of the morrow. . . . As usual in these
Wall Street operations, there was a grim humor in the
situation. Had Vanderbilt failed to sustain the market,
a financial collapse and panic must have ensued which
would have sent him to the wall. He had sustained it,
and had absorbed a hundred thousand shares of Erie.
. . . Vanderbilt had, however, little leisure to devote
to the enjoyment of the humorous side of his position.
The situation was alarming. His opponents had carried
with them in their flight seven millions in currency,
which were withdrawn from circulation. An artificial
stringency was thus created in Wall Street, and while
money rose, stocks fell, and unusual margins were called
in. Vanderbilt was carrying a fearful load, and the
least want of confidence, the faintest sign of faltering,
might well bring on a crash. He already had a hundred thousand shares of Erie, not one of which he could
sell. He was liable at any time to be called upon to
carry as much more as his opponents, skilled by long
practice in the manufacture of the article, might see fit
to produce. Opposed to him were men who scrupled
at nothing, and who knew every in and out of the
money market. With every look and every gesture anxiously scrutinized, a position more trying than his then
was can hardly be conceived. It is not known from
what source he drew the vast sums which enabled him
to surmount his difficulties with such apparent ease.
His nerve, however, stood him in at least as good stead
as his financial resources. Like a great general, in the
hour of trial he inspired confidence. While fighting for
life he could 'talk horse' and play whist. The man-

ner in which he then emerged from his troubles, serene
and confident, was as extraordinary as the financial resources he commanded."

The Commodore now did two things : He at once
sold out all the genuine stock he held, and he put in immediate and vigorous action all the enginery of the law
for the punishment of the conspirators, whom he called
by much harsher names, and threatened with the peni-
tentiary.   He procured attachments against their property and warrants for their personal arrest, and the indignant Barnard sent his most active officers after them.
They had hastily fled to Jersey City, carrying with
them $7,000,000 of the Commodore's money, and there
Fisk, Gould, Drew, and others remained all summer, at
a refuge which became known as " Camp Taylor."

Not only did most of them avoid arrest, but they
visited Albany clandestinely, and by the use of the money
they had got from the Commodore secured the passage
by the Legislature of an act authorizing the issue of bogus
bonds!—similar to an act to legalize counterfeit money.

Courts were appealed to for their protection.   Two
judges became implicated in charges of bribery, one of
whom was impeached, while the other more prudently
resigned.   The attention of the whole country was
aroused by the tumult of the combat.   The Jersey City
exiles tried in vain to compromise ; but all the fighting
qualities of the Commodore were up, and he sent them
word that unless they refunded every cent they had
stolen he would have them in jail if it took his last dollar.

At last he triumphed.   The banishment to Jersey and
the pressure of public condemnation became a double
burden, too great to be borne, and Drew came in one

Sunday and surrendered. He agreed to "do the fair thing," and asked for mercy, making an appeal of the most pathetic nature to the Commodore. As a matter of historic fact, he went to Washington Place and spent half of the night weeping, as usual, over his miserable condition.* It succeeded. About the only soft spot that the Commodore had in his nature was a sentimental willingness to help Mr. Drew out of scrapes. Drew was three years his junior, and was dreadfully ignorant and illiterate, and Vanderbilt regarded with a certain sort of fraternal pride a man who had "made himself," and from a common laborer had got to be worth $18,000,000. So when the unfortunate magnate unlocked the fountains of sympathy and promised to behave and do just what Vanderbilt wanted done, if he would "let up," the overture was received magnanimously. He made restitution, and a settlement was effected. As a witness in court, subsequently, Drew testified, " Vanderbilt allus tole me that I acted very foolish in goin' to Jersey City; I tole him I didn't know but what I wus circumstanced in an ockerd light."

Shortly afterward Gould and Fisk followed his example. They surrendered. Vanderbilt was relieved of 50,000 shares at $70, receiving $2,500,000 in cash and $1,250,000 in bonds of the Boston, Hartford and Erie at $80. He was to receive a further $1,000,000 outright for the privilege thus secured of calling on him for his other 50,000 shares at $70, any time within four months.

This bargain was consummated one morning, while

---

* Daniel Drew's constant premonitions of poverty were at last realized, and when he died he left not a dollar's worth of property.

they were still shadowed by the police. Just before daylight, Gould and Fisk crept across the river with piles of documents and bonds in their buggy, and wended their quiet if not contrite way to Washington Place. As a witness in one of these interminable Erie suits subsequently, Fisk told the story of this early visit in his own droll way. Inferring that the Commodore would not yet be up, Gould counselled a decent delay, but Fisk boldly rang the bell, and went straight up to the Commodore's bedroom.

" The Commodore was sitting on the side of the bed with one shoe off and one shoe on," began this observing and facetious witness. " He got up, and I saw him putting on the other shoe. I remember that shoe from its peculiarity : it had four buckles on it. I had never seen shoes with buckles in that manner before, and I thought if these sort of men always wear that sort of shoe I might want a pair. He said I must take my position as I found it ; that there I was, and he would keep his bloodhounds (the lawyers) on our track ; that he would be damned if he didn't keep them after us if we didn't take the stock off his hands. I told him that if I had my way I'd be damned if I would take a share of it ; that he brought the punishment on himself and he deserved it. This mellowed him down. . . . I told him that he was a robber. He said the suits would never be withdrawn till he was settled with. I said [after settling with him] that it was an almighty robbery ; that we had sold ourselves to the devil, and that Gould felt just the same as I did."

The issue of bogus bonds and the illegal " compromise " by which the conspirators escaped punishment had cost the Erie road in all about nine millions of dollars, and to this amount they were afterward compelled to make restitution.

This Erie venture had cost Vanderbilt a million or two which the above restitution did not cover, and it operated as a warning to him. He declared, in monosyllabic Saxon, that he would never touch Erie again, and " never have anything more to do with them blowers," and he never did. The Legislature, at its succeeding session, passed an act forbidding the consolidation of the Erie and the Central—a rightful and needful prohibition. Thenceforth there was wholesome competition between the two great trunk systems of New York State.

Wall Street looked upon the Commodore as badly crippled before he emerged from this battle-royal, and was greatly astonished to see that he always bore himself with his usual composure and courage, and seemed to have as much money as ever.

5

CHAPTER XI.

TROPHIES OF VICTORY.

Twenty-five Million Dollars in Five Years—William's Way—Consolidation Succeeds—Freight Depot on St. John's Park—Dedication of the Commodore's Monument, the Bronzes—Watering Stock—What is It, and Whom does it Rob ?

THE financial world was disappointed and astonished. The audacious Commodore had not "gone under." On the contrary, he had demonstrated his ability to hold his own against all comers. After he had passed far more than an average life-time in familiarizing himself with marine transportation, and had learned that complicated business to the minutest detail, he had, at threescore and ten, changed the whole purpose of his life and transferred all of his wealth to railroads, in the management of which he had had no experience. Practical railroad men predicted that he would lose ashore the fortune he had made afloat.

He had turned their prophecies to derision. He had learned his new trade as easily as Mezzofanti learned a new language, or Blind Tom a new tune. His hair was silvered, and the crow-step twinkle had come to the corners of his eyes, but in the first five years of his railroad ventures and experiments he had made a clear profit of not less than twenty-five million dollars.

With his son William at his side, now quite established in his confidence and pursuing careful business methods that received his cordial approval, the railroads he had bought rapidly continued to improve. In two years he advanced to the Central road $2,000,000 above the stock he bought. " He burned up its old cars, sold its old locomotives, threw out its old ties, put on new cars, new locomotives, new ties, new rails, and made it what it is to-day, one of the best-regulated and most thoroughly-stocked roads in the State of New York." He believed that the road *must* pay if well equipped and well conducted. And he backed his opinion with his money.

The next fall (1869) he went to Albany again, and asked for the privilege of consolidating the Hudson River and the New York Central Railroads. The "bears," whose claws had been caught in his Harlem scheme, stood off at a very respectful distance, and did not offer their assistance in any way, and the act was passed on November 1st without serious opposition.

About the next thing he did was to buy outright from the city St. John's Park, on Hudson Street, formerly the centre of aristocratic residence. He paid $1,000,000 for it, and he erected there a gigantic freight depot for the Hudson River Railroad. In the western pediment of this imposing structure he erected Albert De Groot's famous bronze *bas-relief*, an ambitious allegory of Industry, emblematical of the Commodore's remarkable career. The artist was the son of Captain Freeman De Groot, who commanded the Cinderella on Vanderbilt's line. The device was erected with a formal celebration, and cost $250,000.

These memorial bronzes, now buried in the business heart of the city below Canal Street, were unveiled on November 10, 1869, in the presence of some ten thousand people. The day was observed in New York by a display of flags on all the public buildings, as well as on the shipping in the two rivers. The exercises at the unveiling consisted of music by the Seventh Regiment Band; a prayer by Bishop Janes, of the Methodist Church; an address by Oakey Hall, Mayor of the city, and a poem by William Ross Wallace. Admirals Gordon and Stringham, of the Navy, were present, and out of compliment to Commodore Vanderbilt, twenty-five veteran sailors from the United States receiving ship Vermont were detailed to haul up the heavy canvas when the bronzes were revealed to public view. When this had been done, and the Commodore's pennant was run up on the flagstaff, it was found that the bronzes consisted of a statue of the Commodore, larger than life, standing in a central niche, flanked on either side with an immense field of bronze devoted to the story of his life, its works and achievements. The figure of the Commodore is rather stiff, and is dressed in the fur-lined coat he was fond of wearing. "As a likeness," says Horace Greeley, in his paper, at the time, "the statue signally fails to do justice to that physiognomy, one of the finest in America, which has never yet been rendered worthily by any photograph, bronze, or picture that we have seen."

The field on the right, or southern side of the statue, is devoted to the marine period of Commodore Vanderbilt's life, while that on the left, or northern side, illustrates his railway life. The *Nation*, speaking of the work, said: " There is about it a curious appropriate-

ness and fitness to the exploits and fame it is to cele-
brate."

While these bronzes, said to be the largest in the
world, do not rank high as works of art, they tell in a
very plain manner the story of the life of Commodore
Vanderbilt. In the marine section there is the image of
the boat in which, as a young man, he carried passengers
from the Battery to Staten Island and back. There is also
one of the vessels of the Pacific Mail line, and a correct
representation of the great steamship Vanderbilt, which
he gave to the United States Government during the civil
conflict. Piled in the foreground, and around the feet of
the statue, are various objects, representing, symbolically,
facts and events in his career, such as a major and minor
engine, anchors, cables, pilot-wheel, cotton-bale, etc.

The northern section of the bronzes contains what may
be called a panoramic view of the Hudson River Railway, with bridges, tunnels, mountains, trains going up
and down the river, etc., with glimpses of the Hudson
and its river boats, all witnesses to his energy and business sagacity. Few men have their statues set up during
their life-time. The Iron Duke and George Peabody
are modern instances. But the courage, tenacity, capacity for toil and energy, crowned with success, won for
Commodore Vanderbilt great respect from his fellow-
citizens during his life. Said the *Tribune* at the time:
" We fully recognize and pay tribute to his broad foresight, patient judgment, and resistless energy of will ; and
in honoring him, we honor the commercial enterprise,
commercial sagacity, and commercial success which
make him the ' realized ideal' of more people than almost any other living American."

Tens of thousands of the residents of the great city have never seen this unique memorial, for it is masked by high business blocks on a street which they never traverse. As a monument for the public eye it might almost as well be in the depths of the Adirondacks.

The Commodore made William H. Vanderbilt vice-president of the consolidated system, and it profited at once from his thorough executive management and attention to details.

The writer in *Fraser's* says: "These roads the Commodore certainly managed with great skill. His administrative ability is immense. He has introduced vigor and thoroughness into every department, and the public are well pleased with the fruits of his labors. He is ambitious of the fame of conducting his roads in the best possible manner, and he takes such a pride in their appearance and appointments as a hunting gentleman takes in his stud."

Then he hastened to dilute the capital of all his roads enormously, pretty nearly doubling his previous wealth. When he was elected president of the Hudson River Railroad its capital was $7,000,000 only; when he became president of the Central it had a capital of $28,000,000. Early in 1869, he declared a tremendous dividend of new stock to all stockholders. No less than eighty per cent. was added in a lump to the estimated value of Hudson River, and one hundred and seven per cent. to the estimated value of New York Central. In other words, the capital stock of the two roads was increased from $35,000,000 to $86,000,000, and then to $90,000,000. As they proved to be worth it, it put colossal profits into the pockets of the president and his friends. One night, at midnight, he carried away from the office of Horace F. Clark, his son-in-law, $6,000,000 in greenbacks as a part of his share of the profits. And he had $20,000,000 more in new stock.

This was the gigantic stock-watering operation which called down on the Vanderbilts the denunciation of a good many who were not partners in the transaction, and which is still regarded by the uninformed and the unthinking as " a pure steal." *

What is stock-watering ? It is simply the conclusion and declaration of a man that his property is worth more to day than it was yesterday. He buys an old, broken-down horse, for instance, and pays $20 for it. He takes some chances. It may die on his hands, but he resolves to save it and make money on it, if possible. He gives the animal the best of care, feeds it well, grooms it carefully, and in a year it recovers from its lameness, acquires a glossy coat, and is sound and well. He then puts a new price on his horse, and asks $200 for it. Noticing that it has spirit and a good form, he speeds it on the track and finds, to his surprise, that it can go in three minutes. He now says, " If any man wants that horse he must pay $1,000 for it." He has " watered " his horse. Has he robbed anybody ? Has

---

* When the Commodore's portrait first appeared upon the bonds of the Central, a holder of some called one day and said ; " Commodore, glad to see your face on them bonds. It's worth ten per cent. It gives everybody confidence." The Commodore smiled grimly, the only recognition he ever made of a compliment. " 'Cause," explained the visitor, " wen we see that fine, noble brow, it reminds us that you never'll let anybody else steal anything ! "

he not a right to charge for it what he pleases, so long
as nobody is compelled to buy ? *

So Vanderbilt bought roads—not to sell, but to improve. They were all crippled when he bought, and
they were afflicted with every pernicious disease that
sick railroads ever have. He administered heroic treatment: He lopped off every extravagance; removed
ornaments from the locomotives; increased the tracks
and the carrying capacity; combined half a dozen short
railroads and made them into a single long one, and
rolled half a dozen Presidents and Boards of Directors
into one; opened new outlets and new feeders; made
every man in his employ do a whole day's work; and
thus, roads which had been the toys of gamblers and the
preserves of bankrupt politicians grew to valuable property in his hands, and showed that they knew their
master.

They had been treated exactly as the broken-down
army horses were treated that were turned out upon the
farms of the State during those same years. He had
bought the roads, and he had put value into them, as
truly as a cabinet-maker puts value into wood when he
makes it into a chair. Was it not his privilege to put a
price on his own property ? It was twice as valuable in
1869 as when he bought it; was it "robbery" for him
to charge twice as much for it ? If he had not bought

---

* In a careful estimate concerning this matter, Charles Francis
Adams computed that in 1870 " $50,000 of absolute water " had been
poured out for each mile of road between New York and Buffalo. In
other words, that Commodore Vanderbilt's brain, brought to bear on
this ramshackle thoroughfare, had added $50,000 a mile to its abso-
lute value.

W. K. VANDERBILT.

it it would not have been worth $50,000,000 in 1869. Was he not fairly entitled to the extra millions, and had he not earned them as truly as a man who wheels sand from a sand-bank earns his daily dollar?

Before he bought the Central, a six per cent. dividend had been nominally paid, but much of the time this had been borrowed. When he had reconstructed the roads on a business basis he made them so serviceable that he more than doubled their value. Indeed, he increased their nominal value from $36,000,000 to $90,000,000, and paid annually eight per cent. on that! If he had not watered the stock their augmented value would have been the same, but instead of paying eight per cent. on $90,000,000 he would have paid twenty per cent. on the $36,000,000. If he had watered the stock without being able to pay dividends on it, the watering would have made no difference in its value. The property was property he had created, and without him the bulk of it would not have existed at all.

5*

CHAPTER XII.

HABITS AND CHARACTER.

Methods of Work—Location in Various Years—Keeping Accounts in
His Head—Punctuality—Close at a Bargain—Whist After Dinner
—Tells a Story of His Mother—Death of His Wife.

His success was not more remarkable than the ease
with which he superintended his extensive affairs. At
ten or eleven in the morning, having glanced through
two or three newspapers, he came out of his house on
Washington Place, and drove in a light, no-top buggy to
his office in Bowling Green. There, in an hour or so,
aided by a single clerk, he transacted the business of the
day, and after giving some hints to his son, William H.,
returned for his afternoon drive up the Bloomingdale
Road. He always despised show and ostentation in every
form. No lackey attended him: he held the reins
himself. With an estate of forty or fifty millions to
manage, nearly all actively employed in iron-works
and railroads, he kept scarcely any books, but carried all
his larger affairs in his head, and managed them without
the least apparent effort or anxiety.

He had already occupied a large number and variety of
offices. Being asked where his first was, he answered,
with a laugh, " On the head of an upturned flour-barrel
on the wharf. I kept my steamboat accounts there for

a year, and took my cold dinner daily on that same barrel."

But as early as 1837 he had an office in South Street. From there he moved the next year to No. 39 Peck Slip, to the little room up the first flight. His agent was D. B. Allen, a son-in-law, and his clerk Lambert Wardell. The Commodore was not much of the time in the office.

He detested the routine of office work; declared that the ledger was a meaningless humbug, and kept his personal reckoning in a little book which he carried in his vest-pocket. He hired men whom he thought he could trust, and then let them do their part of the business in their own way, accounting to him only for net results.

"How much money is there over to-day?" he would inquire of his agent, and ascertaining, would put it in his pocket and carry it away with him.

From Peck Slip he moved to No. 34 Broadway, about 1842, and was burned out by the great fire three years later. Being roofless, and the city being a tumult of ruins and rebuilding, he took possession of an old shanty on an East-side wharf, and kept his office there all winter.

In the spring of 1846 he found fairly comfortable quarters at No. 8 Battery Place, and remained till 1855, when he transferred his office to No. 5 Bowling Green, and thence, at last, to No. 2 West Fourth, in the rear of his house, where he stayed till he left his office for the last time.

At eighty he was still as straight as an Indian, with the elasticity of vigorous manhood in his step, and a face of remarkable beauty and strength.

He owed a good deal of his robust health, doubtless,

to his fondness for driving. He possessed, too, the enviable power of leaving his business absolutely in his office, and never letting it intrude on hours of recreation. Out on the road behind a fast team, or seated at whist at the Club-House, he entered gayly into the humors of the moment. He was rigid on one point only : not to talk or hear of business out of business hours.

He was a good story-teller, and an interesting converser concerning matters within his knowledge, but he could seldom be coaxed or induced to make a speech. After-dinner oratory is mainly the result of practice, and he never practised.

He could express his meaning with force, brevity, and clearness, and some of his letters are models of that sort of composition. He never said a word too much. Wardell, who was at his side for a whole generation, says : " In dictating a letter to a clerk I never saw his equal." But pen and ink always had him at a disadvantage. His English was even worse than Napoleon Bonaparte's French. He always wrote of the reservoir in which steam was generated as the " boylar," and a letter of his is still extant in which he asks a friend to " com down and sea the widdow."

He could not endure the office or office work, and never spent more than an hour a day there, except for conversation. He insisted that most letter-writers were idiots and used ten times as many words as were necessary. If a letter of more than fifteen lines were handed to him he would struggle through three or four lines and then toss it impatiently to a clerk with, " Here, see what this (expletive) fool is driving at, and tell me the gist of it ! "

He never kept money by him in large sums, but almost always invested it the very day it was received, and generally had made the arrangements beforehand. He made it a point never to lose a dollar in interest through lack of promptness.

"On one occasion," says E. H. Carmick, the Commodore's associate in some large transactions, "he and I went to Washington, and lived together at Willard's one winter. We wanted to see John M. Clayton, and arranged to go and call on him on a certain evening. When the night came dense darkness came with it, and it rained pitchforks. I said to the Commodore, 'We can't go now; wait, and if it slacks up we will go over.' I shortly missed him, and inquiring for him, found that he had gone to Clayton's. When it cleared away, about 9 o'clock, I took the stage, and went over to Capitol Hill, where the distinguished Senator lived. I went in and found him, and the Commodore with him, playing whist. 'I didn't suppose you would come in such a pouring rain,' I said. 'Carmick,' he said, 'between you and me, that's the way I got ahead of some of the other boys. I never failed to keep an engagement in my life.'"

He rarely ever alluded to his fortune, and never boastfully; but Mr. Carmick says: "We were sitting in the hotel vestibule one night in 1853, with not much to talk about, when the Commodore said suddenly, 'Who's the second richest man in New York, Carmick?—next after Astor?'"

"I saw what he was thinking of, but I said, 'Stephen Whitney, I guess.'

"'How much is Whitney worth?' he asked.

"'Oh, he must be worth $7,000,000,' said I.

"'H—m!' he exclaimed, 'he'll have to be worth a good deal more than that to be the second richest man in New York.'"

He did not appear to understand the cause of his own prosperity, and perhaps he really did not understand it.

Being asked one day what he considered to be the secret of success in business, he replied :

"Secret ? There is no secret about it. All you have to do is to attend to your business, and go ahead."

He would doubtless have sympathized with the great composer who, being asked to define genius said: "Genius ?—industry ! "

When asked on another occasion to tell the secret of his success, he replied : "Never to tell anything I'm going to do till I've done it ! "

Like Astor, Stewart, Drew, Dean Richmond, and other wealthy men, he was close at a bargain, and watched his pennies more carefully than the average of his fellows. When he was worth $50,000,000 he economized in the same old way, and in making out certificates of stock, would always lump as many shares as possible together, in order to save the twenty-five cents internal-revenue tax on each certificate.

His personal habits of daily life, after his seventy-fifth year, underwent little change. He still rose very early, and took a light breakfast, skimming the morning papers at table. These, indeed, were about all that he ever read, excepting " Pilgrim's Progress," which he enjoyed conning over and over.

After breakfast he would go to his private office, around on Fourth Street, and there stay dispatching busi-

ness and chatting with friends till 11 o'clock. Then he
would inspect his horses in the adjacent stable, and those
whom he liked were asked to attend the inspection.
After this ceremony he returned home, to chat with his
children or grandchildren and dress for dinner. The
afternoon furnished him an opportunity to drive up the
island, and his turn-out was one of the finest on the road.
Supper was served at 6 o'clock.

He ate sparingly at all times, and of the plainest and
most wholesome things; rarely took wine, and generally
retired at 10 o'clock.

At both office and house he was easily accessible; he
never refused to see any caller, however humble, but he
had uncommon discernment, and if the visitor lacked
a sufficient errand he was capable of being sharp, and
even rude, exclaiming: "Come! speak quick and be
off!"

He spent at least half of his evenings at home, but he
was as fond of whist as Talleyrand, and insisted upon
"the rigors of the game" like Mrs. Battle. Therefore
it was that he was a member of three clubs in which
whist was considered the great social duty. The party
at Saratoga, where he spent a portion of every summer,
was very exclusive. A stranger was never taken into
the game, and seldom permitted to watch its progress.

On account of his early association with sailors, pro-
fanity was an established habit of his life. If he did
not swear very wickedly, he swore frequently; indeed,
it was found that he often indulged in forbidden forms
of speech when quite unconscious of it.

Dr. Deems relates a surprising and amusing instance
of this. He was dining there one day, and sitting, as he

usually did, at the Commodore's left, when his host told a story of his early life.

"I had just finished the Caroline, my first steamboat," he began, as he carved the beef, "and I was mighty proud of her, I tell you! When the last bit of paint was dry, I hired a caterer to spread a banquet in the cabin—just a bang-up dinner—nicest he could get. Then I h'isted the flags and went over to the island to see mother. I went and got 'er and fetched 'er down to the wharf—I remember it, Doctor, as if 'twas only last week—and I escorted her aboard and showed her the gay decks and the engine, and the galley, and finally took 'er into the cabin, where the banquet was spread, and set 'er down at the head of the table. I never see anybody so astonished as she was when I told her it was all mine. 'Cornele,' she asked, looking up, 'where the d——l did you git this dinner?'"

"I don't believe a word of it!" exclaimed the Doctor.

"What do you mean?" asked the narrator, flinging down his knife and fork.

"You've got up the yarn," persisted his guest. "I don't believe you had any boat, or any dinner, or that your mother was there, or anything about it."

"You mean to tell me I lie?" exclaimed the Commodore, flushing to the roots of his white hair.

"I am not permitted to use such language at your table," answered the clergyman; "I am your guest. But when you tell me that that pious woman, your mother, on coming on board your boat, said, 'where the d——l did you get that dinner?' I know better, and it throws doubt on the whole story."

"Aw!" exclaimed the raconteur, in disgust; "I'm

mad at myself that I don't break off that mean, low, dirty habit.   It's a shame !   I wish you'd always correct me when I swear, Doctor."

The Commodore met with his greatest earthly loss in the death of his wife, on August 17, 1868.   It occurred at the residence of Horace F. Clark, her son-in-law, where she was visiting.   Her husband hurried to her side from Saratoga, a few days before her death.   She was a noble woman, with strong qualities, supreme affection, frugality, self-denial.   She had borne thirteen children, and had reared twelve of them to adult life.   For more than half-a-century she had been the charm of her husband's home, the sharer of his anxieties and his labors, acquiescent and patient under the sway of his dominant will and in the presence of his trying moods.   The fact that she lived harmoniously with such an obstinate man bears strong testimony to her character.   She was buried in the Commodore's tomb in the Moravian Cemetery at New Dorp,* in the midst of a crowd of affectionate friends.

She was of simple tastes and habits, and never learned to feel quite at home amid the great and splendid city. She clung closely to the acquaintances of her youth, and used to tell those incredulous and amazed hearers that the happiest days of her life were those spent in hard work in the half-way tavern at New Brunswick, and that she liked the house that her husband had built on Staten Island, with all the children romping on the lawn or swarming in to teaze her with their innumerable wants, far, far better than the prim mansion on Washington Place.

* Among the pall-bearers were A. T. Stewart and Horace Greeley.

CHAPTER XIII.

FAMILY MATTERS.

His Grandchildren—Cornelius, Jr., and William K. at Work—The
Thorn in the Flesh—Horace Greeley—"Cornele's Wife"—The
Commodore Marries at Eighty—His Wife's Influence.

By this time most of the eleven survivors of the
thirteen children of the Commodore were married, and
had children of their own to take care of.

William H. had made rapid inroads upon his father's
confidence, until he was completely trusted to carry out
all the details of his schemes. He was not allowed to
share his business secrets: nobody was. Being asked,
two or three years since, if he could furnish much
material for a life of his father, he answered, "No,
none; I knew nothing about him. As to his business
methods, I never understood them, and if he had
thought his overcoat did he would have burnt it up!"

The man who was now his father's predestined heir
lived in a handsome house at Fifth Avenue and Fortieth
Street, with his growing family. His father was regarding anxiously his two oldest grandsons, Cornelius and
William Kissam Vanderbilt, already emerged into manhood. In fact, he had regarded them anxiously and
incredulously for many years, and did not hesitate to
express his opinion that those "youngsters" would be
"spoilt." Spoilt by petting and indolence, he meant.

The Commodore had an idea that most boys were doomed to be ruined, and that nothing on earth could save them except hard and disagreeable work. To put them at some severe service about as soon as they entered their teens, and compel them to support themselves —that was his panacea for the evils that beset youth.

"If a boy is good for anything you can stick him down anywhere and he'll earn his living and lay up something ; if he can't do it he ain't worth saving, and you can't save him." That was his inflexible rule. He had applied it to both William and "Cornele," his sons, and now he urged its application to his grandsons.

Their father was not loth to adopt the rule, for he thought there was something in it, so when the eldest, Cornelius, was sixteen years old, a clerkship was obtained for him in the Shoe and Leather Bank. He served very faithfully and soon mastered the work required of him.

John M. Crane, president of the bank, says: "I do not now see much of Mr. Vanderbilt, as our paths lie apart, but when he was here he was, I think, the most single-minded and conscientious worker I ever saw. He was not merely honest—most bank clerks are that —but he was intellectually precise, and worried if a cent were missing in the accounts. He was thoroughly fair-minded, too, and always did exactly as he agreed, showing, in every way, not only a careful bringing up but a kindly nature."

It is related that one of his uncles, going to Europe for the Commodore, invited the lad to accompany him, and agreed to pay his expenses. It was a rare chance. The young clerk applied to the president for leave-of-absence. "Yes, you can go," was the answer ; "but of

course you will lose your salary for the two months."
Cornelius found that this would be $100, whereupon he
immediately discarded the temptation and remained
through the summer at his desk. Cornelius was in the
Shoe and Leather Bank three years, going into the
Treasurer's office at the Grand Central Depot in 1865,
when he was twenty-one years old. His next younger
brother went to school more, but in 1870 he left the
Academy at Geneva, Switzerland, returned to New
York, and joined his brother in the office. Both were
put at the bottom, and compelled to learn the tedious
routine of the business.

The Commodore's second son, Cornelius Jeremiah,
was a thorn in his flesh and a source of constant annoyance. Since he ran away in his eighteenth year, and
fled to California as a sailor, and his father retaliated
by locking him up as a lunatic, the two had been on the
worst possible terms. Indeed, they scarcely spoke when
they met, except for mutual reproaches. It is not surprising that such a rare specimen of vigorous energy,
thrift, and virility as the father was—a king among men
—lacked patience for this flaccid, nerveless, shiftless,
reckless son ; this sickly epileptic and spendthrift. No
two men could be more unlike. To see each other was
mutually exasperating. The son was accustomed to apply to his father, when speaking of him to others, all
the uncomplimentary epithets in the thesaurus, and the
old gentleman would complain, " I'd give one hundred
dollars if he never'd been named Cornelius ! " A hundred dollars, curiously enough, was usually about the
highest limit of his offers of imaginary bonuses for the
unattainable things which he wanted.

Cornelius Jeremiah was a tall, angular, thin, cadaverous-looking man, with faded eyes, tawny hair, and scraggly beard, nervous, suspicious, petulent, and almost continually in bad health. He was known, more than once, to fall in a fit at a gaming table, recover, and play on.

For nearly a score of years he lived away from home on an allowance, and obtained access to his father only through the intercession of friends—oftenest of the young man's mother. Her heart always warmed toward him, and frequently she gave him money to pay his debts incurred in gambling or other imprudence.

In these straits, when he could no longer get at home the money he needed, he was in the habit of borrowing it of some of the friends of his father. One of these whom he found most useful for his purpose was that careless and generous philosopher, Horace Greeley, who at any time found it more agreeable to give than to refuse, and more easy to give at once and get rid of the suppliant, than to spend time ascertaining what he did with his money. It was difficult for the wayward man to get money from his father in his frequent emergencies, but Mr. Greeley's pocket was always on tap without any unpleasant questions. So the editor of the *Tribune* got into the habit of lending "Cornele" hundreds and even thousands at a time—sometimes ten thousand at a time, when his own family sorely needed the money.

The Commodore heard of this, and supposing, of course, that Mr. Greeley was being deceived and would look to him for reimbursement, determined to put a stop to the outburst of mistaken liberality. So, climbing the crooked little wooden stairs on Spruce Street one day, and marching with heavy tread into the sanctum, which was always open, he greeted the editor abruptly with, " Greeley, I hear you are lending Cornele money."

Mr. Greeley took time to finish the sentence he had begun to write, and then drawled out, " Yes ; I have let him have some."

" Well, now, I give you fair warning that you needn't look to me. I won't pay it ! "

" Who the devil asked you ? " rejoined Greeley. " I haven't, have I ? "

Not another word was said on either side, and the wrathful Commodore stalked out.

When Mr. Greeley died, in 1872, the Commodore relented somewhat—sufficiently to send to each of the editor's daughters a check for $10,000 ; an amount which was found to be much needed.

It is not known that " Cornele " ever did but one thing that pleased his father : that was when he married Miss Williams, of Hartford, a lady whom the old gentleman liked. He not only approved the choice, but he liked the idea of his son's settling down in marriage. He thought that such a step might have the effect of straightening out a career that had been very zigzag, and his youngest son might at last cease to be, as he called him to his face whenever they met, " a disgrace to the family."

But when the young husband ventured to ask for money to build a house in Hartford, it was refused. " No, Cornele," was the answer; " you've got to show that you can be trusted before I trust you." Then the wife was induced to repeat the request. He had some little confidence in her judgment and honesty, and he frankly told her so, adding, " How much can you get along with ? "

" Ten thousand dollars," was the reply.

He drew his check for it and handed it to her, advising her to make it go as far as she could.

A few months later she made her appearance again. He was not surprised, and doubtless said to himself, " Here she is again ; wants $5,000 more."

" Well, what now ? " he said.

" Nothing, papa ; only I've brought back $1,500 ; it was more than we needed, and I've brought you what's left."

The Commodore was thunderstruck. Such a thing had never before happened to him in the whole course of his life. Perhaps it was guileless innocence on her part, and perhaps it was far-sighted shrewdness; at any rate it worked to a charm. Thenceforth " Cornele's wife " could get anything out of her father-in-law.

This lady died ten years before her husband, and left him a very helpless creature. He was confined to an allowance of $200 a week, and spent most of his time complaining of the stinginess of his father for giving him such a niggardly pittance.

Just after the war a Mrs. Crawford moved to New York City from Mobile, Ala., where the fortunes of the family had been badly shattered by the conflict. With her came her daughter, Frank A., a young woman of uncommon intelligence, refinement, and personal attractiveness. She was tall, handsome, graceful, and well educated, and she supported herself here by teaching music. On her father's side she was related to ex-Vice-president Crawford, and one of her great-grandfathers was Samuel Hand, a brother of Commodore Vanderbilt's mother, Phebe Hand.

This last relationship was the cause of an acquaintance springing up with the Commodore and his children. Nothing was thought of it till a year after the death of Mrs. Vanderbilt, when the widower and Miss Crawford encountered each other at Saratoga. It was the old story—a walk on the balconies, a drive in the moonlight, a jocular exchange, a laughable challenge to matrimony from the venerable suitor and at last a serious proposal.

He entertained a good deal of doubt whether Miss Crawford would accept him, and communicated his apprehensions to one or two confidential friends. But she did, after thinking of it a proper length of time. Then he wrote to her with charming naïveté: " You are making a great sacrifice in marrying me. You have youth, beauty, virtue, talent, and all that is lovely in a woman, and I have nothing to give you in return ! "

Miss Crawford said she would marry him if he would send for Dr. Charles F. Deems, her New York pastor. The Commodore telegraphed to him, but he was absent, and it was determined not to make a telegraphic search for him. A trip to Niagara was proposed and agreed to ; they made a rapid journey, crossed to Canada, and in the town of London, half way to Detroit, a young Wesleyan minister was summoned and the marriage ceremony was performed.

Two friends who had accompanied them in their droll elopement, Augustus Schell and Superintendent Tillinghast, of the Central, were witnesses of the marriage. Then they returned to New York. Being spoken to

FREDERICK W. VANDERBILT.

about it, the lively old bridegroom said, " I didn't want to raise a noise in the United States, so I slipped over to Canada and had it done up in a jiffy, and I guess the knot was well tied."

The Commodore never bought a coat-of-arms or even searched for one, and he did not boast of his " blood," yet he seems to have had a strong prejudice in favor of his own, for the ladies whom he selected for his wives were both his cousins.

The marriage was received with surprise and considerable disfavor by other members of his family. They of course thought they knew better than he did about such matters, and they remarked to each other and even to their friends that it was hardly necessary for him to take another spouse. Old saws were quoted to his disadvantage.

But the graceful intruder possessed both amiability and tact, and she brought her whole fund of attractions to bear in winning the hearts of her new relations. It did not take long for her to make herself beloved, as she had always been respected. To be the young wife of the leading millionaire of the country was a trying rôle, but she was equal to its exactions, and she brought to the old man much happiness and solace during his remaining years.

Nay, more; she introduced a new element of Christian gentleness into his home, and even modified his character and habits. For her he yielded to the claims of a wise charity. For her he tried to tone down the rough language which he had picked up about the wharfs in his youth. For her and with her he began to go to church. Dr. Deems has written : " The religious germ

6

planted in his youth was to be developed under the
kindly cultivation of a younger nature, strange to his
long antecedent career. It was the mission of his second
wife to rescue from its burden of worldliness the intrinsic goodness surviving in his soul, and to inspire the
benevolent deeds that crowned his days."

The Doctor tells of an incident illustrating this change
in the old man's moods:

"I went in one day and found him on the sofa in
tears. 'Why, what's the matter, Commodore?' I asked.
'Oh,' he said, 'I've been a-swearing again, and I'm sorry.
I'd ought to stop it, my wife such a pious woman and
you and other religious folks coming to see us, and it's
a shame that I don't.' I told him that such a battle was
about the same as a victory, and that God probably
looked at the heart rather than the lips."

After his second marriage he took more pains about
appearances than ever before. He grew more gentle
and acquiescent and manageable. He acquired some respect for conventionalities. He substituted new carpets
for the old ones which he had hitherto thought good
enough. He ceased to attend spiritualistic "seances"
and to communicate with Captain George and Phebe
Hand through that precarious avenue. He went no
more to the Manhattan Club, and even quitted his card
clubs. After that, his friends of the social quartet had
to come to the house if they wanted to play whist with
him. His children were all married off, and he had
more than thirty grandchildren, to whom, for the first
time in his life, he began to play the part of mysterious
generosity and personate Santa Claus at Christmas.

CHAPTER XIV.

FATHER AND SON.

Buying New Roads Westward—Building the Grand Central Depot—
William H.'s Office Habits—Overwork—A Glance at His Mail—
A Good-Natured Pessimist—The Complacent Commodore.

ALL of Commodore Vanderbilt's railroad interests were
now prosperous under the joint management of himself and his son. In November, 1869, on the consolidation of the Hudson River and Central, he became
President and William H. Vice-president of the system
—one of the largest and most important corporate enterprises in the world. The stock, which ranged from
75 to 120 in 1867, now touched 200, although the amount
was doubled.

The Commodore had always been averse to going
west of Buffalo. "If we take hold of roads running
all the way to Chicago," he was wont to say, "we
might as well go to San Francisco and to China." But
circumstances are stronger than logic, or any one man's
will, and they now compelled him to modify his purpose,
or at any rate his conduct. The same conflict of rival
interests that made it necessary to drive Corning, Pruyn,
and Keep out of the Central, and extend his management to Buffalo, now commanded a union with the
Lake Shore and Michigan Southern to enable him to
hold his own among the trunk lines.

His son-in-law, Horace F. Clark, had made some large operations in Lake Shore as early as 1870, had become its President, and had bolstered up its stock in the market because of his relationship to "the Railroad Emperor." He died suddenly in 1873, and the Commodore finding himself obliged to sustain the property, concluded that the easiest way to do so was to buy it. This, in a few years, made necessary the acquirement of the Canada Southern and Michigan Central, which was accomplished under the immediate administration of his son. These auxiliaries of the New York Central were imposed by the purchase of the Great Western by the Grand Trunk, and they gave "the Vanderbilt system" a needed terminus in Chicago.

During these years, too, the Commodore, now almost eighty years old, began and pushed to completion the vast enterprise by which the northern railroads obtain entrance to New York City. He obtained a charter from the Legislature authorizing the erection of an immense Union depot at Fourth Avenue and Forty-second Street, and giving him the use of the avenue thence to Harlem (previously occupied only by the surface rails of the Harlem Railroad) for an elaborate series of underground or viaduct tracks conducting into the very heart of the metropolis the trains of the Central and Hudson River, the Harlem, and the New Haven and Boston lines. The old man's brain was as accessible to new ideas as ever, as is evident by his adoption of iron trusses springing from the ground for the support of the immense roof of the depot, which was one of the very latest facts in the development of the use of iron in building.

The legislative enactment " allowed " the city to assume one-half of the cost of the spacious subterranean
way, and upon the acceptance of this provision by the
aldermen, the " Fourth Avenue Improvement," as it
was called, was immediately begun. This remarkable
achievement is too recent and too well known to need
particular description. It cost $6,500,000 for the su-
perbly constructed viaducts, tunnels, and bridges. One
hundred and fifty trains pass through them daily, and
the success with which the whole is managed is the
marvel of engineering.

The completion of a side-cut from the Hudson River
Railroad, at Spuyten Duyvel, following the creek of that
name to Harlem, thus furnishing a continuous branch to
the Forty-second Street Depot, was the culmination of
the stupendous project which has its origin in a brain
covered with the silver of four-score years. The Commodore was now ably seconded by the indefatigable
labors and constant vigilance of William H., whom he
had learned to trust implicitly and even advise with,
but he did not relinquish a jot either of his responsibility
or his power.

William H. Vanderbilt had learned a good deal in ten
years. He was not a brilliant original thinker and bold
planner, like his father, but he was, unlike his father,
careful, methodical, and industrious in familiarising himself with routine work. Indeed, this prodigal devotion to
details was his weakness. He resolved, on entering the
office of the Vanderbilt roads as their Vice-president, to
acquaint himself thoroughly with the practical working
of each department. He would not only mark every
check, see every bill, revise every contract, and inspect

every voucher of the finance department, but he would make himself master of transportation, construction, and equipment; he would examine every engine, know every engineer, keep watch of the coal-bin, find out what a new culvert ought to cost, have an eye on the ticket-office, stop all the leakages in the repair-shops, supervise the purchases of steel-rails and chestnut ties, look into the printing-office—in fact, he would find out everything there was to know. He attempted the impossible: a tremendous work, for which the eyes of Argus and the hands of Briareus would have been too few. No one man could do what he laid out for himself.

For a few years he adhered to his determination. He penetrated into every nook and corner of the system. He had become suspicious of others in his management of the Staten Island farm, and now he did not try to keep his suspicion from the knowledge of his employes. He investigated every part of the vast business, moving swiftly, and making his appearance unexpectedly. The immediate result was a steady improvement in the morale of the men, and in the effectiveness of the roads. Trains were on time. There was no hocus-pocusing of contracts. Stealing was reduced to its lowest terms.

Mr. Vanderbilt did not object to desk-work, but he had not that genius for shirking which has saved so many lives—the ability to turn over the easy routine work to other and cheaper men. If there was a letter to write he did not want to dictate it—he wanted to write it. He answered with his own hand all the letters he could. He did his work laboriously, and performed a vast amount of drudgery which executive officers usually assign to clerks. He insisted in reading his own business correspondence, although surrounded by men who had attested their fidelity to his interests by many years of service. He could not be induced to employ a phonographer, or permit others to dictate letters for him. He tried to take up the whole establishment and carry it at arms' length. This making himself a slave of minor details which he might have and ought to have shifted upon others, constantly tended to increase his irritability and to break down his health.

In conversation he was sometimes abrupt and brusque to the verge of rudeness, but he did not possess the power of annihilating an impudent applicant with that imperious scorn and majestic insolence of which his father was a master. He was a pessimist of a cheerful sort, and thought men and women, as a rule, "a pretty bad lot;" generally expressing his opinion of the aggregate in a good-humored, chaffing sort of way, which implied distrust rather than dislike. Whoever has a chance to look into the eleven bulky volumes of bound letters which William H. Vanderbilt preserved as racy samples of their kind—letters from rascals, proposing shady schemes; from charlatans and cranks, offering "valuable assistance;" from "socialists," threatening to kill him at a specified time and place; from women by the hundred, inclosing photographs and asking to see him; from ministers begging for churches, and mendicants of every degree begging for themselves—will come to the conclusion that his low opinion of human nature had a most reasonable foundation. He thought everybody in the world was ready to take advantage of him, and looked upon every stranger as either a foe whom he had yet to meet or a suppliant whom he must yet refuse. But his large fund of buoyancy and bonhommie saved him from falling into a petulent misanthropy.

Both he and his father had the experience of other rich men in encountering flunkies at every turn. Conscious that they did not know everything by a good deal, they wanted to obtain an honest opinion from those with whom they came into contact. Mr. Depew says: "I have frequently seen a look of distress on Mr. Vanderbilt's face when he was talking with a number of friends, because he could see that they were evidently trying to learn the bent of his wishes, so that they might follow him. What he wanted was an honest expression of personal opinion, and he found few men independent enough to give him their real opinions if they differed from his own. He knew that his judgment was not infallible, and he was anxious to learn the real truth about things and to obtain the candid opinions of others in regard to them. He might differ with a man and contest his reasoning, but his own opinion was often modified by what others said."

Like his father, he was perfectly democratic in his instincts. He was easily accessible to any visitor who had a right to his attention, and all were treated alike whether worth millions or nothing at all. He wanted no preposterous coat-of-arms. He never wore jewelry or made any show of his wealth, and always dressed in plain black.

He was anxious above all things to be considered a good fellow; he did not care about being thought a great man, and he did not wish people to humble themselves before him. It was this feeling which made him so popular on the road among horsemen, who considered themselves quite as good as he was, and talked with him on terms of perfect equality. This was, indeed, his safety valve, as there at least he was able to obtain the expression of unprejudiced opinion.

The father and son, at last united in interest and sympathy, now controlled the great northern trunk line to Chicago. They had laid four tracks on the Central, two exclusively for passengers and two for freight, giving the line indefinitely expansive powers. The freight trains could be run continuously, like an endless chain, and carry grain enough to load two hundred vessels a day, while the safety of passenger transfer was brought to a maximum.

Commodore Vanderbilt, now eighty-one years old, looked back at his achievements with complacent satisfaction. "I have made a million dollars every year of my life," he said one day, "and the best of it is that it has been worth three times that to the people of the United States." It was true. If he had put his money at interest when he was seventy, and sluggishly contented himself with the income, he would have benefited the country but little. Instead of that, he aroused to a new youth, began to search for something that needed rebuilding and renovating, laid his hand on the badly-managed railroads of his native State, prostrated by war and crippled by speculators, put together the isolated fragments, reconstructed and equipped them anew, rescued them from poverty and contempt, reduced their passenger and freight rates, and devised and executed improvements that placed his system at the head of the locomotive traffic of the planet. He had one continuous road nine hundred and seventy-eight miles in length,

6*

with side lines greatly increasing this total, representing an aggregate capital of $150,000,000, of which he owned one-half. Old age was on him and death confronted him, but he did not rest. He went on developing, strengthening, maturing, finishing, to the last.

He was, in his eighty-first year, a superb specimen of physical and intellectual manhood. Wherever he moved he attracted as much attention as the President or General Grant. Tall in stature, stately in bearing, his eye as bright as ever, his step still free, a slight consciousness of his extraordinary career expressed in his demeanor, with thirty-three grandchildren around his feet, and increasing tenderness taking possession of his heart and warming his face and his words, he held the foremost place, like some patrician patriarch, among the seniors of the commercial world.

CHAPTER XV.

THE COMMODORE'S CHARITIES.

His Opinion of Beggars—The Way He Gave—Careful About Money
—Meets Dr. Deems—Gives the Church of the Strangers—The
Tennessee University.

COMMODORE VANDERBILT was not naturally a philanthropist. The school of adversity in which he was
trained—penniless boy, boatman, skipper, steamboat
captain, ship-owner—was not calculated to turn his sym-
pathies toward the weak and destitute. A too fierce
fight with Nature almost always tends to harden the
heart rather than to soften it. It was strong men whom
he liked and sympathized with, not weak ones; the self-
reliant, not the helpless. He had always worked hard
and saved every penny that he could, both as boy and
man; "Let others do as I have done," he said, "and
they need not be around here begging." He felt that
the solicitor of charity was always a lazy or drunken
person trying to live by plundering the sober and industrious.

The conclusion was not quite accurate, but the intui-
tion was right. There were important exceptions to his
rule, but he had not time to hunt them up and provide
for them. It was not understood then, as it clearly is
now, that the promiscuous alms-giver on the city streets

does far more evil than good; that hap-hazard charity creates more paupers than it relieves; * and that it is the duty of every citizen to refuse to yield to that wounded emotion, heavenly in its origin but pernicious in its action, that inclines him to drop a nickel into the extended palm as the easiest way of getting rid of a suppliant and gratifying his own untutored moral sense. Darwin's felicitous phrase, "the survival of the fittest," though invented had not yet been popularized, but the Commodore instinctively felt that the average result of charity was to promote the survival of the unfittest, and that about the only way to do any permanent good was by teaching the indolent to be industrious, the unskillful to be expert, the extravagant to be economical, the sluggish to be ambitious—in short, by teaching the weak to help themselves.

He always had an eye to this sort of person among his old acqnaintances, and did not hesitate to give generously where the gift would stimulate the recipient to self-reliance. The people of Staten Island know of scores of instances in which he quietly attempted thus to lend a needed hand. His most persistent applicants for money were clergymen, and for them he felt an aversion not unmixed with contempt. As a rule he dis-

* Gerrit Smith gave so liberally and unreservingly that hundreds lost their self-respect through his largess, and some of his neighbors were turned into beggars. Herbert Spencer tells of a great bequest to an English village, which so demoralized the people that Parliament had to intercede and cancel the gift. It is notorious that as the poor-rates in England increase pauperism increases; and that in those cities where all the able-bodied poor are compelled to work for the public the number of those who solicit alms is reduced three-quarters.

missed them abruptly, sometimes rudely, and once, when he had been annoyed persistently by a needy parson, he presented him with a free ticket to the West Indies and never heard of him again.

One rule the Commodore had that was inflexible. He never put his name to a subscription paper for any purpose whatever. One day E. H. Carmick, his old partner in Nicaragua schemes, met him on Broadway. They talked about affairs in Washington for a moment, then Carmick said, "Commodore, I have something here that you'll be interested in," pulling out a subscription paper. "I want to build an asylum on Staten Island for broken-down merchants, where they can always have a warm home and plenty to eat. Roberts is going to give $10,000. Aspinwall and Astor are in it. We want you to give a lot down on your old place."

The Commodore heard him through, and then said, "No, Carmick; you ought to be about better business! Don't you know that about half the people's 'broken down' one way or another, and that if you was to roof Staten Island right over, it would be filled up before you could turn around ? "

One reason why he gave no more in such reasonable ways as that above mentioned is that the acquisitive habit of a life was so strong on him. He did not see that it was safe to let his expenditures keep step with his increasing wealth. "Something may happen," he kept saying; and, in fact, something in the shape of financial disaster came very near happening two or three times in his life and shipwrecking him. So he kept saving, and denying himself what his money would buy; constantly cheating himself for the sake of others. Only a few years before his death he had some internal trouble for which the doctor recommended champagne. "Champagne!" exclaimed the fifty-millionaire; "champagne! I can't afford champagne! A bottle every morning! Oh, I guess sody water'll do!"

Advancing years, inclining him to stay at home more and more, and the presence of a helpful and intelligent companion in his second wife, effected something of a change in his character. One day he said, "Frank, where is that Doctor Deems I've heard you talk about? —the one that you wanted to have marry us?"

"I haven't seen him since we came back to town," she answered; "he used to preach to strangers around in the University Building."

"I should think he might call on us," said the Commodore.

Somebody told the Doctor. "I have never run after rich people," he said. "I have not avoided them, but when a man, conspicuous for wealth or position, desires to know me, he must seek me. If I am expected I will call."

He was cordially received, contrary to the experience of most clergymen. They talked freely and frankly. The Commodore turned the talk upon the Doctor's work and hopes. They met often after that. One evening the conversation turned on clerical beggars, the host's pet aversion. The Doctor deprecated the whole business.

"Now here I am," he said. "I have been preaching for two years within ear-shot of the Commodore. My little rooms have been overrun. People have said to me, 'Why don't you see Mr. Lenox, or Mr. Stewart, or Mr. Astor, or Commodore Vanderbilt, and get some of them to build you a Church of the Strangers?' Not I. The Commodore will bear me witness that I have never solicited a dollar from him for any object on earth."

"No, he never has, Frank," he said, turning to his wife; evidently thinking the better of his visitor for the abstinence.

"And I never shall, as long as there is breath in my body," said the visitor.

The Commodore obviously did not quite like the remark, but the Doctor went on, "For if he has lived to attain his present age and has not got sense enough to see what I need and grace enough to send it, he will die without the sight." The speaker's impressions of the Commodore were not favorable. He regarded him as an unscrupulous hoarder of money, who merely aimed at accumulating an immense fortune, but had little concern for the human race.

Dr. Deems was at this time thinking of purchasing the Mercer Street Presbyterian Church edifice, hoping to pay for it somehow, and a report of this had got to the Commodore's ears. One Monday evening, at the close of a call, he asked his visitor to come around soon. The reply was that every evening for a week was occupied, but the next Saturday evening he went.

The Commodore offered to buy the Mercer Street Church for him. The Doctor says that he "fired up in a minute," because he supposed the donor had some sinister motive, either wanting a chaplain he could use, or desiring to get hold of the building for business purposes. His benefactor reassured him.

"After the discharge of the lightning of my anger," says the Doctor, "I felt that a sort of April shower

was coming. My eyes were moistening. It seemed a
wonderful Providence, for you know we always think it
is a wonderful Providence if it runs with our ideas. I
extended my hand and said, ' Commodore, if you give me
that church for the Lord Jesus Christ, I'll most thank-
fully accept it.'

" ' No,' said he ; ' Doctor, I wouldn't give it to you
that way, because that would be professing to you a religious sentiment I don't feel. I want to give you a
church. That's all about it. It is one friend doing
something for another friend. Now, if you take it that
way, I'll give it to you.'

" We both rose at the same moment, and I took his
hand and said, ' Commodore, in whatever spirit you give
it, I gratefully accept it, but I shall receive it in the
name of the Lord Jesus Christ.'

" ' O, well,' he said, ' let's go in the sitting-room and
see the women ! ' "

It was some time before the property could be got ;
and one day the Commodore's clerk, Mr. Wardell, called
and said, " Doctor, here is a package containing $50,000
in money from Commodore Vanderbilt." The following conversation took place:

PARSON. " Don't you know what this is for ? "
CLERK. "No, sir ; I don't."
PARSON. " Didn't the Commodore tell you ? "
CLERK. "No, sir."
PARSON. " Shall I give you a receipt ? "
CLERK. "No, sir."
PARSON. " Why don't you take a receipt ? "
CLERK. " The Commodore didn't ask for any."

The Doctor wanted the church given to trustees, but

GEORGE W. VANDERBILT.

the Commodore refused, saying, " No, you hammer away at some of them fellows about their sins and they'll turn around and bedevil you so that you will have to quit. I'm going to give it to you yourself."

" And from that day forth," testifies the Doctor, " he always treated me as one gentleman treats another who has done him a very great favor."

· After the gift of the Church of the Strangers the intimacy between the Commodore and the Rev. Dr. Deems grew.   There is a manuscript memorandum in which the Commodore's wife kept record of his sayings in his last days, in which he expressed his confidence in and love for this clergyman, and his delight that his life had been spared to see the University started, and his hope that he should live to see a wise way to do more. The story of how the University came to exist is as follows :

Commodore Vanderbilt and Dr. Deems were chatting together one evening at the residence of the former in Washington Place, when the conversation turned upon education.   "I'd give a million dollars to-day, Doctor," exclaimed the Commodore, " if I had your education ! "

" Is that your honest sentiment, Commodore ? " gravely asked the doctor.

" It is," was the reply.   " Folks may say that I don't care about education, but it ain't true ; I do.   I've been among educated people enough to see its importance. I've been to England, and seen them lords, and other fellows, and knew that I had twice as much brains as they had maybe, and yet I had to keep still, and couldn't say anything through fear of exposing myself."

During this last remark, Horace F. Clark, son-in-law

to the Commodore, slipped into the room unobserved by the latter, who happened to be sitting with his back to the door.

"Well!" he exclaimed, "I am glad to hear you admit at last, Commodore, that there is some benefit in an education. You've always spoken to me as if you thought it nothing."

The Commodore turned toward him, and, assuming a stern look, replied. "I seem to get along better than half of your educated men."

"Nevertheless, you have made the admission at last," continued Mr. Clark. "Dr. Deems has drawn it out of you for the first time, and I am a witness to it."

With this Mr. Clark prudently withdrew.

"If these are really your sentiments," Dr. Deems went on, "then you must let me tell you that you are one of the greatest hindrances to education that I know of."

"Why, how so?" asked the Commodore with surprise.

"Why, don't you see, if you do nothing to promote education, to prove to the world that you believe in it, there isn't a boy in all the land who ever heard of you, but may say, 'What's the use of an education? There's Commodore Vanderbilt; he never had any, and never wanted any, and yet he became the richest man in America.'"

"Will they say that?" asked the Commodore with evident feeling; and then he added, "But it isn't true. I do care for education, and always have. But what shall I do?"

"Show to the world your true sentiments," replied the Doctor.

"How?" was the response.

"Well," replied Dr. Deems, "here you are proposing to build a monument to Washington to cost a million of dollars. Such a monument will not add one iota to Washington's fame. A monument on every street-corner in America would not do it. Suppose you take that money and found a university."

"A university!" exclaimed the Commodore.

"Yes, why not? The Vanderbilt University, perhaps." This was the first time the name of the new university was ever spoken. The idea was new and valuable—worth considering. After further conversations on the subject the Commodore abandoned the plan of a magnificent monument to Washington, and finally requested Dr. Deems to canvass the question of founding a Moravian University. Naturally his heart turned toward the persecuted Church of his ancestors, and his first thought was to form a great college for its benefit. Dr. Deems took up the task and thoughtfully went over the whole field of the Moravian Church in America. The result was communicated to Commodore Vanderbilt, who found no one in that body to whom he could entrust so great a work. But he did not altogether give up the idea of founding a university. The subject still continued to be occasionally discussed, and gradually the harvest grew ripe for the reaper.

Many years before the incidents narrated above, when Dr. Deems was a clergyman in the South, he had an intimate friend, Rev. Dr. McTyeire, editor of a New Orleans paper. Since Dr. Deems had come to New York Dr. McTyeire had been made a Bishop of the Southern Methodist Church. In early life in Mobile he had been pastor of Miss Frank Crawford—Mrs. Commodore Vanderbilt—and had married a distant relative of hers. Mrs. Vanderbilt had very great affection for this friend of Dr. Deems and knew that Deems had the greatest confidence in McTyeire's ability and integrity. The Bishop was concerned in founding a university in the South. It occurred to Dr. Deems that he was the man the Commodore needed, and that it would help to allay the animosities between the North and the South engendered by the Civil War, if the Commodore would put his college in that section. These ideas were warmly shared by Mrs. Vanderbilt. How to bring the men together was the question. In the Spring of 1870, Dr. Deems had tried to secure an invitation for the Bishop from the Commodore, and was aided by Mrs. Vanderbilt, but it failed. As the intimacy grew between the Commodore and the pastor the time was finally ripe, and the invitation secured. The impression made on the Commodore by the Bishop was such as Mrs. Vanderbilt and Dr. Deems had anticipated. This was in March, 1873. The Bishop one day hurried over to the Doctor's study radiant with the news that the Commodore had offered $500,000 to a university to be founded at Nashville.

He returned home rejoicing and commenced the work, and prosecuted it vigorously. Subsequently the Commodore gave $100,000 more. Then some influence had been brought to bear on him to make him feel that the institution would probably be sectarian. The Doctor showed him how much better it was that a college should be under the care of some Church with a great denomination to back it, and brought him to that view, and showed him that a college with the name of Vanderbilt would be a shabby thing without at least a million of dollars in buildings and endowment. After further thought the Commodore agreed to give the other $400,000, which he arranged before his death. He never regretted it. One of the last expressions of his life was his telling his wife how glad he was that he had done it, and how satisfied he was that he had put it in the hands of men he so entirely trusted.

CHAPTER XVI.

DEATH OF THE COMMODORE.

Taken Ill at Eighty-two—Great Public Interest—The Vigilant Newspapers—Reporters Besiege the Invalid—Death After Eight
Months—A Simple Funeral—The Will.

THE three richest men in America at this time were
Commodore Vanderbilt; A. T. Stewart, who was nine
years his junior, and William B. Astor, who was two
months his senior. Mr. Astor died in November, 1875,
and Mr. Stewart in April, 1876, and less than a
month thereafter, on May 10th, the third and most conspicuous in this triumvirate of wealth was taken ill and
confined to his room.

Great was the excitement. Newspapers published
extras with such bits of fact or rumor as they could
gather. Reporters lay in wait for the doctor and am-
bushed the minister, and newsboys yelled under the
windows of No. 10 Washington Place, "Commodore
Vanderbilt dying!"

The venerable patient felt exasperated that such lib-
erties should be taken with him, and, when a reporter
called next morning, he crawled out of bed and shouted
down the stairs, "I am not dying! The slight local
disorder is now almost entirely gone and the doctor says
I will be well in a few days. Even if I was dying I

should have vigor enough to knock this abuse down your lying throats and give the undertaker a job!"

The protest did no good. The papers had columns daily about his various ailments, about how much he was worth, and how long he would live, and what effect his death would have on the stock market, and who would get his money. Every week some paper announced that he was dead. All summer he lay in the sweltering heat, and lived on. His iron constitution was doing battle for him against a conspiracy of a dozen diseases.

On August 3d he experienced a relapse so radical and severe that even his physicians concluded that his last hours had come. At midnight his life was despaired of, his pulses fluttered feebly, his feet grew cold, his heart intermitted its beats, and the family, brother and sisters, children and grandchildren, gathered around the bed to bid him a long farewell. Then he turned over toward the wall and went to sleep. The next morning's papers recorded his death, but he rallied and got up.

That brigade of enterprising and courteous gentlemen, the New York reporters, had a very lively time of it during the Centennial summer. Every daily had to have a relay, that one might be perpetually on guard at the house.

As wet autumnal days came on, presaging the cold of winter, the score of reporters who had swarmed around the front steps, found the position more and more uncomfortable. They made better arrangements by hiring a large front-room across the street, and thus put the distinguished invalid in a state of siege. One of them has told the curious story of that unique vigil: how they whiled away the weary hours with chess and cards and books; how they tried to establish some regularity of beer and lunches; how they effected an organization to save unnecessary expenditure of effort, appointing a guard to constantly watch the door across the way through the slats of the closed blinds; how they had a picket and a patrol outside, waylaying everybody that emerged from the house; and how impatient they became for a change of some sort—any sort—in the patient's condition.

There was another relapse and another, and a council of physicians was called. Again he rallied, and passed the "golden cycle" of Christmas holidays safely, and emerged upon the New Year. On the afternoon of January 3d he was placed in his rolling-chair and wheeled to the sitting-room, seeming to enjoy the trip. The sick-chamber was on the southeast corner of the second floor, and there he had been for eight months.

At two o'clock on the morning of the 4th a change for the worse took place, and the members of the family were summoned. William H. Vanderbilt arrived at five o'clock, and shortly there were gathered about the bed of the dying man his children, grandchildren, and great-grandchildren. Four able physicians were in attendance, and Rev. Dr. Deems came at nine o'clock. The Commodore comprehended the fact that his last day had come, and spoke to all his descendants, calmly bidding them good-by.

Singing was suggested, and he immediately assenting, Mrs. Crawford led in his favorite hymns, " Come ye Sinners, Poor and Needy," " Nearer, my God, to Thee," and " Show pity, Lord." His face brightened up and he feebly joined in the singing. Just before ten o'clock he asked Dr. Deems to pray with him ; he seemed to follow the prayer, and at the end tried to repeat the benediction. He said, " That's a good prayer," and grasped the Doctor's hand, adding, " I shall never give up trust in Jesus : how could I let that go ? "

At 10.30 A.M. he ceased attempting to speak ; he lifted his right hand and closed his own eyelids, became for a few moments unconscious, or at any rate unresponsive, drew one deep breath and died. He expired peacefully and apparently without pain. Exhausted nature slept the long sleep.

Among those present were his wife, and her mother, Mrs. Crawford ; Mr. and Mrs. W. H. Vanderbilt and their children ; Mrs. Daniel Torrance and husband and daughter ; Mrs. J. B. Allen ; Mrs. George A. Osgood and husband ; Mrs. N. B. La Bau ; Mrs. James M. Cross and husband ; Mrs. William K. Thorn and husband ; Mrs. Meredith Howland and husband ; Mr. C. N. De Forest ; Mrs. S. D. Barton ; Mr. E. D. Worcester, Secretary of the Central Road, and Elliott F. Shephard.

The Commodore's brother, Captain Jacob Vanderbilt, and his sister, Miss Phebe Vanderbilt, were not present, being with another sister, Mrs. Charlotte Egbert, who was lying at the point of death at her home in Tompkinsville, S. I.*

The Commodore had exhibited tremendous vital force, and two of his physicians had died during their attendance upon him.

The funeral was held at 10.30 A.M. the next Sunday,

---

* This was his oldest sister, after whom his first sloop was named, then the wife of Captain De Forest. She died the day after the Commodore.

7

in the Church of the Strangers. In accordance with his express request and direction it was extremely simple, and characterized by a lack of display and parade. He had often condemned the fashionable folly which oppressed the poor with expensive funerals, and had alleged that the rich were responsible for it. He would not have his funeral stir up such pernicious emulation and rob the poor of their hard earnings. So he had said, " No flowers at my funeral; not one! No costly badges of mourning; no crape for showing off!" The injunction was obeyed.

By his express command the Grand Central Depot was not draped in mourning, nor were there any sable trappings or somber festoonery on cars or locomotives.

Among those who attended the funeral were Daniel Drew, Thurlow Weed, Samuel Ward, Gordon W. Burnham, Marshall O. Roberts, ex-Governor Morgan, Peter Cooper, Charles O'Conor, and Frank Leslie, all since dead, though it was only nine years ago.

Dr. Deems said at the funeral that the deceased lacked only two things : early scholastic culture and intimate religious relations during the middle and main part of his life. The last he regretted, but Nature, by giving him a wonderful intellect, compensated for the first in part.

His remains were deposited in the vault of the old Moravian cemetery which his ancestors of the "United Brethren" had helped lay out at New Dorp, and in which most of their bodies lay. He himself had given fifty acres of land to the cemetery.

Commodore Vanderbilt had never connected himself with a church, and was, in his conversation, an irreligious man; but he had never thought about dogmatic theology much, and had never ceased to believe what his pious mother had taught when he was a child. The doctrine of a supreme being, a devil, a heaven, a hell, an atonement, he regarded as settled facts, as undeniable as the multiplication-table. Whenever he spoke of Jesus Christ seriously and deliberately he always alluded to him as " Our Saviour," and he reverently called the Bible " the Holy Scriptures."

He had as great a horror of being thought an infidel as Daniel Drew had, and often declared that he " wouldn't trust with a dollar " a man who doubted the inspiration of the Bible. During his last illness, as he lay on the lounge and Doctor Deems was fanning him one day, he said, " I don't want any misunderstanding about this business. You haven't converted me. I didn't need converting. I always believed in the truth of these things you preach about. You haven't had any more effect on my belief than that fan has ! "

The public had not doubted what would be the general character of the will. William H. Vanderbilt, being the oldest son and the only one fitted by habits and training to take care of it, would undoubtedly inherit the bulk of the property. In this all were agreed. When the will was produced in the Surrogate's Court, four days afterward, it was found that the general conjecture was correct. Not far from $90,000,000 was left to William H. Of the bequests to all other persons, amounting to $15,000,000, one-half went to the four sons of the principal heir, and the oldest son, Cornelius, whose progress the decedent had watched and approved, got much the largest share.*

* See Appendix D.

CHAPTER XVII.

THE COMMODORE'S SUCCESSOR.

Industrious and Prudent—Compromises with Foes—Dealing with Laborers—Contest of the Will—The Quarrel Ended—Generosity and Human Nature—Accurate Business Habits.

WILLIAM H. VANDERBILT, now fifty-six years old, was thoroughly equipped for his new rôle. It involved no radical change in his methods or his life. He immediately took charge of the property, and became president of all the roads, where he had before been vice-president, but his relation to affairs was not materially modified. His service had never been perfunctory. It had been an honest devotion to the interests of his father's property. The only difference seen in 1877 was that his great vigilance and energy in administration were increased; he merely worked harder where he had always before worked hard. He felt the weight of the additional responsibility, and he resolved that his father's apprehension that he would lose the property should not be realized. What he lacked of his father's genius and brilliant audacity he would make up in greater industry and cautiousness.

The first year was signalized by the vigorous warfare in west-bound freight-rates between the trunk lines. Mr. Vanderbilt favored compromise. This was probably the wisest thing to do, but it showed that he did not possess the strenuous temper of his father. The Commodore's energies would have been bent, not to making compacts with rival systems, but to making conquests of them. He recognized no equals. He would have so extended his own system as to make all others confessedly subordinate, reducing them to the rank of local roads. Or, if this were found impracticable, on account of some other possessing better natural facilities for the chief highway across the continent, he would have boldly abandoned his own lines and transferred his capital and his abilities to another as readily as he deserted sails for steam, or ships for locomotives. He was far-sighted and had a broad horizon. He knew no rest and wanted none.

Nor did the son care for rest, but he wanted peace. He was not pugnacious, or happy in the midst of conflict, and about the first thing he did was to put an end to the freight-rate chaos that had lasted for years, and establish an arrangement with his rivals that would enable him to avoid the continual battle, the din of which was one of the pleasures of his father's life.

Truce was hardly declared before the railroad strikes and riots began. One of the results of cutting rates had been that the companies had been unable to maintain their scale of wages, and the Hudson River and Central had in July made a reduction of ten per cent. There were 12,000 men in its employ, and apprehensions began to be felt, in view of the febrile condition of the working-classes, that trouble might result from the reduction. An attack on the Grand Central Depot was threatened. Mr. Vanderbilt was in Saratoga, and call-

ing some directors and officers into conference, a plan
was devised, adopted, and put into execution. He sent
out by telegraph a proclamation that the New York
Central and Hudson River Railroad Company would
give to its employés $100,000 ratably, except to the
executive, departmental, and clerical forces. At the
same time he promised a restoration of the ten per cent.
as soon as the business of the road justified the action.
Out of the 12,000 men less than 500 gave trouble, and
the old wages were eventually restored.

During the early years of his absolute control of the
property, he did all he could to avoid friction, and re-
duce the chances of rate-cutting on the part of rival
roads.

But all did not go smoothly. There were angry mut-
terings about the will. William H. Vanderbilt had received at least $90,000,000, while to the unfortunate sec-
ond son, Cornelius J., the testator bequeathed only the
income derived from $200,000, with the condition that
he should forfeit even this if he began a contest of the
will. For years " Cornele" had been virtually banished
from his father's house, occasional interviews being obtained only through the intercession of his mother or
sisters. Even on his death-bed, the Commodore said
he did not care to see his wayward son. The feeling
was reciprocal, and the latter took apparent pleasure in
rehearsing to knots of listeners the story of his wrongs,
and details of his father's life which were probably the
offspring of a sick man's disordered fancy.

"Why doesn't he give me a chance?" the exiled
epileptic would ask in an angry whine. "Everybody
admits that I know more than Bill does, even if I don't

know very much. Why doesn't father put me in charge of some little branch road somewhere and see what I could do ? "

But the father remained unrelenting, and he had emphasized his distrust in his will. As to the merits of the division of property, public opinion was mainly on the side of the chief legatee, but many who did not know the pensioned son thought that injustice had been done him. There were greedy and needy lawyers to fan the controversy, and the result at last was a contest of the will. For a year the public was regaled with foreshadowings of the evidence at hand to prove the testator's mental incompetency to make a will, and it revealed much of family matters that was not entirely pleasant, and a tremendous inventive faculty on the part of the contestant. The public appetite was whetted, and the public eye on the *qui vive* for scandal when, to his credit, Mr. Vanderbilt compromised by giving to his litigious brother the income on $1,000,000.*

At least two of the sisters had sympathized with " Cornele's " suit, and had given him aid and comfort, neither of them liking the legatee, and one of them not having been for years on speaking terms with him ; but now, in addition to the bequests made to his sisters, William H. voluntarily added $500,000 to each from his own portion.

He drove around one evening, and distributed this splendid largess from his carriage, he himself carrying the bonds into each house in his arms and delivering

---

* A year or two later, on April 2, 1882, Cornelius Jeremiah Vanderbilt was shot dead in his room at the Glenham Hotel, and it was supposed that the shot was fired by his own hand.

them to each sister in turn. The donation was accompanied by two interesting incidents. In one case the husband said, " William, I've made a quick calculation here, and I find these bonds don't amount to quite $500,000. They're $150 short, at the price quoted to-day." The donor smiled, and sat down and made out his check for the sum to balance.

In another case, a husband, after counting and receipting for the $500,000 followed the generous visitor out of the door, and said, " By the way, if you conclude to give the other sisters any more, you'll see that we fare as well as any of them, won't you ? " The donor jumped into his carriage and drove off without replying, only saying, with a laugh, to his companions, " Well, what do you think o' that ? "

The money which " Cornele " had borrowed so recklessly of Horace Greeley had never been repaid, and knowing that the too-generous editor's daughters were in need of it, Whitelaw Reid, his successor on the *Tribune*, began timely and vigorous negotiations which resulted successfully. It was made one of the conditions of the compromise of the law-suit that $60,000 should be at once paid to them, and the condition was fulfilled.

Negotiations for the purchase of the Canada Southern began before the Commodore died, but remained to be completed. Now Mr. Vanderbilt, in consideration of paying the debt resulting from a default on its bond-interest, was given a majority of the stock. A joint committee representing the two companies agreed upon a basis of reorganization, the old bonds being exchanged for new, bearing three per cent. interest for five years and five per cent. thereafter, the interest on the new issue being guaranteed for twenty years by the New York Central road. The Michigan Central was purchased in open market.

Mr Vanderbilt's financial methods showed that he regarded the fortune that had been left him as a trust, and he took good care not to dissipate it. He took few chances. His father was never more careful about interest than he. He allowed nothing to go to loose ends. He compelled strict accounting, and never gave any man with whom he had dealings a dollar that was not his due. He was never penurious, but he always made close calculations.

At one time when he was in Europe, he wrote home, " We are being cheated out of our eye-teeth, and have to pay at least double prices everywhere, because we are supposed to be rich. We have to put up with the overcharges, for it is the only way to get through Europe. But it makes me mad all the same."

When in active control of affairs at the office he followed the unwholesome habit of eating the midday lunch at his desk, the waiter bringing it from a neighboring restaurant.

He paid his bill for this weekly, and he always scrutinized the items with proper care. " Was I here last Thursday ? " he asked of a clerk at an adjoining desk.

" No, Mr. Vanderbilt; you stayed at home that day."

" So I thought," he said, and struck that day from the bill.

Another time he would exclaim, *sotto voce*, " I didn't order coffee last Tuesday," and that item would vanish.

These instances are mentioned as illustrating his care-

7*

ful and accurate business habits, the prime secret of his success as a railroad operator and owner.

All these years the growth of the country was unprecedented. Every day brought across the sea new citizens to cultivate and populate the West, and the incoming ship was a feeder of his roads, and the quarter-section of prairie-land turned up to the sun and planted with wheat increased his revenue.

The vast fortune left him by his father was visibly growing, and he soon began at Fifth Avenue and Fifty-first Street the construction of a palace commensurate with his income, and the establishment of a gallery of modern art adequate to grace so spacious and luxurious a mansion.

CHAPTER XVIII.

THE MANSION.

THE finest and most costly private residence in
America is the brown-stone house on the northwesterly
corner of Fifth Avenue and Fifty-first Street, standing
on a lot fronting 100 feet on the avenue, and extending
back 150 feet. The whole block between Fifty-first and
Fifty-second Streets was secured, and on this Mr. Vanderbilt erected this double four-story mansion.

The southern portion of this was for his own residence, while the northern building he gave to his two
daughters, Mrs. Sloane and Mrs. Shepard. His own
residence is 115×84 feet, and is built in the style of
architecture known as the Greek renaissance. About
three years were consumed in building the mansions, and
the family moved in late in 1881, Mrs. Vanderbilt giving
her first reception on the 17th of January, 1882.

It was Mr. Vanderbilt's first intention to build his
houses of light stone, with colored marble pilasters,
columns and trimmings, but as much of the material
would have to be imported, and the carvings would take
a long time, it might delay the completion of the build-

ings for a couple of years. On this account, even after the foundations were laid, and all the plans completed, Mr. Vanderbilt decided at the last moment to use brown-stone, the material generally used for Fifth Avenue residences. He said that he was not a young man, and that taking the average, he had a life of about ten years before him, and that as he wanted to live in the house, and did not wish to be engaged in building all of his days, brown-stone should be used, as it would not take so long to work as the materials originally proposed.

Mrs. Vanderbilt was contented with her home at 450 Fifth Avenue, and never wished for a better. However rich and opulent her subsequent surroundings, she has still remembered, with never-fading pleasure, the quiet home on the New Dorp farm, and the real friendships formed there. She tried to dissuade her husband from entering the new palace. She once said to a friend, who called upon her while the great residence was in the course of construction:

" We don't need a house better than this, and I hate to think of leaving it, for we have lived so comfortably here! I have told William that if he wants a finer place for his pictures to build a gallery to which he could go whenever he felt inclined; this is too good a house to leave. I shall never feel at home in the new place."

Work was begun in 1879, and was pushed with such energy and rapidity that the new houses were completed in two years. More than six hundred men were em-ployed for a year and a half on the interior decorations, and sixty sculptors brought from Europe were kept at work the same length of time. The cost of the whole

block of houses was over two millions of dollars, two-
thirds of which should be set down to his own residence.
The designing, construction, and furnishing of the house
was left wholly to the artists whom he employed, and he
never made any contracts with them, they having *carte
blanche* to ransack the world and spare no money to get
what they needed.   He took great interest in the work
during its progress, and all the designs were submitted
to him, from the first stone to the last piece of decoration or furniture.   He spent many pleasant hours in the
designing-rooms, and often gave the workmen money to
encourage them.

The drawing-room, the dining-room, and the lower
hall, are the most costly parts of the residence.   The
house is entered by a spacious vestibule which stretches
between the two mansions.   The ceiling of this is of
bronze and stained glass, filled in with a mosaic made
by Fecchina, of Venice, from plans drawn in New York.
The walls are of a light-colored African marble sur-
mounted by a frieze of figures in mosaic.   There are
fixed marble seats in this room, the floor of which is of
marble and mosaic.   The bronze doors at the entrance
are Barbedienne reductions of those by Ghiberti in the
Baptistry at Florence.   These were given to Mr. Vanderbilt by his son-in-law, Mr. Elliot F. Shepard, who
bought them at the San Donato sale for $20,000.   They
were formerly the doors of the palace of the Prince of
San Donato.   A large malachite vase stands in this vestibule.   It was bought for Mr. Vanderbilt, at the same
sale, by Governor J. Schuyler Crosby, then United States
Consul at Florence.   It was given to the first Prince
Demidoff, of San Donato, by the Emperor of Russia.

Passing from this large outer vestibule, one enters the
private vestibule of the Vanderbilt residence, which is
finished with a high wainscoating of marble, and has
three bronze doors—the one on the right opening into
a small dressing-room, the left into Mr. Vanderbilt's
private reception-room, and the third door into the
main hall of the house. The great middle hall or court
extends the full height of the house, and is surrounded
by galleries, tier above tier, leading to the different private living-rooms. It is lighted by nine large stained
glass windows, and is surrounded by a wainscoting
twelve feet high, in carved English oak. Eight square
pillars of dark red African marble, with bronze capitals,
support the galleries. Facing the entrance is a large
and beautiful mantel-piece of red marble and bronze,
over an open fire-place. It reaches to the first gallery,
and has on each side a life-size female figure in bronze
in high relief. The chimney-piece is of massive sculpt-
ured marble, and the effect is very fine. Carved oak
seats are placed on both sides of the door on the eastern
side of the hall, passing into the drawing-room. The
main staircase leads from the north of this hall, and is
lighted by stained glass windows by La Farge, noticeable
for the artist's management of greens and blues.

The drawing-room, which is 25 × 31 feet, has a ceiling
painted by Gallaud, of Paris. The wood-work is a mass
of sculpture, gilded and glazed with warm tints. The
walls are hung with a pale red velvet, embroidered with
foliage, flowers, and butterflies, and enriched with cut
crystal and precious stones. The lights are arranged in
eight vases of stained and jewelled glass disposed at the
corners, at the angles of the large east window, and

at the sides of the door. Some of these vases, upheld by female figures in solid silver, stand on pedestals of onyx with bronze trimmings, while the lights in the corners are backed by mirrors, to add to their brilliancy, and rest on black velvet bases. The carpet was woven in Europe from special designs.

At the north of the drawing-room there is a door opening into the library, a room 26 × 17 feet. The wood-work of this room, composed of mahogany and rose-wood, is inlaid with mother-of-pearl and brass in an antique Greek pattern. The book-cases, mantels, and doors are treated in the same manner. A large table in the same style stands in the center of the room, and all the furniture corresponds. The ceiling is set with panels containing small square mirrors.

In Mr. Vanderbilt's private reception-room the walls are fitted with a high wainscoting of mahogany, the space above being covered with stamped leather. The ceiling is of massive mahogany.

South of the drawing-room there is a Japanese parlor. In this room the ceiling is of bamboo, picked out with red, green, and yellow lacquer-work. The rafters are exposed. A low-toned tapestry, with panels of Japanese uncut velvet in curious designs, cover the walls and fur-niture. A low cabinet of Japanese pattern extends around the room, containing innumerable shelves, cup-boards, and closets. At various points there are bronze panels, picked out in gold and silver. There is a large open fireplace in this room. The dimensions of this room are the same as those of the library, 17 × 26 feet.

To the west is the handsome dining-room, in Italian Renaissance, 28 × 37 feet. It contains an arrangement

of glass-faced cases, supported by rich consoles, that rest
upon a beautiful wainscot of English oak, of a deep
golden hue, delicately carved. These cases are filled
with silver, porcelain, and glass. The elliptical arched
ceiling is divided into small oblong panels, carved in
relief, representing fruit and foliage decorated in various
tints of gold. The spaces at each end of the room, between the wainscot and ceiling, and the large center
panel of the ceiling, are filled with paintings by Lumin-
ais, of Paris, representing hunting-scenes, etc. The furniture is of English oak, with brass ornaments, and covered with stamped leather.

The great picture-gallery is to the west of the main
hall, and occupies the entire rear of the building. The
dimensions are 32×48 feet. The ceiling is thirty-five
feet high, and is chiefly formed of a sky-light in opalescent and tinted glass, leaded in quaint designs. A mon-
umental mantelpiece of red African marble, with cone
of glass mosaic-work, occupies the western wall. The
woodwork of the room is black oak, with San Domingo
mahogany for the caryatides and pilasters. The floor is
inlaid with the same mahogany, and bordered with a
mosaic of Sienna and black marble in the Pompeiian
style. The walls above the wainscoting are covered
with a dark-red tapestry, to set off the pictures. Over
the doors on the north, east, and south sides are balconies
connecting with the second story of the house. The gallery has a separate entrance from Fifty-first Street, and
the vestibule is entirely—floor, walls and ceiling—of
marble mosaic-work made in Venice. North of the gallery is the aquarelle room. This is finished in Circas-
sian walnut, Moorish style, touched here and there with

bright colors. The conservatory opens into the gallery from the west.

After ascending the staircase, with its bronze banisters, to the first landing, the room in the northeast corner of the house is the family parlor. It is finished in ebony, inlaid with ivory. The walls are covered with a dark-blue silk brocade, and the ceiling is divided in small panels, with paintings of children at play.

The next room on Fifth Avenue is Mrs. Vanderbilt's bedroom, furnished by Alard, of Paris. The walls are of white marble, hung with silk, and the ceiling is covered with the painting, "Awakening of Aurora," by Lefebvre. The frieze is of rosewood and mahogany. The room is twenty-six feet square.

Mr. Vanderbilt's room, adjoining, is the one in which he died. A large Turkish rug covers the polished oak floor, in the center of the room, and richly embroidered hangings of golden-brown are draped from the windows and doors of the apartment. The furniture is of polished ebony, artistically inlaid with satin-wood, and from the canopy of the bed hang heavy silken curtains. Carefully selected paintings from the brushes of master hands grace the paneled walls at intervals.

Adjoining the bedroom is a dressing-room. This is wainscoted eight feet high in glass opalescent tiles of blue, gold, and silver tints, and gilded on the backs. The bath-tubs and basins are of mahogany and silver, and are concealed by sliding plate-glass mirrors. A well appointed dressing-table and a luxurious barber's chair, comprise the furniture of this room.

The large room on Fifty-first Street is a library, fitted up in mahogany and stamped leather. The bedroom intended for Miss Lelia, now Mrs. Webb, is fitted with rosewood, inlaid with mother-of-pearl. The mirrors are painted with an imitation of lacework through which peep children's heads.

Mr. Vanderbilt had expressed the hope that he would be able to live in his palace ten years, but when five years had barely elapsed he was buried from its spacious vestibule.

CHAPTER XIX.

THE ART GALLERY.

Modern French Art—Best Collection in the World—A Good Investment—Mr. Vanderbilt's Tastes and Fancies—His Visits to Artists—Abuse of Hospitality.

ONE of the most enduring monuments of William H.
Vanderbilt is the collection of art treasures which he
made. The value of these pictures is estimated at a million and a half of dollars, and it is known to be the most
complete collection of works in the world representing
the best modern artists of France. The canvases number
a little over two hundred, and many are the best examples of the masters who painted them. They were
not purchased as a commercial speculation, although the
money is well invested, since they constantly increase in
value with age, and especially after the death of the artists, for Mr. Vanderbilt included a provision in his will
which should forever continue the gallery and the house
in the possession of some male descendant of his bearing
the name of Vanderbilt.

Mr. Vanderbilt had learned to enjoy and appreciate
works of art long before he was able to purchase the
best. Even when he went to Europe with his father in
the memorable North Star excursion, he brought
back with him for his farm-house on Staten Island a

couple of small but good Italian paintings. Later in life, after he had become associated with the Commodore in business, and was living on Fifth Avenue, he was fond of going down to the Tenth Street Studio Building, in New York, and purchasing works by such well-known American artists as Samuel Coleman, James Hart, J. F. Cropsey, J. Brown, Tait, Beard and Guy. He was especially fond of Mr. Guy, and finally gave him an order for a large picture representing the interior of his residence at the corner of Fifth Avenue and Fortieth Street, with himself surrounded by his family. At the request of Mr. Guy he allowed this picture to be exhibited at the National Academy. There it was seen by a horde of irresponsible newspaper critics, who permitted themselves to write many things which were personal to Mr. Vanderbilt and his family, and which proved very annoying. Some critics forget to be judicial regarding the work under review, when they happen to know the artist or author. After this experience Mr. Vanderbilt said he would never loan another picture for public view, and he never did.

Mr. Vanderbilt did not continue to make a collection of American pictures after he had come into possession of his fortune, since he was able to buy the best and most costly in the world. He decided, at the outset, to procure nothing that was not important. Many of his fine pictures were painted to order. He visited Paris frequently, became acquainted with the artists, and took a personal interest in them. When he gave a commission, it was not unusual for him to offer a higher price than was proposed, telling the artists at the same time that he wanted them to do the best they could. He

often made the artists presents in addition to the stipu-
lated price. In 1878 he had four pictures painted to
order by Meissonier, Gérôme, Detaille, and Rosa Bonheur. These are, in the order of the artists named
above, "An Artist and his Wife," 18 × 15 inches; "Reception of the Prince of Condé by Louis XIV.";
"The Arrest of an Ambulance, Eastern Part of France,
January, 1871," 46 × 32 inches; and "A Flock of
Sheep."

In 1879 the following pictures were painted to order
for him, "Down by the River," by Alma-Tadema, of London, a work 32 × 68 inches; "The Portrait," by Louis
Leloir; "A Fête During the Carnival," by Madrazo;
"Ready for the Hunt," by Rosa Bonheur, and "Ready
for the Fancy Ball," a water-color by Alfred Stevens.
In 1880 Meissonier's portrait of Mr. Vanderbilt was
added to the collection; Antoine Seitz, of Munich, added
"Homeless," and Detaille and Vibert contributed two
water-colors. In 1881 new pictures were painted to
order by Professor Knaus, of the Berlin Academy, and
Defregger, of Munich. In 1882 Jules Lefevre, of Paris,
painted his great picture, "Attiring the Bride," a canvas 69 × 94 inches.

Mr. Vanderbilt, like most other men of decided
character, liked to do things in his own way. He was
not niggardly in his dealings with artists, acting toward
them with the same generosity and lavishness he always
showed in the building and furnishing of his house.
But he had an independent judgment of his own, and,
regardless of the reputation of the artist, he would not
buy a work which he did not like and comprehend. If
his attention was called to a certain picture, he was apt

to reply, "It may be very fine, but until I can appreciate its beauty I shall not buy it." For many years Mr.
Vanderbilt would not buy a Corot, since he did not see
the beauty of his work, but in the end he purchased two
small examples, because, he said, he was tired of being
told that he must have a Corot! He liked pictures
which told a story, with either strong or cheerful subjects, such as appeal to the imagination of the ordinary
individual, and of these the bulk of his gallery is composed. In this he seems to have had the spirit of the
Greek artists of two thousand years ago, the chief characteristic of whose work was simplicity. According to
Professor Waldstein, of Cambridge, England, "Their
works were meant to be gazed upon, and not to be the
subject of learned commentaries ; they were intelligible
to the people, appealed to their senses, their feelings,
without the need of a verbal explanation."

He had no affectation regarding the fine arts, or anything else, but was frank and simple in his manners and
conversation. He would not purchase a picture of a
nude subject, and he had a natural delicacy which made
him dislike anything bordering on the doubtful or pru-
rient, hence there are no such pictures in his gallery.
He was fond of brilliant historical pictures, and obtained
many of them. Mr. Vanderbilt may have intended, as
has been asserted in some quarters, to use his collection
for the public good, and especially for the benefit of
American artists, but since no such arrangement is con-
templated by his will it would be profitless to discuss
what he might have done. Soon after taking possession of his house in 1882, he gave several large receptions to his gentlemen friends, who were invited to

inspect the picture-gallery. And on a few occasions he opened his gallery to those who had been invited by card.

An anecdote is related of Mr. Vanderbilt, while in Paris, which shows that he was always guided by common-sense. A French nobleman wrote to him that he had many articles of *vertu* which he wished to sell, such as Louis XVI. furniture, Sèvres china, Marie Antoinette tables, etc. Mr. Vanderbilt went to the house and saw the nobleman and his articles of *vertu*. When he returned, he said,

"There are those who are supposed to know all about these things and their intrinsic value, and of the associations connected with them. Well, I do not know all that, and I am too old to learn. If I should buy these things and take them to New York and tell my friends this belonged to Louis XVI. or to Mme. Pompadour, and should relate all the other things which make them valuable, I should be taking them from a field where they are appreciated to a place where they would not be. Perhaps I should know less about them than any one else. It would be mere affectation for me to buy such things."

During his visits to Paris Mr. Vanderbilt became acquainted with many of the foremost French artists, among others Meissonier, whom he liked well, and of whom he purchased altogether seven pictures, at a total cost of $188,000. The artist, in turn, appeared to like his great patron, and the two got on well together. One day in 1880 Mr. Vanderbilt requested Meissonier to paint his portrait. "I do not often paint portraits," was the reply, "but I will paint one for you."

While sitting for this, Mr. Vanderbilt asked the artist which picture he considered to be the finest he had ever painted. "The Information—General Desaix and the Captured Peasant," was the reply.

"Where is it?" asked Mr. Vanderbilt.

"I have not seen it since 1867, when I painted it," said the artist sadly. "It is in Dresden, and belongs to the collection of Mr. Meyer. It is lost to France," he added, as if he felt sore that such a fine work should be owned by a German.

Immediately, without letting the artist into the secret, Mr. Vanderbilt requested his agent to ascertain from the owner the price for which he would sell the picture.

"Fifty thousand dollars," came in reply.

"Get it," was the answer, and he drew a check upon his banker for the full amount. Mr. Meyer objected to the check, and wanted the cash, so the next day Mr. Vanderbilt went to the bank and drew the money, and in a few days the picture was delivered in Paris. Then he prepared a surprise for the artist. He had the picture placed on an easel in a room adjoining Meissonier's studio, and at the close of one of his sittings for the portrait, said,

"Meissonier, I want your judgment on a picture I have just purchased."

"Certainly, with pleasure," was the reply. "Where is it?"

"In the next room," said Mr. Vanderbilt.

So they went into the room, and Mr. Vanderbilt's attendant uncovered the picture, and behold! it was Meissonier's masterpiece. The effect was electric. The

W. H. VANDERBILT'S RESIDENCE.

artist threw up his arms, uttered exclamations of delight, got down on his knees before the canvas, sent for his wife, and danced about as only a mad French artist can. Mr. Vanderbilt heartily enjoyed the little comedy, and in due time had the picture sent to New York.

For Meissonier's picture, "The Arrival at the Château," Mr. Vanderbilt paid $40,000. He made very liberal offers to Mr. Delahaute, of Paris, for Meissonier's "1814," representing Napoleon with his marshals, all on horseback, at the head of his army, plodding on through a deep snow, but that gentleman declined to part with his treasure.

Mr. Vanderbilt bought his own pictures, as everything else. Two or three middlemen, known as "dealers," tried to enhance their reputation and increase their business by allowing it to be understood that they were doing his buying for him; but this was a mistake. He knew what he was about, and employed them as seldom as possible. In their stead, he called to his sympathetic assistance several friendly connoisseurs in art, who helped him gratuitously and impartially. He began to buy pictures quite early in life, before he could well afford to do so, which shows that he had a natural love for art, as he had for horses. A little picture which Mrs. Vanderbilt prizes more than any of the rest is a souvenir which her husband gave her more than thirty years ago, and which cost in the neighborhood of ninety dollars. One day, when the pictures were being rearranged in his new house, he pointed out this one to his son George, who remarked : " I suppose, father, you would not take $800 for that now." "No, nor $8,000, or even $80,000," he replied.

He had learned to love it, and it had given him and his wife an immense amount of enjoyment when they lived in the seclusion and retirement of the New Dorp farm. It was this same life on a farm which enabled him to have some sort of judgment regarding at least two of the valuable pictures he bought; and even when in Paris, at the Palais Royal, or in the studios of the most famous artists, he did not hesitate, if occasion demanded, to acknowledge with frankness and simplicity his former humble life. He once made a visit to Boucheron, a famous French picture-dealer, to see a work by Troyon, which was for sale. The subject is a yoke of oxen turning to leave the field after being taken from the plow. While connoisseurs spoke highly of the work they were inclined to take exceptions to the action of the cattle, thinking it forced and unnatural.

"Well," said Mr. Vanderbilt, "I don't know as much about the quality of the picture as I do about the truth of the action of the cattle. I have seen them act like that thousands of times." So, too, when he bought the "Sower," by that celebrated artist, J. F. Millet, the thing that pleased him the most was the fidelity to nature of the attitude and action of the man in the field, flinging broadcast the seed.

Once, while in France, Mr. Vanderbilt went out to Fontainebleau, to visit Rosa Bonheur. He arrived early in the morning, and took breakfast with her. The artist and the American millionaire seemed at once to feel in sympathy, although their conversation was carried on through an interpreter, for he could not speak French, and she was unable to converse in English. He gave her a commission for two pictures, when she replied that he could only have one in a year, and the other in two or three years, perhaps.

"Tell her," said he, "I must have them. I'm getting to be an old man, and want to enjoy them."

With a woman's ready wit she laughed at him for calling himself old, for she had discovered that they were both of the same age? The result was that Rosa Bonheur painted both pictures within the year.

Mr. Vanderbilt always sought for the best pictures money could buy. Once, when visiting the collection of M. Barbedienne, in Paris, who did the bronze-work for his house, he saw the large and beautiful "Autumn Sunset," by Dupré, which he persuaded the owner to part with, although he had made his will, which left all his pictures to the Louvre. M. Barbedienne sold the work to Mr. Vanderbilt, and is said to have regretted it ever since.

Upon another occasion, in 1880, he visited in London a collection, and there saw the original picture of Gérôme's "Sword Dance." He purchased it at once, and sold a less important picture with the same subject, by the same artist, which he owned. The collection finished, and the gallery filled, he took great pride in the fact that it contained so many fine examples.

"If I were to begin to buy to-day," he frequently remarked, "I could not within a few years gather such a collection if I were to spend all my fortune." He was once asked by a famous sculptor of New York which of his pictures he liked the best.

"I enjoy them all," was the reply.

The only private collections in America which can at all rank with the Vanderbilt, are the Stewart and Belmont in New York, and the Walter in Baltimore. There are no finer private collections of modern works in Europe. Those of Defoer Bey and M. Secretan in Paris, and of Baron Schroeder and Sir Richard Wallace, in London, are the most valuable in Europe.

Some of the more important works in this unrivaled collection are as follows: "Arrival at the Château," "Information," and the "Ordinance," by Meissonier; "Champigny," and the "Ambulance Corps," by Detaille; "The Sower," "Water Carrier," and other examples of Millet; "Fountain of Indolence," by Turner; "After the Chase," by Sir Edwin Landseer; "Odalisque," by Sir Frederick Leighton; "Bourget," by De Neuville; "The Two Families," by Munkacsy; "The Sword Dance," by Gérôme; "A Study from Nature," and "Gorges d'Apremont," by Rousseau; "Rainbow," by Jules Breton; "Picture Gallery," "Sculpture Gallery," "The Entrance of the Theatre," and "Down by the River," by Alma-Tadema; "Fête During the Carnival," and "Masqueraders," by Madrazo; "Arab Fantasia at Tangiers," by Fortuny; "The Village Fête," by Professor Knaus; "Midday," by Jules Dupré; "The Bride of Lammermoor," by Millais; "Arab Plucking a Thorn from his Foot," by Bonnat; "The King's Favorite," by Zamacois; "A Dream of the Arabian Nights," and "Christening," by Villegas; "Blindman's Buff," the "Bathers," and an oriental scene, by Diaz; three cattle pieces by Troyon; a fine river view by Daubigny; "The Good Sister," by Bouguereau; "Forbidden Books," by Vibert; "Game of Chess," by Leloir; a cattle piece by Van Marcke; "A Hunting Scene," and other works, by Rosa Bonheur; fine pictures by such artists as Clays, Ziem, Fromentin, Edouard Frere, Schreyer, Hamon, Williams ; a fine example of Thomas Faed ; a figure piece by Boldini ; Leopold Muller's "Oriental Market Place," two lovely fan designs in water-colors, by Jacquemart ; a sepia by Rosa Bonheur ; "Twilight in Scotland," by Gustave Doré ; "The Young Mother," by Béranger ; "The Reaper's Return Home," by Becker ; "Paying the Rent," by Erskine Nicol ; "Rubens in His Studio," by Sir John Gilbert ; "The Monarch Oak," by Linnell ; "Returning from the Fair," by Bochmann ; the "Hungarian Volunteers," by Pottenkoffen, and a picture by Gérôme called "Reception of the Prince of Condé by Louis XIV." A description of it was given by the artist to Mr. Vanderbilt. "The reception takes place," says the artist, "on the grand staircase at Versailles. This staircase no longer exists. It was destroyed under Louis XV., but there remains an engraving of it, very well executed, which has enabled me to reconstruct it with truth. In the year 1674 Condé had returned to court, where he was received with triumph. The King came forward to meet him on the grand staircase, which was not his usual habit. The Prince was going up slowly, on account of the gout, which made him almost helpless. As soon as he saw the monarch, 'Sire,' said he, 'I beg your Majesty's pardon, to make you wait so long.' 'My cousin,' answered the King, 'do not hurry. When one is loaded with laurels as you are it is difficult to walk quickly.' By the side of Louis XIV. stands his son, the Duke of Burgundy, whom they called the Great Dauphin, at that time thirteen years old. Behind him is his perceptor, Bossuet, Bishop of Meaux."

For two winters Mr. Vanderbilt endeavored to share his treasures with the public of New York. He opened his gallery to the inspection of lovers of art during certain days of each week, and was very generous in responding to requests for cards; but some of the more vulgar and intrusive of his visitors insisted on helping themselves to flowers from the conservatory, and inspecting the private rooms of the mansion on other floors, and this annoyance became at last so pronounced that cards were granted only on satisfactory identification. During the last year access to the gallery was very difficult.

CHAPTER XX.

THE VANDERBILT FAMILY.

Captain " Jake "—His Wealth and Habits—His Children—The Sisters of William H.—His Widow and Children—Their Homes and Families.

CAPTAIN JACOB VANDERBILT more nearly resembled the Commodore than any of his other brothers or sisters. Like him, he was a sea-captain, and for years commanded some of the largest and best-known steamboats on the Sound. He was Captain of the ill-fated Atlantic, which was lost on Fisher's Island some forty years ago, and had he not been detained in Stonington by a matter of business would have had charge of her on the night on which she was wrecked. Having amassed a comfortable fortune, he virtually retired as a captain about 1857, and then turned his attention to the affairs of the Staten Island Railroad and Ferry Company, in which his brother had been more or less interested, and which he, representing his brother, with some other prominent gentlemen, purchased of George Law. Building a handsome house on Grimes' Hill, Staten Island, he has resided there ever since, and has been President of the Staten Island Railroad Company almost uninterruptedly from 1863, when William H. retired, until Mr. Erastus Wiman obtained control of the corporation in 1883.

Captain Vanderbilt is now about seventy-seven years of
age, is spare and of medium height, with gray whiskers,
and keen, piercing eyes, having all the features of his
brother. During the "flush" years of the war he
made considerable money in Wall Street, but has never
speculated on any large scale, and has been content to
live modestly and quietly in his Staten Island home.
He is probably worth about seven hundred thousand dollars.

His absorbing and almost sole amusement is driving,
and he has owned some famous trotters in his day, one
pair, a gift from the Commodore, standing at the head
of the 2.20 class for several years. There was nothing
the old Commodore loved better than to pass his brother
the Captain, on the road, and the rivalry between the
two was very great. Many Staten Islanders remember
vividly the days on the old race-track at New Dorp,
when the Commodore and the Captain would speed their
fleet steeds around the course, and the excitement that
these brushes occasioned.

The Captain himself tells a story of how one day
while he was flying behind his fleet steeds along a narrow Staten Island road he heard the sound of wheels
and the regular hoof-beats of a pair of trotters behind
him. Faster and faster did his horses go, but nearer
and nearer did his pursuer approach. At length there
appeared in the near distance a bridge with only room
enough for one team to pass at a time. With true horse-
man instinct, not looking round, he felt that he had now
the advantage of his opponent; but success was not to
be, for just as he entered upon the bridge two horses
and a driver dashed past him, taking off both wheels of

his buggy, and the familiar form of the Commodore was discerned guiding the reckless steeds. As he dashed ahead, he turned slightly and remarked, "You mustn't try to beat your brother, Jake."

Captain Vanderbilt married a Miss Banta, an estimable woman, who died some six years ago. He was exceedingly happy in his domestic relations. His children have all received a thorough education, his two daughters being accomplished musicians. The eldest, Miss Ellen Vanderbilt, married Captain Sparrow Purdy, from whom she was divorced in about three years, and who afterward died in Egypt in the service of the Khedive, after having proved himself a gallant officer. She married for her second husband a Mr. Herman Cæsar, who also died about four years ago, leaving her a widow with three children. She now resides at New Brighton, Staten Island, and is very much esteemed and liked by her cousin's family.

His second daughter, Miss Clara Vanderbilt, married Mr. James McNamee, of the firm of Work, Davies & McNamee, which has figured so largely in the Grant & Ward case. With her husband, who is an able lawyer and a leading politician on Staten Island, she resides in a handsome house on the summit of Grimes' Hill, about half a mile from that of her father. Jacob H. Vanderbilt, Jr., the Captain's youngest child, is now about thirty-two years old and a widower, his wife, Annie Hazard, having died three years ago, leaving two children. Mr. Vanderbilt and his children reside with the Captain.

Miss Phebe Vanderbilt, the last-surviving sister of the Commodore, died a year ago aged seventy-five.

8*

She never married, and her sweetness of character
and disposition made her greatly beloved by all who
knew her. She was the favorite sister of both Commodore and Captain Vanderbilt, and was widely known in
her later years as " Aunt Phebe." She was well provided for in the Commodore's will, and W. H. Vanderbilt also left her a legacy in his, which in consequence
of her death reverts to the estate. Miss Vanderbilt
lived for many years on Staten Island, but for the ten
years preceding her death she made her home in New
York with her niece, Mrs. Read. The other sisters
of the Commodore were Mrs. Barton and Mrs. De Forest, both of whom left large families of children, who
have all been remembered in the famous will.

The sisters of Mr. William H. Vanderbilt who are
still living are, Mrs. Torrance, Mrs. W. K. Thorn, Mrs.
D. B. Allen, Mrs. LaBau, now Mrs. Berger, and Mrs.
Osgood. Mrs. Cross, Mrs. Lafitte, who first married Mr.
Smith Barker, and Mrs. Robert Nivens, who first married Mr. Horace Clark, are dead. The daughters of the
Commodore were all women of fine physique and remarkable strength and force of character. Mrs. Allen,
who has a leading social position in New York, is an exceedingly handsome woman, with fine form and features
and beautiful gray hair. Her expression strongly resembles that of the Commodore. Mrs. Torrance is also a
striking and attractive woman. Two of her sons are
prominent in Parisian society, and one married Miss Anthony, who was soon divorced from him, and married Mr.
Frederick Vanderbilt, her cousin. Her daughter married Mr. Meredith Howland, a member of the old New
York family of that name. Mrs. W. K. Thorn is very

well known in Murray Hill society. Her eldest daughter
married first Mr. King, and on his death, Mr. Daniel
Parrish. Mrs. Parrish's daughter, Miss King, was recently married to Mr. Alexander Baring, son of a member of the celebrated banking firm of Baring Brothers.
Mrs. Thorn's second daughter, Miss Lena Thorn, was for
some years a great belle in New York society, and recently married Mr. Gustave Kissell.

Mr. Vanderbilt's third sister, Mrs. Osgood, is widow
of the millionaire yachtsman George Osgood, who was
the owner of the famous yacht Fleetwing. Mrs. La-
Bau, Mr. Vanderbilt's fourth sister, who at the death
of her first husband married a Mr. Berger, has three
daughters, and is now living abroad. She is well remembered from her contest of her father's will. Mrs. Lafitte left a daughter who died unmarried. Her second
husband is also dead. The death abroad of Mr. Robert
Niven, who was the second husband of Mrs. Horace
Clark, the fifth daughter of the Commodore, was
announced a few weeks ago. Mrs. Clark had a daughter
by her first husband who married Mr. Clarence Collins,
from whom she was soon divorced. She afterward
married an Englishman, and is now living in England.
An invalid sister died unmarried on Staten Island a few
years since.

These five sisters of Mr. William H. Vanderbilt are
all of them wealthy in their own right, while some of
them married exceedingly rich men. Mrs. Allen, Mrs.
Torrance, Mrs. Thorn, and Mrs. Osgood are probably
the richest, Mrs. Osgood having been left a fortune by her
late husband of some two or three millions.

But it is with the immediate family of Mr. Vanderbilt himself that this volume has most to do. So frequently are their names mentioned in the public press, so prominent have they become by reason of the great wealth that is now theirs, and so greatly will their lives, their personality, and their daily doings continue to be of public interest, that some description of their personal appearance and characteristics may serve to dispel many confused ideas regarding them.

Mrs. William H. Vanderbilt is rather slight of figure and of medium height, has dark hair, hardly as yet tinged with gray, dark hazel eyes, and a very sweet and refined expression. Exceedingly simple in her mode of life she rises early, devotes several hours to her household duties, and afterward visits some of her grandchildren or has them brought to see her. She generally drives in the Park in the afternoon, accompanied by one of her daughters, and after a quiet family dinner and evening chat with her friends retires at an early hour. She is regular in her attendance at church, and faithful to charitable duties. Her name does not appear prominently in the list of the leading charities, although she contributes largely to them in a quiet manner, and generally requests that her name should not be mentioned with these contributions. Comparatively few persons know her intimately, although her circle of formal acquaintances is necessarily a large one. She is exceedingly constant to her friends, and has especial affection for those of her early married life. She has never cared for society : devoted to her children and to her home it has been only on account of her daughter, Mrs. Seward Webb, that she has entertained at all during the past five years. Since she has had so handsome a home in

New York, Mrs. Vanderbilt has never cared to assume the charge of a country-house in summer, and with her husband has spent the warm months at Sharon Springs and Saratoga, returning to the city early in the autumn.

Mrs. Vanderbilt has three brothers residing in Brooklyn. They are Benjamin P. Kissam, who lives at 73 First Place; Samuel H. Kissam, of 240 Carroll Street, senior partner of the banking house of Kissam, Whitney & Co., 11 Broad Street, New York, and Peter R. Kissam, of 76 First Place, who is a banker at 19 New Street, New York. They are the children of the Rev. Samuel Kissam, who died in Brooklyn in 1869. He was a minister of the Dutch Reformed Church, and occasionally preached in Brooklyn, but had no charge. Before going to reside in Brooklyn he lived at Cedar Hill, near Albany, of which place he was a native, and where he preached for about twenty-five years.

"Our money doesn't make us any better than anybody else," is a maxim on which Mr. and Mrs. William H. Vanderbilt always insisted. So they did not try to dictate to their children in regard to their marriages, except to insist that the spouses should be honest and decent. They sedulously avoided those preposterous misalliances which are often made in our wealthy families. They kept foreign noblemen at arms-length. "Avoid all pretenders and people who put on airs," Mr. Vanderbilt used to say to his children. "Avoid adventurers and humbugs of every sort. Don't be fooled by appearances. We have money enough for ourselves and for the husbands and wives you will marry, but we haven't respectability enough, for no family has any to lend." So all the children seem to have married sensibly.

The New York *World* says : "The most interesting feature of the democratic side of Mr. Vanderbilt's character, however, is illustrated in the marriage of his children. His sons all have honest American wives ; his daughters all have plain, unpretending American husbands. There has been no attempt on either side to connect titles with the family name by means of a wedding-ring. Mr. and Mrs. Vanderbilt have not followed the example of the American aristocracy of wealth, and put their daughters up at auction to be bid for by seedy and needy European titles. Their boys and girls have fallen in love and been married like the boys and girls of any honest American mechanic. For this both father and mother are entitled to credit."

Cornelius Vanderbilt, the eldest son, the present head of the house, to whom his father left a fortune of $62,-000,000, is now forty years of age. He is of medium height, well-built, with an open, frank countenance, framed by dark whiskers, and has a clear, rosy complexion. His hair is brown and he has the steely gray eyes of the Commodore. He received a very thorough education from tutors and at private schools, and his habits of life have always been most correct. He is greatly interested in charitable matters, and is much liked both in business and society. He married about twelve years ago Miss Alice Gwinn, of Cincinnati, and they have four children, three sons and a daughter, of whom the eldest son is named Cornelius, and was left a special bequest of $2,000,000 by his grandfather. Mr. Vanderbilt resides in a beautiful house on the northwest corner of Fifth

Avenue and Fifty-seventh Street, the interior decorations
and furnishings of which surpass in some ways even those
of his father's palace further down the avenue. Mrs.
Cornelius Vanderbilt is very petite, with a rather pretty
face, not exactly handsome, whose chief charm is a most
gracious and winning smile. She is thoroughly domestic
in her tastes, and while not averse to society does not
care much for it. Her manners are simple and unaffected, and she possesses much quiet dignity, and is an
affectionate, devoted, and loyal wife. Some of her costumes show remarkable taste and have been greatly admired. Mr. Vanderbilt's summer home for some sea-
sons past has been at Newport, and his recent purchase
there of Mr. Pierre Lorillard's magnificent country-seat,
"The Breakers," will probably insure the permanent
location of himself and family there during the warm
months.

William Kissam Vanderbilt, the second son of the
late millionaire, is about thirty-six years of age, stoutly-
built and inclined to corpulency. His face is an open,
full one, framed in English whiskers, and his complexion
is ruddy and high-colored. He is what would be called
a handsome man, and his figure was, until the last few
years, a decidedly athletic one. He is fond of horses,
although not so much as his father, or the late Commodore. He may often be seen driving a fleet pair of
roadsters on the macadamized avenues that surround his
country-place at Islip, and he indulges in yachting at
times. As a man he is less popular with his fellows
and associates than any of his brothers. He is of a
somewhat morose disposition, but his wife thoroughly
understands him, and he is greatly dependent upon her

strong character and will-power. In 1875 he was married to Miss Alva Smith, a daughter of Mr. Smith, a
wealthy merchant of Savannah, and later of New York
City. Somewhat grave and reserved in temperament,
and consequently not particularly fond of society, Mr.
Vanderbilt has been induced to go out more or less by
his wife, who is an accomplished woman of the world,
and devoted to gayety. Mr. and Mrs. Vanderbilt reside
in winter in a white marble house, built in the style of
an old French château, at the northwest corner of Fifth
Avenue and Fifty-second Street, while in the summer
they occupy a beautiful country-house near Islip, L. I.
They have three children, who are all still quite young.
Mrs. Vanderbilt, with her sisters, Miss Amide, Miss
Jennie (now Mrs. Fernando Yznaga), and Miss Mimi
Smith, are all well known in New York society. Mrs.
Vanderbilt is tall and slight, and is neither a blonde
nor a brunette, while her hair, although she is a young
woman, is tinged with gray. Her conversational pow-
ers are rather remarkable. She is quick at repartee,
witty, and somewhat sarcastic, and this has made her
much admired and to some extent feared in society.
Her intimacy with Lady Mandeville, formerly Miss
Consuela Yznaga, has been of long standing.

Mr. Frederick W. Vanderbilt, the third son, now
about twenty-seven years of age, is of medium height,
has a somewhat spare figure, with slightly reddish hair
and small mustache, and rather sallow complexion. He
is passionately devoted to yachting, and finds his chief
pleasure in outdoor sports, caring little or nothing for
society. His fine steam yacht, Vidette, is one of the
fleetest and most elegant in every appointment in the

flotilla of the American Yacht Club. He is considered by his associates a thoroughly good fellow, entirely devoid of any snobbishness or nonsense. His business habits are good, and he is looked upon as an able and safe financier. His office is in the Grand Central Depot, and he has charge of the interests of the Nickel Plate Road. Very popular among his employés, he is generally known as Mr. Fred.

His marriage was something of a romance. In the early part of this chapter mention has been made among the sisters of William H. Vanderbilt of Mrs. Torrance, and it was stated that one of her sons married a Miss Anthony, of Rhode Island, a relative of the late Senator Anthony. She lived with him but six months, and then obtained a divorce on the grounds of desertion. Mr. Frederick Vanderbilt immediately became an ardent suitor for her hand, and a year afterward married her, greatly against the wishes of his father and mother, who were not reconciled to the match for some time. The young couple lived for months after their marriage in an apartment house at Park Avenue and Fortieth Street, but on the completion of the Vanderbilt palaces, Mr. Vanderbilt, Sr., who had meanwhile become not only reconciled but devoted to his daughter-in-law, presented the young couple with his old house at Fifth Avenue and Fortieth Street. Mrs. Vanderbilt is herself fond of society, and last winter entertained considerably, giving several handsome receptions; but her husband's aversion to the gay world keeps her at home a great deal.

The youngest and only unmarried son is George W., now about twenty-three years of age. He is undersized, of rather frail physique, and somewhat thin and pale, but

he is not in as delicate health as his appearance would
indicate.   The student and litterateur of the family, he
spends much of his time with his books, and delights in
delving among musty tomes in old second-hand book-
stores.   He has a large and complete library of his own
on the second floor of the Fifth Avenue palace, and by
his father's death becomes virtually the manager and
head of this house.   He takes great pride and delight
in the art gallery, and is thoroughly acquainted with the
history of the paintings and the distinguishing characteristics of the artists.   Devoted to music, he is an almost nightly attendant at the opera.   The child of his
father's mature age, he was always his favorite and constant companion, entering into all his plans, and sharing
all his hopes and fears.   It is understood that his father
had very ambitious views for him in a literary way, as
some writings of his evinced much promise.   Shortly
before his father's death he was given almost all the
Staten Island family property, and Staten Islanders
look to him with hope as a future and liberal patron.
George Vanderbilt is by no means an avaricious man,
and does much good in an unostentatious way.   The
$1,000,000 that the old Commodore left him was
doubled by his father and presented to him on his
twenty-first birthday.   The portrait we present was
taken five years ago, but he has an aversion for the
photographer, and declines to have any more taken.

The daughters of Mr. Vanderbilt are Mrs. Elliott F.
Shepard, formerly Miss Margaret Vanderbilt; Mrs.
William D. Sloane, formerly Miss Emily Vanderbilt;
Mrs. H. McKay Twombly, formerly Miss Florence
Vanderbilt, and Mrs. Dr. Seward Webb, formerly Miss

Eliza Vanderbilt. Mrs. Shepard is the eldest of the daughters, and was in Europe with her husband and children at the time of her father's death. She is tall and dark, and while not handsome has a very agreeable face. Her family consists of three daughters and one son, of whom the eldest is now about fifteen years of age. These children have been admirably educated, and have been brought up in princely style, having tutors and governesses by the dozen. While in Europe they travelled with as much ceremony and privacy as would a royal family, and never dined at the table d'hôte in any hotel. Mrs. Shepard is a thorough Vanderbilt in her domestic tastes, and rarely goes into society, except to dinners, where her husband's professional position makes attendance necessary.

The second daughter, Miss Emily Vanderbilt, to whom Mr. Vanderbilt left the upper one of the two Fifth Avenue palaces, married about fourteen years ago Mr. William D. Sloane, one of the members of the large carpet firm. She has a family of several young children, to whom she is greatly devoted. In appearance she is tall and frail-looking, with light hair, auburn in tinge. Mrs. Sloane's chief diversion is the opera. As this book goes into type Mr. and Mrs. Sloane offer to build and endow a Maternity Hospital in connection with the College of Physicians and Surgeons, and the offer is accepted. It will be located between Ninth and Tenth Avenues, on Sixtieth Street, and will cost with the endowment about a quarter of a million dollars.

The third daughter, Miss Florence Vanderbilt, now Mrs. Hamilton McKay Twombly, was married in 1879. She is a brunette of medium height, and by many considered the handsomest of the women of the family. Her marriage was a good one, and met with Mr. Vanderbilt's warmest approval. Indeed Mr. Twombly was from the beginning his favorite son-in-law. He leaned upon him, and relied greatly upon his business judgment and ability. Mr. and Mrs. Twombly occupy a house built for the latter by her father at Fifth Avenue and Fifty-fourth Street, and its interior decorations and furnishings are surpassed only by those in the houses of her brother Cornelius and her father.

Miss Eliza, or "Lelia" Vanderbilt, as she is familiarly known, has been married three years to Dr. Seward Webb, a son of the late General James Watson Webb. The courtship was a long and romantic one. Mr. Vanderbilt never looked with favor upon it, and it was only after the most determined persistence on the part of the young people that he consented to it. After their marriage, following his usual custom, Mr. Vanderbilt aided Dr. Webb in every way, and finally persuaded him to abandon his precarious profession and become president of the Wagner Sleeping-car Company. The marriage thus far has been a happy one. It is a proof of old prejudice, however, that Mr. Vanderbilt's will provided that Mrs. Webb should not obtain control of the $10,000,000 left her until she was thirty years of age. Dr. and Mrs. Webb occupy the house on Fifth Avenue next to Mrs. Twombly's. In appearance Mrs. Webb is short and dark, and has a decidedly interesting and pretty face. She went a good deal into society before her marriage, but since that time has led rather a quiet life.

These are the children of the two-hundred-million-

millionaire, and such are their individual appearances and characteristics. As has doubtless been noticed, they are all, both sons and daughters, strongly domestic in their tastes. This is all the more strange as they are possessed of vast wealth which would so easily enable them to shine as society leaders. But perhaps they have found out, what many even younger than they are know, that there is not on earth a more hollow and profitless and tiresome relation in which intelligent human beings can mingle than that which is called modern society. They are all well-informed, and abreast of the best thought and aspiration of the age. The excellent education and bringing-up that they have received is well attested by the fact that there is not one among them who seems to have done anything " off color," a rare concurrence of merit in so large a family in these lively days. They are affectionate and devoted to their mother and to each other, and constitute in every respect an exemplary family.

CHAPTER XXI.

SOCIAL POSITION.

THERE has always been some sort of aristocracy on earth, and never, save in the case of Arthur's mythical Round-Table, has it been composed of the most worthy people of a community. An ideal aristocracy should be a classifying of the noblest, most self-denying, and most helpful men, and the most generous and refined women, and they would be so modest as to be quite unconscious of their pre-eminence. The aristocracy of the old world is mostly composed of families who have attained their prominence, either recently or remotely, by successful pillage; and their coats-of-arms are merely the pictures of the castles, banners, and weapons by the skillful use of which they won their wealth and rank.

American aristocracy has a different basis. Civilization had taken such deep root when the country was founded that brigandage had become unfashionable. Even the most gallant pirates were considered disreputable; and Robert Kidd, instead of being given a dukedom, as he would have been in England three centuries earlier, perished miserably and in disgrace. So in this country aristocracy has, by a tacit understanding, come to be founded on money rather than on war. Yet it is not the making of money, as one would suppose, that is considered honorable and meritorious, but the possession of money which somebody else made.

It is chiefly the inheritors of wealth, not the accumulators, who are the artificial social leaders. When Cornelius Vanderbilt was born, John Jacob Astor was a baker's errand-boy on the corner of Pearl and Frankfort Streets, and he spent most of his time as an itinerant vender of bread and doughnuts, peddling the baking from door to door in a basket. Peter Lorillard had not yet built his little snuff-factory on the Bronx. A patrician, in this country, is any man of good manners and out of jail, whose plebeian father made money enough for him to live on.

New York society has become of late years so essentially a plutocracy, or aristocracy of wealth, that very naturally the Vanderbilts, with their enormous possessions, have come to be looked upon by the world at large as leaders of the Metropolitan society world. That they could have become so by the least effort on their part several years ago admits of not the slightest doubt, and that they are not so to-day will be generally received with a feeling of incredulity. Yet such is the case. With the single exception of Mrs. William K. Vanderbilt, who was a leading society belle before she married, the Vanderbilt women have during the last five years been rarely mentioned in connection with the winters' leading entertainments, and their names are not found as often in the public prints as patronesses of this or that ball, rout or party, as those of Mrs. Astor, Mrs.

Belmont, Mrs. Iselin, Mrs. Schuyler, and a score of others. This is due to the reasons given in the preceding chapters. All the daughters of the house as well as the sons, and daughters- and sons-in-law, with the one exception of Mrs. William K. Vanderbilt, are such lovers of home that the gay world has little or no attraction for them.

By the curious custom and tradition by which the society world decides that the children of the millionaire of 1850 are much further advanced in the social scale than the children of the millionaire of 1880, the Astors, Belmonts, and other leading families have assumed to take precedence of the Vanderbilts. They can do so no longer, even according to their own flimsy law of superiority, as the death of the millionaire father admits his children into the ranks of the social leaders of the metropolis. Thoroughly qualified and thoroughly competent to assume this position they are in every way. Well educated, with polished manners, and all the refinement that wealth, luxury, and beautiful and artistic surroundings can give, their homes palaces, their business sway powerful and extensive, they bid fair to place themselves at the head of our untitled social nobility.

The Vanderbilts obtained their first secure foothold in New York's leading society by the great fancy-dress ball given by Mrs. William K. Vanderbilt in her beautiful house at Fifth Avenue and Fifty-third Street on the evening of March 26, 1883, which was an event never before equaled in the social annals of the metropolis, and one that interested the whole country. It is impossible to give here more than a brief outline of this truly marvelous entertainment, which surpassed in splendor, in

CORNELIUS VANDERBILT AND WIFE IN FANCY BALL COSTUME.

beauty, in brilliancy, and in luxurious and lavish expense any scene before witnessed in the new world.

For weeks beforehand the costumers, milliners, and dressmakers, not only of New York, but of all the larger eastern cities, were engaged in preparing the richest and most varied of garments for this wonderful entertainment. Histories, novels, and illustrated books of all periods were ransacked by the expectant guests to obtain either suggestions or models upon which their own costumes could be patterned. All else was forgotten in society during the forty days of Lenten penitence which preceded the event, and the most improbable and fantastic tales and rumors of the forthcoming splendor were constantly circulated in the community. Even the daily press became affected by the prevailing excitement which the ball occasioned in the atmosphere, and assigned their ablest and most skilled reporters for two weeks beforehand to the preparation of lists of the costumes of the guests and more or less accurate foreshadowings of the event. In fact they devoted more attention to it, than they have ever done before or since to any purely social affair.

Although Mrs. W. H. Vanderbilt had already given a ball in her own palace which was largely and fashionably attended, and although the names of two or three of her daughters and daughters-in-law had already figured as patronesses of the distinctive society balls of the metropolis, two or three of the leaders of New York society, notably Mrs. William Astor, had never called upon any of the ladies of the Vanderbilt family. It was Lady Mandeville, who with her family had been making Mrs. W. K. Vanderbilt a visit of a year, who first suggested

9

the entertainment to her hostess, and it is largely due to
her society experience, cleverness, and tact that the ball
was in every way the grandest ever given on this continent, and one which fully established the Vanderbilt
family as social leaders.   According to the generally accepted story in society, soon after the first announcement of the ball Miss Carrie Astor, the only unmarried
daughter of Mrs. William Astor, organized a fancy-dress
quadrille to be danced at the ball by several young ladies
and gentlemen.   Mrs. Vanderbilt heard of this, and
stated in the hearing of some friends that she regretted
that she could not invite Miss Astor to her ball, as her
mother had never called upon her.   This reached Mrs.
Astor's ears, and soon afterward she called upon Mrs.
Vanderbilt and they were invited.   Thus did the ball
break the last barriers down.

The brilliant scene was well framed in one of the most
beautiful of New York houses—the reproduction of one
of those fascinating chateaux of the French renaissance which are the pride of Touraine.   Seen, as it was
on the night of this entertainment, under a blaze of light,
and kindled into splendor everywhere by masses of
flowers and a moving throng of varied and magnificent
costumes, it was the most fitting frame-work an artist
could have asked for a succession of pictures so hetero-
geneous, so incongruous in detail, yet in their general
effect so dazzling and so attractive.   The guests, on arriving, found themselves in a grand hall about 65 feet long,
16 feet in height, and 20 feet in width.   Under their
feet was a floor of polished and luminous marble, and
above them a ceiling richly paneled in oak, while over
a high wainscoting of richly carved Caen stone hung

antique Italian tapestries. Over this hall, to the right, rose a grand stairway of the finest Caen stone, carved with superb delicacy and vigor, to the height of fifty feet.

By eleven o'clock the members of the six organized quadrilles assembled in the gymnasium, on the third floor, a beautiful apartment, 50 feet in length by 35 feet in width. These quadrilles, six in number, comprised in all nearly a hundred ladies and gentlemen, and, having formed in the gymnasium in order, they moved in a glittering processional pageant down the grand stairway and through the hall into a room in the front of the house fitted and furnished in the style of Francis I., 25 feet in width by 40 in length, whose whole wains-coting of carved French walnut was brought from a chateau in France, and whose ceiling was painted by Paul Baudry. Thence the procession swept on into the spacious dining-hall, which was converted for a night into a ball-room, and the dancing began.

The first quadrille was the "hobby horse," led by Mr. J. V. Parker and Mrs. S. S. Howland, a daughter of Mr. August Belmont. The horses took two months in construction. They were of life-size, covered with genuine hides, and were light enough to be easily and comfortably attached to the waists of the wearers. The costumes for the men were red hunting-coats, white satin vests, yellow satin knee-breeches, and white satin stockings. The ladies wore red hunting-coats and white satin skirts, elegantly embroidered. The other quad-rilles danced were the "Mother Goose," led by Mr. Oliver Northcote and Mrs. Lawrence Perkins, in which the famous characters of Mother Goose were personated; the "Opera Bouffe," the "Star," the "Dresden China," and the "Go-as-you-please." In the "Star" quadrille, which was organized by Mrs. William Astor, the ladies were arrayed as twin stars, in yellow, blue, and white. The "Dresden China" quadrille, in which the dancers personated those dainty porcelain figures of the famous pottery, was perhaps the most notable of the evening, and even the photographs in costume of those who appeared in it are cherished as household treasures to-day. The dancers all wore ivory-white satin costumes, every appurtenance of which was pure white; their hair was powdered and dressed high. The gentlemen wore the old German court costume of white satin knee-breeches and powdered wigs, while the two crossed swords, the mark of the Dresden factory, were embroidered on all the costumes.

Among the hundreds of striking and unique costumes only a very few can possibly be noted. Mrs. W. K. Vanderbilt herself personated a Venetian princess, as painted by Cabanel. The underskirt of her dress was of white and yellow brocade, shading from the deepest orange to the lightest canary, while the figures of flowers and leaves were outlined in gold and white and iridescent beads; her white satin train was embroidered magnificently in gold, and lined with Roman red. The waist was of blue satin covered with gold embroidery, and on her head was a Venetian cap covered with magnificent jewels, among them a peacock in many-colored gems.

Lady Mandeville, who received the guests with Mrs. Vanderbilt, wore a costume copied from a picture by Vandyke of the Princess Marie-Claire Decroy.

Mr. W. K. Vanderbilt appeared as the Duke De

Guise ; Mr. Cornelius Vanderbilt as Louis XVI. Mrs. Cornelius Vanderbilt went as the Electric Light, in white satin trimmed with diamonds, and with a superb diamond head-dress. Miss Amide Smith, Mrs. Vanderbilt's sister, came as a peacock, in a dazzling costume of peacock-blue satin, and Mrs. Seward Webb, Mr. Vanderbilt's sister, as a hornet, with a brilliant waist of yellow satin with a brown velvet skirt and brown gauze wings. Other notable costumes were those worn by Miss Work, as Joan of Arc; by Miss Edith Fish, as Marie Antoinette ; by Miss Turnure, as an Egyptian Princess, and by Mrs. Bradley Martin, as Marie Stuart. The Duc du Morny wore a court dress; Madam Christine Nilsson a mourning costume of the time of Henry III.; Mrs. Pierre Lorillard appeared as a Phœnix, and Mr. Hurlburt as a Spanish knight.

It was a royal entertainment, which had never before been equaled in the social annals of America, and which it is probable will not be surpassed for many years to come. It was the wonder not only of the year but of the decade, and the Vanderbilt ball will be remembered when other events much greater in their significance and in their bearing on the time have been quite forgotten.

CHAPTER XXII.

HORSES AND STABLES

Love for Horses—Fondness for Fast Teams—Excellent Amateur
Driver—Perils of the Road—Maud S.—Summer Recreation—
The Derby—His Stables—Resigns the Reins.

WILLIAM H. VANDERBILT really loved his horses. He
not only admired their performances, as his father did,
and liked them because they enabled him to go ahead
of other people's horses, but he felt and showed a warm
interest in other qualities besides their fleetness—in
their beauty, docility, and affectionate disposition. Unlike his father, he was fond of petting and handling his
horses, and while on Staten Island he usually insisted on
taking care of the horses himself.

His penchant for fast horses increased after he moved
to New York. It was not until about 1865 that he rode
behind a really fast horse, although at that time he
owned a fair pair of his own which could make a mile
in three minutes. At that time there was a private
driving-club near Macomb's Dam Bridge, on the upper
end of Manhattan Island, frequented by such men as
Commodore Vanderbilt, Robert Bonner, and Colonel
John Harper. Mr. Bonner was the owner of the mare
Peerless, and noticing that Mr. Vanderbilt seemed interested in her, he invited him to drive round the

track. He was astonished at her speed, and from
that day manifested a growing desire to possess good
horses.

Before his father's death he made no pretence of
being one of the leaders on the road, but was content to
ride behind horses of considerable speed. The highest
price ever paid by the Commodore for a horse was
$10,000, for Mountain Boy. A year before he died he
bought a fast horse named Small Hopes, and this fine
animal he left to his son and heir.

After the death of the Commodore, Mr. William H.
Vanderbilt took his father's place on the road. He
bought Lady Mac, to match with Small Hopes, and
astonished the trotting public by driving the team to a
top road-wagon a mile over the Fleetwood Park course
in 2.23¼. This was about the beginning of the craze
for fast teams.

Other men purchased fast teams to compete with Mr.
Vanderbilt, and the excitement on the boulevards and
avenues above Central Park, and on the Fleetwood
track was unprecedented. Among the most notable of
these was Edward and Dick Swiveller, driven by Mr.
Frank Work, the most persistent and formidable rival
Mr. Vanderbilt had on the road; Blondine and Mill
Boy, Maxey Cobb and Neta Medium. Mr. Vanderbilt
soon discovered that his team, Small Hopes and Lady
Mac, would not be able to maintain his prestige on the
road, and he secured another team composed of the bay
mare, Aldine, and the chestnut mare, Early Rose. This
was in 1882. The team was driven in Hartford, Ct.,
a mile in 2.16½. Shortly after this Mr. Work's famous
team beat the record, and great was the excitement

among the road men.   Mr. Vanderbilt now determined
to be his rival for the team record.

Maud S. had made her appearance in Kentucky, and
was developing great speed.   When the mare was but
four years old Mr. Vanderbilt offered to give $20,000
for her if she would show a mile in public in 2.20.   The
trial was made in October of that year at Lexington,
where she made a record of 2.17½.   Mr. Vanderbilt
then gave $21,000, the extra thousand going to her
driver.

On June 14, 1883, over the Fleetwood track, Mr.
Vanderbilt took his fastest wagon-ride, behind Aldine
and Maud S., a mile in 2.15½.   The road-wagon, with
Mr. Vanderbilt, weighed nearly four hundred pounds.
This performance has not been equaled by any team. No
professional driver even ever drove a team as fast as that.
He seemed, in driving, to have a special control of his
horses.   When his friends were congratulating him upon
the result, he quietly replied : "It is pretty good for
an amateur."   He wanted his horses to be fast, was always anxious to see what they could do and he treated
them well.   Of late years he paid less and less personal
attention to the stabling and feeding of his horses.

Having beaten the record of his rival, Mr. Work,
Mr. Vanderbilt appeared to be satisfied, and the feeling
between the two gentlemen subsided.   Among the other
horses with excellent records which he owned, were
Leander and Lysander; Bay Dick and Charles Dickens.

Fast driving has its perils, especially in the crowded
thoroughfares of a great metropolis, and Mr. Vanderbilt experienced his share.   On November 7, 1878,
while he was speeding along Jerome Avenue at

the rate of a mile in 2.40 his team knocked down and
fatally injured a man named Riley. In giving an account of the accident afterward Mr. Vanderbilt said :

"On pleasant afternoons from fifty to a hundred
gentlemen congregate on Judge Smith's stoop to witness
the driving of fast horses on what is known as the speed-
ing-ground of Jerome Avenue. I was driving along on the
afternoon of November 7th, when, after coming around
a turn in the road, I saw a man about sixty feet ahead
of me and about twenty-five feet from the gutter. I at
once shouted to him, being scared at seeing him so near
in front of me. He hesitated and seemed confused.
Although I tried my best to pull up my team, it was too
late, and my right horse struck him. I could not turn
my horse out any further than I did, for I cracked my
wagon in turning as it was. When I stopped my team
and looked back I never had such a sensation pass over
me before. Such an accident never before occurred to
me. I had him taken to Judge Smith's hotel, and tried
to have the man given all the attention possible."

On October 17, 1883, Mr. Vanderbilt met with a
severe accident on the track at Fleetwood Park. He was
driving Maud S., and came in collision with a sulky.
He was thrown violently to the ground, and for a while
remained senseless. He suffered a severe shock, but no
serious injury. His first question on recovering consciousness was to ask whether the mare was hurt.

In the spring he was at Fleetwood Park nearly every
day, taking a deep interest in the trials made there by
horses belonging to his friends, or else speeding his
favorite team. The pull of the reins seemed to inspire
him, and he appeared his best when sitting behind

9*

Maud S., or his trotting team, Aldine and Early Rose, a brisk breeze blowing his long English whiskers back of his head, a flush on his good-humored Dutch face, and a cheery tone in his voice.

He always took his horses with him to Saratoga and Sharon Springs, where he usually spent the summer season; and every afternoon he went to the Lake, and there met the men with whom he loved to associate. This daily drive seemed to be his greatest delight, and if the weather prevented he did not hesitate to express his disappointment to his friends. Like all classes of the English people he loved the excitement which driving on the road affords. He went to Fleetwood because he liked the track. He was fond of the excitement of a pleasant brush, and the fresh air did him good.

He had a good deal of respect for his horses, and, as is well-known, would never use them for money-making purposes on the track. Indeed, he thought so much of his famous Maud S. that when he had decided to sell her, she was offered to Mr. Bonner for $40,000, although other men stood ready to pay $100,000. Mr. Vanderbilt said at the time, "If I sell her to the syndicate the public will think I still own her, while if I sell her to Robert Bonner it will be known that there is no collusion between us. Then, she will never be trotted for money, and will be sure of good care." Thereafter he frequently spoke of Maud S. with affection and enthusiasm.

He did not give up the practice of driving daily with his own hands until his health was impaired, and then he would go out with a man in his employ, who was careful and trustworthy. To use the words of Mr. Bonner : " For one who had such varied interests to look after, and naturally could give but limited time to his horses, he was an excellent judge of an animal and frequently surprised his friends by his intelligent criticisms of well-known track performers that he had seen. In a word, Mr. Vanderbilt loved horses, and could drive them well."

When at Saratoga, in 1874, Mr. Vanderbilt made the acquaintance of a clerk at Congress Hall, Matthew Riley, since a broker on the street. Riley always liked a good horse, and knew something about horse-flesh, so the two used to " talk horse," and in the end a feeling of congeniality sprung up, which ripened into a friendship that lasted as long as Mr. Vanderbilt lived. Every afternoon, when the clerk could get away from the hotel, Mr. Vanderbilt would come around with his horses and take him out for a drive. Says Mr. Riley: "The minute Mr. Vanderbilt got his hands on the ribbons he left all care behind him, just as Maud S. shows her heels to a common horse. He was full of jollity, and though he did not often tell stories himself, he would pull up his flyers as we jogged along and listen with a relish to a good story from one of the boys, and when it was good he had a hearty laugh for it. He had a wonderful faculty for controlling horses better than any non-professional I ever saw, and he was, in my opinion, the best double-team driver in America, amateur or professional. In 1883 we met every day on the road, and used to jog out to Fleetwood and then race back down Seventh Avenue with the boys. He was driving at that time, among other horses, Leander, his favorite, and he tried to match him but could not. Leander is a fine fellow, and out of fifty-four races he has won thirty-four first prizes. He is fourteen years old now, 1885, and hasn't a blemish on him."

Until a few years ago Mr. Vanderbilt was very fond of witnessing a well-contested trot, and generally on the first day of the Buffalo Grand Circuit meeting, in August, he would take a party of friends from Saratoga by special train, witness the trotting, and return at once to the Springs. On these occasions he royally entertained his guests.

In 1877 he visited England to witness the Derby, and said that the sight of three hundred thousand people looking at a horse-race was worth in itself a trip across the ocean. When in Europe during the trotting season he sent many cablegrams to his agents in this country, asking about his horses. When St. Julien and Maud S. trotted in Rochester, he had the details of the race reported to him by cable, a dispatch being sent after every heat.

Up to about a year before his death, Mr. Vanderbilt usually attended the trials of fast trotters, and could be seen on the steps of the New York Driving Club house, watching with interest all that was going on. He was fond of Dan Mace, the trainer, and would spend much time in his company talking about horses. The last year of his life he did not go out much, on account of poor health, and when he did it was simply for a drive to Macomb's Dam Bridge, and home early.

He built magnificent stables on Fifty-second Street, near Madison Avenue, at a cost for the building alone of some $60,000. Its walls, floors, ceilings and stalls, of which there are sixteen, are all finished in polished cherry, ash, and black walnut. At the north end of the stable is a large box stall, 18 × 12, built for Maud S., but now occupied by Aldine. The carriage house is light and airy, with a high ceiling. Arranged in rows here stand a Victoria, a square coach, a landau, a d'Orsay, a Brougham, and a small Victoria, two cutters, a family sleigh, five light road wagons, and a tilbury. The harness room is 12 × 12, and contains a large number of harnesses arranged in glass cases with oak frames. The entire area, 100 × 75 feet, is given up to the purposes of the stable, which includes a carriage-room, 40 × 57, and a riding-ring, 38 × 51. In this last the horses were exercised when not in use out of doors. This room is covered by an iron and glass dome ; beneath this is a marble floor, and around the outside edge is a track of tanbark. The stable is lighted by gas, the jets shaded with porcelain globes, decorated with horses' heads. About the walls are hung pictures of English racing scenes.

Almost all the exercise that Mr. Vanderbilt took was behind his horses, and it is probable that they actually prolonged his life for years.

CHAPTER XXIII.

WILLIAM H. VANDERBILT'S DONATIONS.

His Method of Giving—The Tennessee University—The College of
Physicians and Surgeons—The Grants—Minor Gifts—The Obelisk—Public Ingratitude.

WILLIAM H. VANDERBILT had no ambition to be regarded as a philanthropist. He had held his own
against a scheming world, to his father's astonishment,
and he had in seven years doubled his father's bequest,
to the world's astonishment. With that he was measur-
ably content.

He recognized the fact that he had obligations, and
he met them without hesitation when they presented
themselves before him in unquestionable shape. Old
friends who were needy ; old associates of his father
who had been unfortunate ; employés of the Central,
suddenly disabled or afflicted—these he helped without
stint, and what he gave was given encumbered with no
tedious restrictions. He shunned subscription papers
instinctively, like his father, but if a case of suffering
was laid before him by anybody whom he knew to be
trustworthy he did not hesitate.

The Commodore, like those other illiterate men—Cor-
nell, Vassar, and Johns Hopkins—had borne fervent
testimony in favor of learning, by founding a university,

and the son was not slow in adding to the million dollars the father had given. He added $200,000 to the endowment, and gave $100,000 for the Theological School. The hall built with this latter gift was dedicated on May 8, 1881, the birthday of its patron. Only two weeks before his death, he gave his check for $10,000 toward the formation of a library for the University.

Mr. Vanderbilt was pleased with approval, and far more sensitive to public opinion than his father was; but he was shy of any conspicuous honors, and always gave when he could, as above, to institutions already founded and christened, so that his name might not be coupled with the donation. In this spirit he made his largest gift. In 1864 he cast about to see where he could most wisely bestow half a million dollars where it would minister to the sick and suffering. It would build and magnificently endow a new hospital, to be forever known as the Vanderbilt Hospital, and to stand as a defence and answer the slanders of Socialists. But no; he did not want a monument—he merely wanted to give the money where it would do the most good. So he gave it to an admirable institution already founded the College of Physicians and Surgeons. It was a superb endowment. And a year afterward, his daughter, Mrs. Sloane, added to the gift a quarter of a million from her own resources.

The letters which he wrote to General and Mrs. Grant after their financial disaster, generously offering to cancel their obligation of $150,000 to him, and pressing his offer with delicate insistance, won for him many grateful expressions from all parts of the country.* The

* For these letters, see Appendix D.

incident extorted a sort of patronizing tolerance and churlish admiration even from those millions who were in the habit of denouncing every word he spoke and disparaging every generous deed he attempted.

Among William H. Vanderbilt's minor gifts may be mentioned, $100,000 distributed among the employés of the New York Central Railroad ; $50,000 toward paying the debt incurred by the Church of St. Bartholomew when it moved to its present situation on Madison Avenue, and $10,000 to the Deems Fund for the education of poor young men at the University of North Carolina.   He has also contributed to the University of Virginia, and made almost innumerable private donations, of which the public has no knowledge.

He was plain, simple, and unostentious in his manner of giving, and did not care to have his charities bruited in the public prints.   When Dr. Deems explained to him the plan he had devised in relation to helping poor young men who wished to get an education, he said, " I like the scheme, and will give you $10,000 for your fund."

Within two years afterward over fifty students had been helped through the university by the aid of this gift.   It is known that he was very kind to his father's old friends, and he gave pensions to many superannuated employés.   The last check he signed, three hours before his death, was for the benefit of a charity in a distant city.

When the Suez Canal was opened, in 1869, there was a large gathering of notable people from all parts of the civilized world.   Among the representatives from America was Mr. W. H. Hurlburt, then editor of the

New York *World*. He met the Khedive of Egypt, Ismail, and this functionary was the first to make the suggestion looking to the removal of the obelisk at Alexandria to America. He offered to present the monolith to the United States, as he had given its prostrate companion to England. Mr. Hurlburt became deeply interested in the project, and cast about for ways and means for its accomplishment.

It was ten years later, in June, 1879, that the attention of Commander Henry H. Gorringe was called to the subject. He became interested in the matter, made a careful development of original plans, and an estimate of the cost of executing them, which resulted in an offer to undertake the work. A couple of months later he received the following letter :

NEW YORK, August 4, 1879.

LIEUTENANT-COMMANDER H. H. GORRINGE, United States Navy.

DEAR SIR : I have learned that you have or can procure the facilities to remove to the city of New York the obelisk now standing at Alexandria, in Egypt, known as " Cleopatra's Needle."

As I desire that this obelisk may be secured for the city of New York, I make you the following proposition : If you will take down and remove said obelisk from its present position to this city, and place it on such site as may be selected with my approval by the Commissioners of Parks, and furnish and construct at your own expense on said site a foundation of masonwork and granite base of such form and dimensions as said commissioners and myself may approve, I will, on the completion of the whole work, pay to you $75,000.

It is understood, however, that there is to be no liability on my part until the obelisk shall be so received and placed in position in the city of New York, and the same to be in as good condition as it now is. It is understood further that this agreement binds also my executors and administrators ; you to accept this proposition in writing on the receipt thereof, and agree to execute the same, and complete the work fully in every respect within one year from the date hereof.

Very truly yours,
W. H. VANDERBILT.

To this proposition Commander Gorringe replied :

NEW YORK, August 6, 1879.

MR. WILLIAM H. VANDERBILT.

DEAR SIR : I hereby acknowledge the receipt of your letter of August 4, 1879, relating to the removal of the obelisk from Alexandria, Egypt, to New York, and its erection on a site to be selected with your approval, and I accept the proposition and the conditions named therein.

Very truly yours,
HENRY H. GORRINGE,
Lieutenant-Commander, U.S.N.

Commander Gorringe had much difficulty in getting a vessel adapted to the novel transportation, and when he reached Egypt he found that no one, not even the Khedive, believed that the great obelisk would be or could be taken to America. At last the monument was turned over to a horizontal position ; an iron steamer was obtained ; its bow was removed, and the vast mono-lith was introduced to the hull endwise. On June 25, 1880, the ship Dessong was afloat with her unprece-dented cargo, and amid the cordial acclamations of the Egyptian populace she started for America. A fortnight later, in mid-ocean, the after crank-shaft broke, and she had to lie still a week, Neptune conducting himself in a most kindly manner during that period. The Dessong anchored off Staten Island on July 20th, and in the afternoon of the same day she was moored in the Hudson River, off Twenty-third Street.

It took one hundred and twelve days to move the obelisk overland from the foot of West Ninety-sixth Street, to the pedestal erected for it in Central Park, a distance of two miles. The corner-stone, of polished syenite, was laid with masonic ceremonies, and on January 22, 1881, the colossal stone was re-erected at noon, in the presence of ten thousand people. On the first claw of the fourth crab, beneath the obelisk, is the inscription:

The cost of removing from Alexandria and placing on this spot this obelisk, pedestal, and base, was borne by William H. Vanderbilt.

Mr. Vanderbilt paid $103,732 for the entire removal and re-erection. The obelisk is of fine syenite of the Assouan quarries. It was formerly the companion of the obelisk now standing on the Thames Embankment. The pair were originally erected by Thothmes III., B.C. 1591–1565, before the famous Temple of the Sun at Heliopolis. While at Alexandria, this obelisk was usually the first and last of Egyptian monuments to be visited by travelers. Owing to the gradual sinking of the land of that part of Egypt the sea came to within eighty feet of its base. It was already inclining toward the water, and in a few years must have fallen and been broken.

Commander Gorringe lived to write a history of his achievement, dedicated

To William H. Vanderbilt, in recognition of the enlightened munificence to which New York is indebted for the possession of one of the most interesting monuments of the Old World, and of the most ancient record of man now known to exist on the American Continent.

In the preface of this work, Mr. W. H. Hurlburt says : " But no man knows as well as I do the discouragements and difficulties through which success was won, and it appears to me to be my duty, therefore, to bear witness here, once for all, to the absolute simplicity of purpose and single-minded public spirit to which New York is indebted for the possession of the great obelisk of Alexandria. No arguments were needed to commend the project to Mr. Vanderbilt, whose liberality made it practicable."

Mr. Vanderbilt's wealth was so extraordinary that his relation to society was peculiar. His charities were never received with a hearty good grace. When he gave $300,000 to the University, the act was coarsely greeted with " That's nothing for him ! " When, with royal courtesy, he offered to forgive General Grant a great debt of honor, there were ingrates who said " Well, he stole the money, as every millionaire does, and it would be only just if he were to give up ten times as much." When he donated half a million to the surgeons' college, and another half million to other equally needed institutions, they expressed their gratitude in " Huh ! It isn't a quarter of what he ought to give ! "

CHAPTER XXIV.

THE MAUSOLEUM.

Original Design Rejected—Too Grand—Moravian Thrift—The Site
Secured—The Plan Adopted—A Romanesque Tomb—Granite,
Limestone, and Bronze—The Interior—Allegorical Sculptures.

WHEN Mr. Vanderbilt determined to build a tomb for
his last resting-place, and for the members of his immediate family, he consulted the architect of the Vanderbilt houses, Mr. Richard M. Hunt, and desired him
to prepare the plans. Mr. Hunt, being acquainted with
many of the most magnificent mausoleums in Europe,
drew elaborate designs for a grand and pretentious
chapel above-ground, very ornate, since he understood
that the cost would not be considered.

When these were submitted to Mr. Vanderbilt, he
said : " No, Mr. Hunt ; this will not answer at all. You
entirely misunderstood me. We are plain, quiet, unostentatious people, and we don't want to be buried in
anything so showy as that would be. The cost of it is
a secondary matter, and does not concern me. I want it
roomy and solid and rich. I don't object to appropriate
carvings, or even statuary, but it mustn't have any unnecessary fancy-work on it."

The architect began again, and toned down his origi-

nal intention to something far less ornamental, and the
mausoleum now being finished on the lower end of
Staten Island is the outcome. It is undoubtedly the
finest and most costly private tomb in America, and will
rank high by the side of the royal tombs of Europe.
The structure stands near the brow of a hill just back or
west of the old Moravian Cemetery at New Dorp. Mr.
Vanderbilt originally intended to place it in the cemetery, where so many of his ancestors are buried, but the
trustees asked more for the requisite plot of ground than
he thought it was worth. As Commodore Vanderbilt
had given the fifty acres of land constituting the cemetery, they were unable to come to an agreement, and
the result was that fourteen acres of land were purchased just outside of, but adjoining, the cemetery. A
much more suitable site was thus procured, and the
fine structure is placed where it can be seen to advantage, and not upon level ground, with commonplace
surroundings. The tomb has a front some forty feet in
height, by sixty in breadth, and is placed against a bank
of nearly the same height, so that the sides, rear, and
most of the roof are not seen, being covered with earth
and green turf. The sides are also effectually masked
by retaining walls curving outward, each nearly a quar-
ter-circle, and heavily buttressed. The result is, therefore, that as the visitor approaches he sees merely a
gabled front, rich in carved work, forty feet high,
made of Quincy granite, divided laterally into a center
projected some six feet from the front walls of the
aisles.

Standing upon the steps in front of the central door-
way, an extensive and lovely view is obtained. The lit-

tle hamlet of New Dorp, with its quaint and scattered farm-houses, including the village post-office and the blacksmith's shop, lies at the foot of the knoll; beyond are the extensive flatlands which gently slope to the south shore of the island, which merges into the blue waters of the lower Bay of New York and the silver gray of the broad Atlantic. At the right can be seen a sapphire strip of land known as Sandy Hook, with a stretch of the Jersey coast beyond, while at the left there is a full view of Coney Island, with the highlands of Long Island stretching toward Greenwood and the city of Brooklyn.

Every steamship and sailing craft which enters New York Harbor must pass in sight of this mausoleum. It will be the first prominent object seen on Staten Island by those who come from Europe to America. The farm where Mr. William H. Vanderbilt spent some twenty odd years of his life lies spread out below the tomb like a map. It is fitting that his last resting-place should dominate the landscape he knew and loved so well.

The style of architecture followed in the tomb is Romanesque. Each of the three divisions of the façade has a door-way, in which is hung a double bronze door. The upper part of the door is grated, to admit light to the vestibule. The chief feature of the front is the great central door-way, an arch of some seven feet in diameter inside and twenty outside. It is splayed inward, together with its supporting piers, in a curve of nearly a quarter of a circle, to the depth of five feet. The tympanum of the arch is filled with sculpture cut in the solid granite, representing the emblems which signify the writers of the four gospels, with a figure of Christ in the center. A richly-wrought string course traversing the entire front is continued across the opening as a transom, and the whole field of the wall of the central front is decorated in diaper. Another string-course divides this from the gable above, which is decorated with a mock arcade the height of the openings, conforming to the line of the roof, after the manner of the façade of the famous Cathedral of Pisa.

In front of the main door is a semicircular platform, eighteen feet in diameter, on a level with the floor of the vestibule, and gained by an ascent of six steps. The vestibule is eleven by fifty-one feet in area, and opens through a single door-way at the center into the tomb proper. Each side of this door-way are large tablets of polished Quincy granite, and two of the same size at either end of the vestibule. There is a deep arched recess opposite each side-door, opening into the vestibule, which contains a huge vase of polished granite standing upon a pedestal. These can be used for holding flowers. Either side of the main door, in the front wall of the vestibule, there are small doors, at the foot of bronze staircases, which lead to the ventilating chambers above the catacombs.

In the tympanum over the great door-way opening into the tomb proper is a bas-relief showing a figure of Christ, with angels and scroll-work, and the words, in English text, " I am the door." This is seen from the vestibule, as the tomb is entered. Inside the tomb another bas-relief over the same door-way shows Christ in the act of pronouncing a blessing, with the words " Pax Vobiscum " on a scroll.

The great room of the tomb proper is sixty by forty-five feet, and fully forty feet high from the floor to the top of the arches. It resembles a church built of solid stone and richly carved, only that the side-walls are filled with open catacombs. This room is composed of two bays nearly square, and a semicircular apse, or chancel, covered with a half-dome. The apse is raised above the main floor of the tomb, and contains an altar of stone, to be used in religious services for the burial of the dead. The bays are covered with vaulted ceilings resting upon arches turned between the bounding piers, and terminating in open rings, protected by open lanterns visible from without, and through which alone, with the glass nine inches thick, light is admitted to the interior.

The great interior is an unobstructed space, and occupies the breadth only of the central part of the front. The sides of the room contain the cells or catacombs, for coffins. Beneath each of the large arches which support the vaulted ceiling on each side are two subordinate arches springing from a central column. There are eight compartments thus formed, each containing nine cells, or seventy-two in all. A ventilating pipe runs from each cell to the air chambers above. The cells are about 2 feet 7 inches in width by 2 feet 2 inches in height, and 8 feet deep. The heads of the arches above the cells are filled with semicircular bas-reliefs, about 8 feet by 4, illustrating scriptural subjects. Beginning with the first, at the right of the apse, they are as follows : " The Creation of Man ;" " The Fall of Man ; " " Giving the Law to Moses ; " " David Praising the Lord ; " " Solomon sitting in Judgment ; " " The Virgin

10

and the Christ Child ; " "The Crucifixion," and "The Ascension." Rich bronze gratings, costing $60,000, and requiring twenty tons of standard bronze, protect the cells from intrusion. These gratings, or gates, are very artistic and elaborate in design. They were made in America by artisans brought from Paris. Each piece had to be cast separately, after which all were put together. New moulds were made for every piece for each of the screens, or gates. The effect of so much bronze work is wonderfully rich, and gives the interior of the tomb a strange appearance. The color harmonizes with the deep-toned and gloomy surroundings. This bronze work renders both the tomb and the cells within burglar proof. The whole interior of the tomb is made of light-colored Indiana limestone, the floor consisting of large slabs of it. The structure was over a year in building, and is supposed to have cost not less than $300,000.

CHAPTER XXV.

CLOSING LABORS.

As year followed year, Mr. Vanderbilt withdrew more
and more of his attention from the roads, leaned more
and more upon his sons, and took longer and more frequent vacations. Sometimes he went to Europe just for
the ocean voyage, returning upon the same vessel which
carried him out.

He was widely condemned as "a dangerous monopolist" by all agrarians, and by others who were moved
by similar feelings without, perhaps, proceeding to the
extreme conclusions; and the illustrated papers constantly put forth vile caricatures of him representing
him as a colossal dragon on wheels, rushing across the
land with bloody claws, yawning jaws, and breath of
flame. He was vehemently denounced as the enemy
of the people, the oppressor of the poor, the robber of
the industrious.

It was partly to silence this senseless clamor that he
resolved to sell $35,000,000 worth of his Central stock.

How to do it without breaking the market and causing a depreciation of all securities was the serious question. Negotiations were carried on for weeks with great secrecy. A journey was made to Europe in the interest of the scheme. In the last week in November, 1879, the bargain was closed.

To a syndicate representing chiefly the Wabash system, but also a number of foreign capitalists, he sold 250,000 shares of Central stock. He was known to hold at the time at least 400,000 shares, which, as the market then stood, represented a wealth of $52,000,000. The stock had not been seen on the London Board for nearly fifteen years, and it was felt that it was desirable that it should be there. Besides, there was danger of a rupture in the traffic agreement between the Central and Wabash systems, the latter system having been extended a short time before, and through freight being a prize for which an active competition among the trunk lines was to be expected. The purchasing syndicate was composed of J. S. Morgan & Co., of London, Drexel, Morgan & Co., August Belmont & Co., L. Van Hoffmann & Co., Morton, Bliss & Co., Winslow, Lanier & Co., Edwin D. Morgan, Cyrus W. Field, Jay Gould, Russell Sage, and others. This syndicate took the 250,000 shares at 120, which was 10 below the ruling price in the market. It was agreed that the syndicate should have a corresponding representation in the directory of the Central, and that Vanderbilt should not place any of its stock on the market for a year.

The news of the consummation of the sale reached Wall Street early on November 26th, and the effect was promptly visible in the advance of the Vanderbilt and Wabash stocks. New York Central and Hudson River rose from 129¾ to 134¼, and Wabash common from 39 to 43½, preferred from 63 to 68. The rest of the list being affected by sympathy, Erie closed at 38⅜, that being the highest price of the day. The advance was due to a general conviction that the arrangement was one of the highest value to the two systems, inasmuch as it was a guaranty of at least temporary harmony in traffic relations between them. Mr. Vanderbilt admitted that one of the considerations that entered into the sale was that it would relieve him and his road of the embarrassment growing out of the public distrust of great power in a single man.

The $35,000,000 which he received for the stock he at once reinvested in government bonds, and within a year it was reported from Washington that he was receiving interest on bonds amounting to $53,000,000.

Chauncey M. Depew, speaking of this colossal transaction, said: " Mr. Vanderbilt, because of assaults made upon him in the Legislature and in the newspapers, came to the conclusion that it was a mistake for one individual to own a controlling interest in a great corporation like the New York Central, and also a mistake to have so many eggs in one basket, and he thought it would be better for himself, and better for the company, if the ownership were distributed as widely as possible. . . . These syndicates afterward sold it, and the stock became one of the most widely-distributed of the dividend-paying American securities. There are now about fourteen thousand stockholders. At the time he sold there were about three thousand."

Mr. Vanderbilt had done all he could to prevent the

completion of that "piratical" road, the Nickel Plate,
cutting rates desperately to that end, but to his discomfi-
ture it pressed on mile after mile, and he felt compelled,
early in 1883, since he could not break it, to buy it.
His second son carried on the negotiations with a good
deal of ability, and on the reorganization of the company was elected its president.

On May 3, 1883, Mr. Vanderbilt finally resigned the
presidencies of the various roads of which for six years
he had been the head. His health had been gradually
failing, and he felt that he owed all his care to its recu-
peration. The retirement had been anticipated for some
time, but it caused considerable surprise. In surrender-
ing his position, Mr. Vanderbilt said:

"GENTLEMEN: The companies of which I have had
the honor to be president for many years past are now
about to elect new officers for the ensuing year. The
meetings of all of them have been called at this office at
this time to thank you as the directors and officers, and
also the shareholders of the several companies, for the
confidence they have always reposed in me as their president. It is my belief that these corporations are all
in sound condition, and that all the prominent positions
in them are filled by gentlemen who understand their
duties, and who will discharge them to the satisfaction
of the stockholders. This fact has had great influence
with me in determining the course of action which I
have, after due deliberation, decided upon.

"In my judgment the time has arrived when I owe
it as a duty to myself, to the corporations, and to those
around me upon whom the chief management will de-
volve, to retire from the presidency. In declining the

honor of a re-election from you I do not mean to sever my relations or abate the interest I have heretofore taken in these corporations. It is my purpose and aim that these several corporations shall remain upon such a basis for their harmonious working with each other, and for the efficient management of each, as will secure for the system both permanency and prosperity. Under the reorganization each of them will elect a chairman of the Board, who, in connection with the Executive and Finance Committees, will have immediate and constant supervision of all the affairs of the companies and bring to the support of the officers the active assistance of the directors. The plan of organization now adopted and inaugurated will remove the business of the companies from the contingencies of accident to any individual, and insure a continuance of the policy which has heretofore met the approval of the stockholders."

The various Boards passed complimentary resolutions in response.

Mr. Vanderbilt, accompanied by his son George and his Uncle Jacob, immediately sailed for Europe, which he had visited many times since that first celebrated voyage on the North Star. James H. Rutter was elected president of the Central, and retained the position until his death, his successor being Chauncey M. Depew. The system laid out by Mr. Vanderbilt, which is based on the English system of railway management, has since been maintained.

A thousand sarcastic changes have been rung, and a thousand indignant editorials written, and hundreds of satirical cartoons printed, concerning the notorious saying attributed to him, " The public be d——d ! " His utterance of it was at first denied by those desiring to defend him, but Samuel Barton, his favorite nephew, was one of the party at the time, and he confirmed the report of the exclamation having been made. But the vicious story of the reporter was virtually false, notwith-standing, for he omitted all the context and the surround-ing circumstances which explained the malediction.

The thing under consideration was the fast Chicago mail-train, which Mr. Vanderbilt was about to take off.

"Why are you going to stop this fast mail-train?" asked the reporter, whom Mr. Vanderbilt had received on his special car with every evidence of cordiality.

"Because it doesn't pay," was the answer. "I can't run a train as far as this permanently at a loss."

"But the public find it very convenient and useful. You ought to accommodate them."

"The public?" rejoined Mr. Vanderbilt; "how do you know they find it useful? How do you know, or how can I know, that they want it? If they want it, why don't they patronize it and make it pay? That's the only test I have of whether a thing is wanted—does it pay? If it doesn't pay, I suppose it isn't wanted."

"Mr. Vanderbilt," persisted the reporter, determined to get a column interview somehow, "are you working for the public or for your stockholders?"

"The public be d——d!" broke out the irritated man—"I am working for my stockholders! If the pub-lic want the train, why don't they support it?"

That is the way it happened. Mr. Vanderbilt often spoke freely to reporters—sometimes too freely. He did not seem to realize the weight which people placed on anything that fell from his lips.

CORNELIUS VANDERBILT'S RESIDENCE.

Great were his indignation and disgust when he found that his casual words in defence of the stockholders whose agent he was had been tortured into a brutal speech—a malevolent imprecation aimed at the whole American people, to whom he owed his fortune. Nothing, he alleged, was further from his thoughts.

Steadily, during these years, Mr. Vanderbilt's two eldest sons, Cornelius and William Kissam, had grown from being assistants to being associates and practical allies. They had neither found nor sought to find places that were sinecures in the great establishment. Cornelius had, on his grandfather's death, become First Vice-president and chief of the Finance Department, and his younger brother had become Second Vice-president and head of Transportation. The duties of these positions were exacting, but the young men who occupied them had been trained to work, and they had been taught by both father and grandfather that constant work was their only salvation.

After his resignation of the presidency, William H. Vanderbilt had, on the advice of his physicians, withdrawn almost entirely from office-work, and even from active superintendence. He had resigned his directorship and sold his stock in the Western Union Telegraph Company, and in the Union Pacific. His latest operations were purchases and dealings in Chicago and Northwestern, Omaha, and Philadelphia and Reading, and a few other minor transactions. During a year or two, a project which had gradually assumed tremendous physical proportions, known as the West Shore Railroad, had been a very pronounced thorn in Mr. Vanderbilt's flesh, by reason of its continuous opposition to the great

10*

system of which his father was the founder. It was pushed to completion by its reckless and desperate projectors, and soon went into the inevitable bankruptcy. Mr. Vanderbilt did not hesitate vehemently and frankly to denounce the promoters as a gang of thieves and blackmailers, who had stolen the money of duped stockholders in order to obtain the chance of stealing his; but the rivalry was too immediate and disastrous, and something must be done. Mr. Depew undertook negotiation at the solicitation of Mr. Vanderbilt, which resulted within the week in an absolute transfer of the West Shore to the New York Central on terms calculated to discourage those who build competing roads for the sole purpose of selling out.

At all times Mr. Vanderbilt entertained positive views as to discriminations and rate-cutting, and he did not hesitate to express them.

On February 28, 1878, the New York Chamber of Commerce held a meeting to hear the Railroad Transportation Committee report on "Freight Discriminations and the Effect upon the Commerce of the City." At this meeting the following letter from Mr. William H. Vanderbilt was read.

PRESIDENT'S OFFICE,
NEW YORK CENTRAL AND HUDSON RIVER R.R. Co.,
GRAND CENTRAL DEPOT,

NEW YORK, February 21, 1878.

DEAR SIR,—You ask me to give you my views upon the peculiar difficulties and disadvantages attending the receipt and shipment of merchandise at this port. Cities, like railways, must offer equal facilities with their competitors for business. Within the past ten years Philadelphia and Baltimore have made rapid progress in competing for foreign and home trade. They have granted to their railroads the most liberal privileges in the use of streets, docks, and water-fronts, and have furnished them every assistance for the erection of warehouses and elevators, and the establishment of steamer and other lines. As a natural sequence, the imports and exports at those cities are constantly increasing, and will continue to increase, at the expense of New York, until New York shall see its danger and fully offer the same facilities for commerce. The New York merchant is subjected to a terminal charge of from seventy cents to one dollar per ton, a burden from which his Philadelphia and Baltimore rivals are free. It is clearly to the interest of the Baltimore and Ohio, and the Pennsylvania Railway, carrying goods upon a pro rata of the Baltimore or Philadelphia mileage, to take them to those ports, rather than to New York, and deliver them to the consignee, without this terminal charge; and, from this cause, leaving out their other and local influences, it is to their interest to divert trade from this port; for here comes always this exceptional tax, in the shape of a terminal charge, affecting every ton of freight delivered in the city, and amounting to about ten dollars a car in excess of the same freight delivered in either Philadelphia or Baltimore.

The land under water around this city has been granted to it by the State for the purpose of improving, increasing, and extending the commercial facilities of the metropolis. This property is a trust, to be used, not to secure a temporary income, but to be so administered as to enlarge and cheapen the business of this port. But the city, relying upon its natural and other advantages, has always appropriated, improved, and rented this gift, as if it was held only for the immediate revenue which could be collected, without regard to the effect of such a policy upon our future prosperity. Public sentiment has heretofore sustained this view, but the time has come when both the city government and the merchants must see that any revenue derived from this source is insignificant compared with the damage inflicted. While steamships at other and rival ports land at comparatively free wharfs, the rental of a dock owned by our city is about equal to seven per cent. per annum upon the cost of a first-class ocean steamer, and at the same time our railways are prohibited from reaching these docks, though the distance is only a few feet, the expense trifling, and the connection would to that extent put us on an equality with rival cities. When the railroad desires to use city property for the building of depots, and the increase of facilities, it pays at the same rate as to a private individual. When it wishes to erect piers over the land under water, and applies for a permit, the city expects a large yearly rental for this ground, covered by fifteen or thirty feet of water, and that the pier built by the company at great expense shall revert to the city, after a few years, as its absolute property.

Every burden of this description is paid directly by the railroad, but necessarily reimposed upon its traffic. The property of the city, otherwise useless, is improved at the cost of the company, and the improvement increases our terminal facilities, adds to our commercial advantages, and cheapens the expense of doing business at this port; but the terms imposed neutralize most of the benefit. In all these matters the true interests of the city, the railroads, and the merchants are identical. We have the same competitions, and we must live on profits so small that volume of business becomes a necessity. It is short-sighted policy which prompts an increased terminal expense at New York, making it to the interest of any road to carry its traffic elsewhere. The natural advantages of this city, and its large control of the channels of trade, ought to be so supplemented by its liberality and wisdom as to induce all lines to seek New York.

I appeal to the merchants to arouse the municipal authorities on this question, and to encourage and sustain every effort looking to relief and improvement. Trade once lost is hard to gain. The New York Central and Hudson River Railroad is ready at all times to bear the burdens and make the expenditures necessary to compete with roads in other seaboard cities. With thorough harmony of action, as there is of interest between the municipal government, the merchants, and the railroads, the financial and commercial supremacy of New York can be maintained.

Very truly yours,

W. H. VANDERBILT.

CHARLES S. SMITH, ESQ.,
Chairman of Committee of Chamber of Commerce.

In October, 1884, at the commencement of the railroad war, cutting rates to the West, Mr. William H. Vanderbilt said :

" I can tell you one thing : our old road will not be behind any of its rivals, whether they are young or old. The rates to the West may be any figure that the other lines may choose to make them . . . The fact is that there has got to be a further liquidation. Some companies among the trunk lines have confessed that they were not making much money, but others have not . . . Everybody has lost money in the last year or two, and it is fortunate that the losses have fallen on the richest men. I feel the depreciation, and perhaps in proportion to my wealth, but on some of the rich men it is telling pretty hard. It is ridiculous to suppose that politics will change the process of liquidation. The success of one candidate or the other will not add a cent to what I already have. But I decline to discuss politics ; I take an interest in it, but I have not given anything to either side.

" One of the troubles in this country just now is the relation of wages to the cost of production. A skilled workman in almost every branch of business gets every day money enough to buy a barrel of flour. I don't refer to ordinary laborers, but to men skilled at their trades.

The man who makes the article receives as much wages, in many instances, as the article is worth when it is finished. This is not exactly fair, in my opinion, and must be adjusted. Until wages have a truer relation to production there can be no real prosperity in the country."

The following letter, written by Mr. Vanderbilt just afterward, explains itself.

THE HONORABLE GROVER CLEVELAND :

MY DEAR SIR—I congratulate you and the people of the whole country upon your election to the Presidency of the United States. You owe your election, in my opinion, to the fact that the people believed you to be an honest man, and not to any particular efforts made by any faction of either the Democratic or Republican parties.

Independent men who care more for good government than for parties or individuals have made you their choice, because they were convinced that your administration would not be for the benefit of any political organization or favored persons, but for the interest of the whole people. This is just the result which is most desired. We have reached a time when party amounts to little ; the country is above all, and wants an honest government by honest men. The belief that we will find it in you has led to your election.

Yours very truly,

W. H. VANDERBILT.

NEW YORK, November 7, 1884.

Mr. Vanderbilt voted generally the Republican ticket, but in late years the Democratic. His sons are all Republicans, excepting William Kissam, who is an enthusiastic Democrat, approving, usually, of both the measures and methods of his party.

CHAPTER XXVI.

W. H. VANDERBILT'S DEATH.

Worry and Anxiety—His Declining Health—Morning of the Last Day—At Ward's Studio—Conference with Mr. Garrett—Paralysis and Quick Death—Effect on the Public Mind—Simple and Inexpensive Funeral—The Vault at New Dorp—Home Again.

MR. VANDERBILT was a much more comfortable and happy man upon his Staten Island farm than in his Fifth Avenue palace. Like many farmers, he knew that the story of Antæus, the giant son of Neptune, said to have been strongest when he touched the earth, was not a fable, but the poetical expression of a rugged fact.

After he left the farm and came to the city to live he complained of a feeling of suffocation, and every pleasant Sunday for years saw him behind a brisk team driving to the ferry to seek the free air of his former home. These visits became less and less frequent with the flight of years, until sometimes months would pass and find him chained to the city. It told upon his health—the confinement and care of his great and growing property.

William H. Vanderbilt never learned his father's knack of turning off business rapidly and easily. Whatever he had to do he generally did in the hardest way. He could not acquire the habit of shifting his burden.

Of course, this injured his general health. His ap-

petite failed him. He was anxious about himself, and
wanted the doctors to see him often. His anxiety was
increased by an attack of paralysis which the doctors
called "insignificant" while living in the house at the
corner of Fortieth Street, but the effects of it soon
passed away, and he pretty nearly recovered his confidence that he might possibly enjoy a long life. "If I
can only pass my sixty-fourth birthday!" he would exclaim; "that seems to be a dangerous period in our
family." So the result proved it to be.

His death on December 8th was sudden and dra-
matic. He had no note of warning. He died instantly, as he had often wished to die, not sympathizing
with the prayer of the litany. The day had been without excitement. He rose at the early hour of seven, as
was his custom, and breakfasted at eight and a half with
his family. He showed little appetite for food, but this
was not unusual, as he had been suffering from indigestion for years. After the morning meal the "boys"
dropped in to see him, as they were wont to do—Cornelius, William K., and Frederick W.—and consulted with
him about the management of the properties that the
family controlled, and in the direction of which they
were active. About half-past nine this conference was
held, and Mr. Rossiter, the treasurer of the Central
road, and the custodian of many of Mr. Vanderbilt's
business confidences, was also present. At eleven o'clock,
some matter being under consideration that required
the presence of Mr. Depew, he was sent for, but he returned word that he would be unable to answer the call
before one o'clock, and an appointment was made for
that hour.

Considerable business had been transacted by this time, and Mr. Vanderbilt, remembering that he had an appointment, left the house and walked briskly to the studio of J. Q. A. Ward. He gave the sculptor about an hour's sitting for the bronze bust of him which had been ordered by the trustees of the College of Physicians and Surgeons, that notable beneficiary of his bounty.

Returning to the house, he had luncheon at 12.30, sitting at table with his wife, his youngest son, George, and his daughter, Mrs. Twombly. It was afterward remarked that he was in a cheerful mood and chatted in a jocund manner with the family. At one o'clock Mr. Depew arrived, but finding that Mr. Robert Garrett, president of the Baltimore and Ohio Railroad Company, had just called to have a talk with Mr. Vanderbilt, he waived his own engagement till later in the day, and insisted on Mr. Garrett taking his place. The arrangement was accepted, and Mr. Garrett began to talk over the project of bringing the new trunk line into the city *via* Staten Island and Mr. Vanderbilt's old home.

The two men were seated in the study, a capacious room on the north side of the house. A brisk fire was burning on the hearth. The greater millionaire sat in his favorite easy-chair, one with a deep seat, low back, and soft arms ; at his left, his table scattered with papers ; behind him, his desk. The smaller millionaire sat on a sofa just opposite, under the front window, and here and thus for an hour they conferred. Mr. Garrett unfolded his plans for establishing terminal facilities ; Mr. Vanderbilt leaned eagerly forward and listened, and made suggestions.

No one who heard their quiet conversation could have

inferred that Mr. Vanderbilt was talking to the son of
his old antagonist in transportation, with whom he had
had more than one desperate rate-cutting battle. Mr.
Vanderbilt was speaking, when suddenly his visitor
perceived an indistinctness of utterance. Leaning forward to catch his meaning, he saw the muscles about
the mouth twitch slightly. Then they were violently
convulsed, and a spasm shot through the frame. In another instant the stricken man plunged forward, without a cry, headlong to the floor. Mr. Garrett caught
him before he struck, but before he could lay him on
the rug and put a pillow under his head he had ceased
to breathe, and in a moment the pulse was still. The
family were summoned; doctors were sent for; restora-
tives were tried; in vain—the man was dead.

When Dr. McLean, the family physician, arrived, he
found that apoplexy had done its work—a blood-vessel
burst in the head, a clot of blood upon the brain, and
that was the end. Mrs. Vanderbilt fainted when she
heard the news from the physician.

It was generally agreed that Mr. Vanderbilt had been
subjected to no peculiar annoyance or fatigue during the
day—no special nervous pressure. Mr. Ward said:
"Mr. Vanderbilt was somewhat out of breath when he
came in, though he had not been exerting himself more
than to get out of his carriage and walk into the house
here. At each of the former sittings he was in excellent
spirits, and while I worked on the clay model he talked
about horses and various artistic subjects, especially
paintings. He never seemed to tire of relating his
amusing and unusual experiences in buying the works of
art now in his residence. To-day, however, Mr. Van-

derbilt was rather silent, and after a few minutes seemed to grow drowsy. I asked him whether he was feeling well, and he said that his head felt a little queer, but that he supposed it was the result of sitting up rather late last night, and would therefore soon wear away. After about half an hour he grew very restless.

"He took a short nap in his chair, then roused himself and asked how I was getting along. To interest him, I brought out a picture of Maud S. and asked his opinion of it. He thought it not very good, and said he had a much better one. From this we began discussing horses and fast records, and the possibilities of the future. Mr. Vanderbilt was now much more wide awake, but as he was not feeling his best, I suggested that he cut the sitting short, and I could do very well with what I had. He lingered a few moments to discuss the clay, and I asked him if that was his first bust. He laughingly asked if I hadn't heard about the one at the Eden Musée, and went out."

The news of the death spread with marvelous rapidity. By dusk everybody in town knew it. By dark it had been telegraphed to the ends of the continent. The sons and daughters hurried home. Cards and messages of condolence poured into the saddened house by the hundred. Telegrams came from remote cities. Scores of friends stopped at the house to inquire and to leave messages. There was no attempt to intrude on the suddenly-afflicted household.

Curiosity and interest caused crowds to gather in front, and to prevent too great a throng an officer was detailed to patrol the walks. He had no trouble in preventing collections of people, but men and women paced up and down, watched the bright vestibule and darkened windows, talked in bated breath of the sad affair, and wondered what he had done with his fortune.

All night that ghostly policeman walked his short beat in the somber shadows. Scores of people came and whispered together under the gas-lamp, noiselessly made inquiries of the sentry, gazed up at the drawn curtains, watched the callers—some of them closely-veiled ladies—coming and going on foot and in carriages, and listened to the newsboy's dissonant cry, not five rods away, "Extry! Extry! Death of William H. Vanderbilt!"

Within three blocks a meeting of magnates was held for the purpose of preventing a fall in prices, and it was agreed by the syndicate to buy three hundred thousand shares, if necessary, to sustain the market. It was said that $12,000,000 was pledged for the use of the pool. The solitary patrol marched to and fro. The hoarse announcement of the newspaper came up the street, and now and then a messenger boy darted out of the darkness and back again, and vanished on his way.

The funeral was very simple—as simple as his father's —as simple as the last rites over the body of a man of such plain tastes should have been. No needed expense was spared, but nothing was wasted. Friends were requested not to send flowers. The body was not embalmed. The coffin was exceedingly plain, of cedar with elliptic ends, draped in black English broadcloth, and lined with white satin.

On the morning of the 11th the family assembled around the remains of the dead for a farewell and a brief prayer. Then the undertaker closed the casket, the pall-bearers removed it to the undecorated hearse, and the cortége moved through the crowd to St. Bartholomew's Church, where the most simple public ceremonies were held by Bishop Potter. Upon the casket was a bank of fresh violets, a bunch of palms, and a wreath of myrtle, and a cross of white roses was at the foot. The regular burial service of the church was read, and there was no eulogy of the deceased. The following gentlemen served as pall-bearers: Chauncey M. Depew, Samuel F. Burger, J. Pierpont Morgan, C. C. Clarke, Charles A. Rapallo, John R. Brady, William Turnbull, William L. Scott, William Bliss, D. O. Mills, George J. Magee, Stephen D. Caldwell.

From the crowded church down crowded streets again moved the procession to the foot of Forty-second Street, where the ferry-boat Southfield was in waiting—the same boat that had taken the remains of Commodore Vanderbilt to the same destination. Again the boat was crowded with mourners; again the pilot rang his bell, and they moved out into the stream, carrying the remains of the dead millionaire from the city where he had lived and labored and doubled the enormous fortune that had been left him, to the lovely island where he had spent so many years, and which now was to be his final resting-place on earth.

The body was placed in the public vault of the little Moravian cemetery at New Dorp, and a simple service was said by the local clergyman. Everything was quiet and unpretentious. A stranger passing by and looking over the low wall would never have imagined that the simple rites that were taking place were over the remains of the richest man in the world, nor have dreamed of the immense wealth represented by the sorrowing group.

When the family and friends returned to the city, a watch of armed men was set over the vault, and they paused in their solemn pacing to and fro in the cold night, turned a bull's-eye lantern on the faces of curious strollers, and answered their questions. For several months this armed guard will be on duty night and day protecting the body of the dead from the hyena rapacity of the living, until the completion of the mausoleum on the adjoining hill which Mr. Vanderbilt began some months since as the final home of the Commodore and his descendants.

CHAPTER XXVII.

THE WILL.

Two Hundred Million Dollars given Away—The great Burden Distributed—Widow, Children, and Relatives well provided For—The " Residue " of a Hundred Millions—Charities—The Testator's Purposes and Dreams.

How the great property had been divided by the will was the question that now excited unusual interest. The bequest of $200,000,000 was unprecedented in the history of the world, and for three days the public discussed all the possibilities with eagerness, and the newspapers of all the land published every fact and rumor that could tend to the solution of the mystery.

It was well known that the Commodore had been an advocate of primogeniture—the special advancement of the eldest son—not because he cherished the old feudal superstition that the eldest-born had superior rights, but because he believed that, if equally capable, such a single heir would be more likely to keep a vast inheritance intact, and thus the better to maintain the power of the family. It was obvious that the Commodore had carried this conviction into effect in devising the bulk of his estate to William H., giving to his other children only enough to insure their comfort; and it was further known that he had discriminated in his will in favor of his young namesake, the eldest son of his eldest son, and had indicated him as the future head of the house.

This son, Cornelius, was understood to have weathered the financial storm of 1883 more safely than his brothers, and to have retained and augmented his inheritance in a way that indicated shrewdness and thrift. This was quoted in support of the assumption that he would now inherit one-half, perhaps three-fourths, of the tremendous wealth which his father and grandfather had accumulated. Moreover, it was alleged, by those who thought themselves in a position to know, that at least one will had been signed and attested within five years which executed the Commodore's wish to have the estate entailed in a direct line. And it was not known that this will had been destroyed and superseded. When the legal will was brought from the Safe Deposit Vaults and read—the last of nine wills that had been made in six years—great was the public astonishment. It overthrew primogeniture, by dividing half of the property equally between the two eldest sons.

The family were not surprised. They knew that the testator had honestly experimented with primogeniture and had been himself a victim of it. His doctor alleged that he had died of overwork. Originally equipped with a superb constitution, fine physique, and extraordinary muscular power, his health and strength had declined from the day that he took charge of his father's business. His appetite had failed him. Dyspepsia had assailed him. His sleep was broken. Pleasure had lost its zest. In eight years he had lived twenty. Constant worry had laid the foundation of arterial changes that resulted in a rupture of a large vessel in his brain and sudden death.

He felt a premonition of his doom, and he said to his

family : "The care of $200,000,000 is too great a load for any brain or back to bear. It is enough to kill a man. I have no son whom I am willing to afflict with the terrible burden. There is no pleasure to be got out of it as an offset—no good of any kind. I have no real gratification or enjoyments of any sort more than my neighbor on the next block who is worth only half a million. So when I lay down this heavy responsibility, I want my sons to divide it, and share the worry which it will cost to keep it."

On the day succeeding his funeral, Saturday, the 12th, the will was carried to the Probate Court by Chauncey M. Depew and the four sons of deceased. It covered nineteen pages of foolscap, type-written, and contained about six thousand words. A petition for probate was signed by the four sons and verified by their oath, setting forth that the will was signed September 25, 1885, in presence of the required witnesses ; that it bore no codicil ; that the names of the heirs-at-law and next of kin were, in the order of age, Marie Louise Vanderbilt, the widow, living at No. 640 Fifth Avenue ; Cornelius Vanderbilt, a son, living at No. 1 West Fifty-seventh Street ; Margaret Louise Shepard, a daughter, living at No. 2 West Fifty-second Street ; William Kissam Vanderbilt, a son, living at No. 660 Fifth Avenue ; Emily Thorn Sloane, a daughter, living at No. 642 Fifth Avenue ; Florence Adele Twombly, a daughter, living at No. 684 Fifth Avenue ; Frederick W. Vanderbilt, a son, living at No. 459 Fifth Avenue ; Eliza O. Webb, a daughter, living at No. 680 Fifth Avenue ; and George W. Vanderbilt, a son, living at No. 640 Fifth Avenue.

Provision is first made for the widow. To her de-

11

cedent gives for use during life the house in which he
resided at the time of his death, the pictures and other
works of art, the horses, carriages, and stables, and he
leaves to her an annual allowance of $200,000, and the
privilege of disposing of $500,000 absolutely, by will, to
any one whom she may desire thus to benefit.

To each of his four daughters he leaves the houses in
which they are now living, near his own residence; but
he adds a condition which shows that he shares his
father's incredulity as to the business ability of women,
directing that the portion intended for his youngest
daughter shall not be delivered to her till she attain the
age of thirty, and if she die childless before that time
her portion shall revert to the estate.

The testator sets apart $40,000,000 of certain specified
securities, and directs that it be divided into eight equal
parts and distributed to his children, giving to each one
five million dollars absolutely.

He then sets apart another $40,000,000 of railroad
and other securities as a trust fund. This is to be divided into eight equal parts, held by trustees, and each
child is to receive the interest on $5,000,000 during life,
in addition to the $5,000,000 absolutely given. This
makes an annual income of about $500,000 for each.
The principal goes to the children of the eight, as each
of them may direct by will. If any son die without
leaving children, his portion of the trust fund is to be
divided among surviving brothers or their children.
The same direction applies to the daughters' shares.

After the death of the widow, the works of art (excepting the marble bust of Commodore Vanderbilt,
which is given to Cornelius), the family residence,

stables, etc., in which she has a life estate, are bequeathed to her youngest son, George Vanderbilt, or to
his children if he be dead. If he die without issue,
William H. Vanderbilt, the eldest son of Cornelius, will
receive this property, and $2,000,000 besides. The tes-
tator further gives $1,000,000 to this favorite grandson,
absolutely, on attaining the age of thirty years. If he
be not living at the time when such bequests would fall
to him, then they shall go instead to the next son of
Cornelius, who bears the same name as his father.
" My object being," the testator says, recurring to the
spirit of the Commodore, " that my present residence
and my collection of works of art be retained and maintained by a male descendant bearing the name of Vanderbilt."

Mr. Vanderbilt also gives $2,000,000 to his eldest son
Cornelius in addition to all other bequests; $30,000 to
William V. Kissam, a nephew; to his brother, Jacob H.
Vanderbilt, the dividends during life on 1,000 shares of
New York Central; an annuity of $2,000 to his Aunt
Phebe and each of twelve other relatives, and of $1,200
to others; and to his secretary, E. V. W. Rossiter, $10,-
000.

He gives $200,000 to the Vanderbilt University, of
Tennessee, which his father founded. To the follow-
ing, $100,000 each is bequeathed. To the Domestic and
Foreign Missionary Society of the Protestant Episcopal
Church; St. Luke's Hospital; the Young Men's Chris-
tian Association of New York; the Protestant Episco-
pal Mission Society of New York; the Metropolitan
Museum of Art, and the Moravian Church at New
Dorp. The following get $50,000 each : The General

Theological Seminary; the New York Bible and Common Prayer Book Society; the Home for Incurables; the Protestant Episcopal Church Missionary Society for Seamen in the City and Port of New York; the New York Christian Home for Intemperate Men, and the American Museum of Natural History.

Thus about half the property is disposed of. The vast remainder is divided and given in two equal shares to the two eldest sons, Cornelius Vanderbilt and William K. Vanderbilt, giving them about $50,000,000 apiece in addition to their present large fortunes. It is estimated that Cornelius Vanderbilt cannot have less than $80,-000,000—nearly as much as his father received from the Commodore.

The widow and the four sons are made executrix and executors, and each son is made one of the trustees for all the trust funds except those for his own benefit. If they qualify they shall serve without compensation.

The New York *Sun*, alluding to this will, said:

"Never was such a last testament known of mortal. Kings have died with full treasuries, Emperors have fled their realms with bursting coffers, great financiers have played with millions, bankers have reaped and sowed and reaped again, great houses with vast acres have grown and grown and still exist; but never before was such a spectacle presented of a plain, ordinary man dispensing, of his own free will, in bulk and magnitude that the mind wholly fails to apprehend, tangible millions upon millions of palpable money. It is simply grotesque.

"The numerical significance of a million is incomprehensible; it can only be measured relatively and by illustration, and when it comes to dealing with hundreds of millions, the understanding is overwhelmed and helpless. Mr. Vanderbilt gave them right and left, as if they were ripe apples."

For a week after the publication of the will, its provisions were a leading topic of popular discussion throughout the country. It was taken up and picked to pieces, approved and criticised, with as much spirit as would have been manifested if the parties to the dispute had all been legatees. One thought the property should have been equally divided among the children ; another that Cornelius should have had almost all of it, to carry out the Commodore's dream ; another that it should have been distributed among the whole population of the country, " and it would have given $4 to every man, woman, and child in the United States ; " another that it should have been directed more to objects of public benevolence. In this last, many concurred.

To those who knew him best, it seemed a wonder that the testator was not so wholly embittered as to refuse to make any provisions in his will for public charities. He had been harried and abused by the press, whenever he had tried to do any generous action. Every announcement that he had made a donation to science or medicine, to art or music, was met by the churlish comment, " It's nothing for him ! " and " Why didn't he give ten times as much ? " Instead of gratitude, he got sneers ; instead of decent treatment, insults. The demand of the loudest-talking, if not the most influential, of the press of the city, seemed to be that he could atone for the heinous crime of being rich, only by giving away all of his property at once to anybody who chose to ask for it. So it is a marvel that he did not become wholly hardened and cynical, and refuse to consider any schemes for the special benefit of the public.

On the contrary, his mind was busy with such purposes, trying constantly to give permanent form to the
liberal thought. " The great trouble of our time," he
was in the habit of saying, " is that there are too many
people idle. There are few skilled mechanics among
them; most of the tramps and loafers are those who
are unskilled, who have not been trained to do any
difficult thing, and do it well. What is especially
needed, is to have all boys and girls of all classes of
society taught some sort of difficult trade—given special
training, so that they can fall back on work whenever
necessary." To this end he considered the expediency
of establishing some great tool-house, where poor children might be taught trades; but he gave it up because
he came to think that such training should be conferred
by a modification of the public school system.

But inquiry shows that Mr. Vanderbilt wished and
meant to associate his name with some great gift to the
city of New York which should be at once unique and
pre-eminent; and this generous ambition at last, two or
three years before his death, took the form of a public
Museum, like the British Museum, to be, like that, of
incalculable value as an educator of youth. He decided
to build such a museum of magnificent dimensions on
the block opposite to his house on Fifth Avenue, and to
endow it with $5,000,000. This would be a far greater
endowment than that possessed by any other museum
in the world, and it might be expected in a few years to
excel all others in the extent and value of its collections.

The delay in realizing this superb vision, and finally
its failure through death, resulted from the impossibility
of obtaining the land. It belongs to the city, but is

rented to the Roman Catholics for an orphan asylum, for 999 years, at the rental of $1 a year. The asylum people would not relinquish the advantages of their fine bargain, and the city was helpless; so, after persisting for two years, Mr. Vanderbilt suspended the plan till he could find another acceptable site, and New York lost one of the most valuable monuments of industry and art that it was within the power of man to rear.

CHAPTER XXVIII.

ESTIMATE OF HIS CHARACTER.

Temperate Habits—Abstemious—Domestic—Tribute of the Directors
—Opinions of Jay Gould and Russell Sage—Letter to Matthew
Riley—A Much Abused Man—Fond of Opera—The Student
Waiters—The Undelivered Apple-Jack.

THE general habits and personal character of Mr.
Vanderbilt will not be doubtful to those who have
attentively read the preceding pages.

He used no tobacco in any form. He was abstemious
at table. Few men ate less, he taking no meat sometimes for days together. He never partook of rich foods
or hot breads. He was fond of shell-fish and of the
cereals in a coarse form, with milk. He retained simple
tastes, and seldom drank wine or liquor of any sort. He
was not in any sense a high liver.

He weighed about one hundred and eighty pounds,
and often complained that he did not get enough physical exercise. His chief recreation was the opera, of
which he was fond. His physician, Dr. McLane, said:
"I did not think he needed medicine when I first diag-
nosed his case in 1870, and I have never thought so since;
therefore, I prescribed as little as possible. My theory
was that he needed rest and relaxation. I believed he
had too much to think of, and that under the weight of
such important cares as his great interests involved his

health had been affected in such a way that only complete rest and freedom from worry would restore it. I saw him on Sunday, and congratulated him on his appearance. He seemed to be in excellent health, and in fine spirits over the successful transfer of the West Shore property and the solution of that puzzling and annoying problem. The suddenness of his death shocked me. Those who saw him shaking with laughter over the 'Queen of Sheba' at the Metropolitan Opera House last Wednesday night will agree with me that his appearance indicated quite a lease of life on earth."

In his home life Mr. Vanderbilt set an example worthy of emulation by many men of less affairs. He was exceedingly domestic, and devoted to his home and family. It was a very pressing matter of business indeed which got him out of his home at night. He used to stay at home and play whist every evening after dinner. He was passionately fond of a good rubber, and played with considerable skill.

Unlike the iron Commodore, he always felt that his children had rights. He was kindly, conciliatory, and indulgent in his relations with them, and in the midst of the greatest affairs always found time to look after their welfare and enjoyment, to bend to their humors and fancies, and to make their hours happy. Instead of fearing him, they loved him. As a host he was always cordial to friends and acquaintances, affable to strangers, and approachable and accessible to all. He did not bring his shop to the fireside.

He was a fair story-teller, and while not a picturesque or poetical talker, he was fluent and vigorous of speech, and capable of conveying a vivid impression of his ex-

11*

periences. He was fond of recalling the amusing incidents of his travels in Europe before any of the family
spoke French or German, and when favorably launched
upon the after-dinner tide he could agreeably entertain
a table-full.

Perhaps there is no better way of conveying an adequate idea of Mr. Vanderbilt's character as it was understood by those who worked with him and saw much of
him than by copying here the following expression of
their regard uttered by the directors of eleven railroad
companies assembled together on the day after his death.
Cynics can, if they choose, make some grains of allowance on the ground that this estimate was uttered by his
associates and beneficiaries—but, in the main, the words
are no doubt true:

"His sudden death in the very midst of the activities
whose influence reached over the entire continent has
startled the whole country, and in the hush of strife and
passions the press and public give tender sympathy to
the bereaved family and pay just and deserved tribute
to his memory. But to us, who were his associates and
friends, endeared to him by the strongest ties and years
of intimacy, the event is an appalling calamity, full of
sorrow and the profoundest sense of personal loss, while
officially we feel that his sagacity, his strong common
sense, his thorough knowledge of the business, his willingness to lend of his vast resources in times of peril, and
his counsel and assistance, were of invaluable and incalculable service in conducting and sustaining these great
enterprises.

"He came into the possession of the largest estate ever
devised to a single individual, and has administered the

great trust with modesty, without arrogance, and with generosity. He never used his riches as a means of oppression, or to destroy or injure the enterprises or business of others, but it constantly flowed into the enlargement of old, and the construction and development of new works, public in their character, which opened new avenues of local and national wealth, and gave opportunity and employment directly and indirectly to millions of people. In keeping together and strengthening, during a period of unparalleled commercial depression and disintegration, the combination of railways known as the Vanderbilt system, which he inherited from his father, greatly extended, and transmitted to trained and worthy successors, he performed a work of the highest beneficence to the investors and producers of the whole country.

"None of his accumulations were derived from his injustice to others, from conspiracies against associates, from crushing out the weak, but the humblest stockholder shared in equal proportion in whatever benefited the common property.

"But it is not alone for his sense, judgment, and justice in the vast business with which he was connected that he will be remembered. His many and unostentatious charities are known only to the beneficiaries, but the Vanderbilt University, the Egyptian Obelisk in the Central Park, and the Medical College in New York will remain among the enduring monuments of his public spirit. When he had gathered in his galleries the largest and best collection of modern art in the world it was his greatest gratification to invite the public to enjoy, in equal measure with himself, those priceless treasures.

"To the employés of his railroads he was exacting in discipline and the performance of duty. He was merciless to negligence or bad habits in a vocation where millions of lives were dependent upon alertness and fidelity. But within these limits he was a just and generous employer and superior officer. He knew how to reward faithfulness and remember good conduct, and always held the respect and allegiance of the vast bodies of men who called him chief. The successful administration of the railways under his management and the affairs of his life was largely due to his rare knowledge of men and his ability to recognize the qualities needed in the control of great trusts.

"With all the temptations which surround unlimited wealth, his home life was simple, and no happier domestic circle could anywhere be found. The loved companion with whom he began his active life in the first dawn of his manhood was his help, comfort, and happiness through all his career, and his children have one and all honored their father and their mother and taken the places which they worthily fill in their several spheres of activity and usefulness.

"In performing this last and saddest of duties, we who were his associates, advisers, and friends remember not the millionaire, but the man. His frankness, his unaffected simplicity, his deference to the opinions of others, his consideration for the feelings of all, his tenderness in suffering and affliction, and, his whole-hearted manliness, were to us precious privileges in his life, and are loving recollections in his death."

Arrangements had been made by heavy holders of stocks to buy freely if the market showed a decline on

Wednesday. Early in the morning there was an excited crowd in the vicinity of Wall and New Streets, and when the corridors and galleries were opened at 9.30 there was a wild scramble of those eager to obtain entrance. The scene has not been paralleled since the panic of '73, and in fifteen minutes every available foot of room was occupied. In the *mêlée* hats were knocked off, clothing torn, and a few persons slightly injured. On the floor the throng was thickest about the Vanderbilt properties, and when the first roll of the gong was heard, announcing the hour for business, the Lake Shore corner resembled a bear-pit, being filled with a jostling, yelling crowd of frantic men. The first recorded quotation was at 85, as against 88, the closing figure of Tuesday afternoon, for stock sold half an hour after Mr. Vanderbilt was dead; but the collusion of the large operators was instantly apparent, for purchases were rapid, and the stock rallied and rose to 86, then to 87. The behavior of New York Central and the other Vanderbilt stocks was about the same. At first, for an hour, they went off, but the strong hand of Gould, Sage, and Field was felt, and they all rapidly recovered their ground. And when the great gong rang again at 3 o'clock brokers looked at each other with a sigh of relief, and said: "It wasn't much of a shower after all."

Jay Gould said, shortly before the close of business: "This rapid recovery demonstrates to me very clearly the wonderful growth of this country. Its richest man is dead, but in spite of the calamity the stock market is likely to close higher than yesterday, when his death was not anticipated. A few years ago the result might have been very different."

Russell Sage, one of the shrewdest men in America, and himself the possessor of a fortune of not less than $50,000,000, said: " Mr. Vanderbilt was a very remarkable man, of far more original force and financial ability than any one imagined when he succeeded to his father's millions. I don't know that any one ever thought of comparing him to the Commodore, whose genius in finance was really beyond comparison. He was to finance what Shakespeare was to poetry and Michael Angelo to art. But William H. was certainly an able successor. He doubled the colossal fortune that was left him, and that proves an executive skill that only one man in a million possesses. I have had more or less to do with him, and the three qualities I observed as most striking in his character were his readiness, his reliability, and his courage. That is to say, he always met an emergency with a plan ; he always kept his word to the very letter, and he possessed such a fund of decision and persistence that, having undertaken to do a thing, and having made up his mind how it was to be done, he went right ahead and. put it through on the lines he had laid down. I think that his rare success in manipulating his great fortune was due to these qualities."

The relations of Matthew Riley, the broker, to the dead millionaire throw some interesting side-lights upon his character. Mr. Riley is a lover of horses, and he and Mr. Vanderbilt were for years warm friends. In 1876 Mr. Riley went to Philadelphia and became manager of the Exposition Hotel. Of this he says:

" I was quite successful with the house, and everything going smoothly, when one day I got one of his regular monthly letters that always brought sunshine and encouragement to me. It stated that Dan Mace had that day driven his team, Rutledge and Dickens, a mile in 2.20. I sat right down and wrote him, offering congratulations on the team, asking him if he was coming to Philadelphia that summer, and urging him to be my guest if he did come; also telling him of a fast horse I had seen that would please him. The letter brought this reply from Mr. Vanderbilt, written from 452 Fifth Avenue, the house the Commodore had given him. It was not dated, but you will see from the contents that it was the summer of '76."

The letter referred to was as follows :

M. RILEY.

DEAR SIR : Your very kind note of yesterday is just received, and I assure you I am very much pleased to hear that you are so prosperous in your business. Let me give you a word of good advice. These are hard times, and but very few are prosperous. Don't let this opportunity slip. Give up your horse and all other unnecessary expenses, and put away for a rainy day every dollar that you can save from your business. This summer is your harvest. You know what it is to struggle against adversity. Now is the time to save something ahead. Don't neglect it, and you will always thank me for pressing it upon you. Your account of the horse—he must be a good one. If he was here I would try him a week or two, and if he suited me would buy him at a fair price. My team, Rutledge and Dickens, are fine, but I want a third horse to come in with them. Father's health is such that I can make no plans for this summer. I am afraid he will not get out again, but we must hope for the best. He is of so much vitality and game that he may outlive the disease. I am really glad you are doing well. Now, take my advice and lay up a good nest-egg. Do away with luxuries that are really of no use until you get in position where the enjoyment of them can be indulged in from your interest money rather than from the principal. Don't laugh at this. You know I would like to see you do well and prosper. Now while you are young and in health is the time to provide for old age. Yours very truly, W. H. VANDERBILT.

A postscript follows on the first page, showing how sincerely the writer had his friend's interest at heart:

Don't think I have preached to you a sermon. I have said so much because I want you to improve the present opportunity.

"Another thing Mr. Vanderbilt did for me," continued Mr. Riley, "that was almost as good as that. One day about two years ago I was driving Kitty S. and met Mr. Vanderbilt behind Little Fred. We had a friendly brush down the road, and I beat him. About ten days later we were jogging together after a spin. I had heard that he was angry because I had beaten him that day, and told him so. Said he: 'My dear Riley, if you pay attention to the words of every envious sucker you'll have a hard row to hoe in this world!' After a minute's silence he said: 'I don't know any better way to kill off these bilious fellows than to make you a present. What horse is there in my stable that you want?'

"I thought him joking, and said: 'Are you in earnest?'

"'Yes,' he answered, 'I am.'

"I said: 'Leander is the best horse you own.'

"'Well,' said he, 'Leander is your horse.'

"That was two years ago, and ever since I've used Leander. Mr. Vanderbilt was very fond of him, and I value the gift not so much for its worth as for the giver."

Mr. Vanderbilt was the most thoroughly and cordially abused man in this country—probably in any country. His great wealth and the investments he made brought him into contact with the public and subjected him to a good deal of honest criticism. He was also the object of malicious denunciation by many who, only understanding that he was immensely rich, and unable to understand how his riches could possibly benefit anybody but himself, looked upon him as a buccaneer or highwayman, who had aggrandized himself at their expense. These men hated him because they were covetous of his possessions. In every mail that came to his desk were denunciations of his opulence. His daily mail was a museum. He was promised fortunes by future millionaires on the condition that he would merely help them to start. These were the commonplace letters. Then came the grotesque ones. From the impecunious person who claimed relationship. From the ambitious dynamiter who was about to put in motion a mysterious machine for the annihilation of the whole Vanderbilt family. From the energetic Socialist who demanded money and threatened assassination in case of refusal to pay. Skulls and cross-bones, daggers and black coffins, were common features of decoration, and occasionally a suspicious-looking package was opened with care and found to be a badly-constructed "infernal machine." On three occasions Mr. Vanderbilt's mail assumed a really dangerous aspect.

In April, 1882, such a dastardly contrivance was sent to him, but it was intercepted before it reached him, through the premature explosion of a similar one addressed to another distinguished magnate, Cyrus W.

Field. The machine was a clumsy device, and it was contained in a box lined with a German Socialistic newspaper.

Thus, Mr. Vanderbilt was made at times to feel that the reputation of being the richest man on the globe could not be worn with impunity. But the menaces did not much alarm or agitate him, and he never went out of his way on account of them. "What's the use of dodging?" he would say to his secretary, laughing; "I am a good-sized target, and if the cranks are bound to kill me, they can do it. But they can't scare me to death, anyhow." He believed that he would die when his time came and not before, and, beyond taking ordinary care against treachery, he did not bother himself about those whom his prosperity made natural enemies.

Mr. Vanderbilt was a church-member, having connected himself with the Episcopal Church, which for many years he attended on Staten Island. But he was warmly interested in secular enterprises of a public nature. If not an enthusiastic lover of classical music, he enjoyed modern operas keenly, and felt all the responsibilities of his position as a patron of the lyric drama. He was always a liberal subscriber, and on the occasion of Henry E. Abbey's benefit, at the close of an opera season that is unique in the musical history of the world, he sent to that enterprising and spirited manager his check for $5,000.

He was fond of the drama in general, and kept himself surprisingly well posted on theatrical news, so that in conversation with one of the profession he well knew what he was talking about. Mr. Vanderbilt was the first supporter that Mr. Dion Boucicault found for his theatrical insurance scheme that he so vigorously agitated.

Mr. Jay Gould gave the following estimate of his dead compeer :—" I have for many years considered Mr. Vanderbilt as a man of unusual ability in the management of large financial interests. When his father died and he came into possession of his large fortune, Mr. Vanderbilt was not long in demonstrating his ability to manage the property which had been intrusted to his care. He made no move upon the checker-board of finance until he felt satisfied that the move was a safe one to make. He would not run a great risk unless he were absolutely compelled to by force of circumstances, which I assure you was not very often. His judgment upon values was always sound. Few men have made so few mistakes in the handling of moneyed interests as Mr. Vanderbilt. He was not a bold venturer or operator. He seemed to be satisfied with a small, or, at least, a fair, return from his investments, so long as they were sound."

Isaac P. Chambers, controller of the New York Central Railroad, said : " I acted as the private secretary of Mr. Vanderbilt in connection with the auditor's duties from 1865 to 1883. During all those eighteen years I was never further away than in the next room to his, and I never saw a man of more amiable disposition. He was not understood by the public. He thought of their interest in every respect, and in considering any new movement or change in policy, would say : ' We must look out for the public first, for you know that we are their servants.' He was a very generous man, and was constantly overrun with applications for assistance, and one would be surprised at the character of many of the applicants.   Doctors of divinity, lawyers, and even judges who had become entangled in speculations would ask him to help them out of their troubles.   I remember one letter he wrote in reply to a request for advice in December, 1878, in which he stated substantially this : That he never speculated in stocks and never recommended any one else to do so, for he had seen too many people ruined by ventures of that kind ; that stocks in Wall Street did not sell on the merits of the properties, but were subject to the whims and caprices of a few men ; that he wrote this much in the hope of influencing one man to be satisfied with an honest livelihood obtained in a legitimate business, for thousands of people had lost the savings of a lifetime in one day of speculation ; that the writer had asked for his advice and there it was."

Mr. Depew said, alluding to his dead friend : " A peculiarity of the man was his fearlessness.   He was constantly in receipt of letters informing him that at a certain hour and place he was to be shot, stabbed, or otherwise killed, and under what circumstances.   It would have been an easy matter to do this, for he always drove over the same roads, went the same way to the office, at the same hour, and back again at fixed hours and over fixed routes.   He used to hand me these letters. Many of them were from cranks, others from that class of adventurers who make a living by preying on the fears of their fellow-men ; some of them contained threats, others apparent disclosures.   Some I thought were real : but he would never allow me to investigate them further.   On the contrary, when informed that he would meet death at a particular hour and place, he never failed to go there on time. He said that he wanted to enjoy life, and that if he were to be watched and protected it would become a burden to him. If death had to come, it would come whatever he might do, and he would go right along. He was in this a philosopher, and so when he was abused in public or in the press. He held this idea: that in consequence of his wealth and the character of his investments, that gave him constant public prominence, he was necessarily subjected to constant criticism that to a certain degree was justified. He got used to abuse, and while he was not much affected by it, I know that he was mightily pleased when the newspapers said anything complimentary of him."

Mr. Vanderbilt spent some months of the summer of 1883 driving with his family among the White Mountains. At the Glen House students from Bates and Bowdoin Colleges were employed as waiters, and he at once began to inquire of them about their college life and experiences. He ascertained that the students were in most instances the sons of parents who were not burdened with an abundance of wealth, and were therefore depending in a large measure upon their own efforts in securing money with which to meet the expenses of their college course, and some helped to support their parents besides. Mr. Vanderbilt thought this very plucky and creditable, and on going away he left $3,000 with Charles Milliken, the landlord, for the promising and ambitious young students in black jackets and white aprons. Each of them returned to school $100 richer through his thoughtful generosity. This is only one instance of scores of similar ones.

Only a week before he died, when he visited the farm for the last time, to inform the resident farmer of the change in ownership, he said, sitting in his carriage: " Well, I am no longer master here. I have given it all to George. He will look after the place hereafter. I cannot be bothered with it any more. After all, I have enjoyed more peace of mind and quietness here than I ever have in the big city yonder." And then he rode back to New Dorp, and entered the old Moravian Cemetery, and drove through it, and up the hill, to the magnificent family mausoleum in course of construction. He was anxious to know if the workmen would be able to get it enclosed before winter came with its frosts and snows.

And thence he drove down to the ferry, where he met and saluted his old neighbor, Tyson Butler, who had " given him a lift" a quarter of a century before. In that early time before the war, when Vanderbilt was a farmer at New Dorp, he sent his crops to the city market on schooners, and brought back manure, which was hauled up the sandy beach by oxen.

Once Vanderbilt's cart got stuck in the sand and his oxen could not draw it out. His farming neighbor, Tyson Butler, going by with a yoke of oxen, sung out: " Vanderbilt, your oxen are no good. I'll bet you a half-gallon of applejack that mine can haul that load up the beach."

" Agreed ; I'll take that bet," was the reply.

The oxen were hitched on, and they hauled the load out without great difficulty.

" The applejack is yours ! " said Vanderbilt. But he forgot to deliver it.

So on this pleasant day in December, 1885, returning from the cemetery, this same Mr. Vanderbilt, become the richest man in the world, stood on the ferry-dock at Clifton chatting right and left with all he knew—and he seemed to know everybody. Mr. Butler drove his oxen by, hauling the great blocks of Quincy granite for the Vanderbilt mausoleum at New Dorp, and seeing his former neighbor, he shouted: "I haven't got that apple-jack yet, Vanderbilt; I'm getting thirsty."

"And you've remembered it twenty-five years!" exclaimed Mr. Vanderbilt. "Well, Butler, you shall have it."

The next week the rich man was dead and laid to temporary rest in the cemetery vault, and the old teamster went on hauling stones for his monument.

CHAPTER XXIX.

THE SONS AND THEIR HERITAGE.

The New Residences—Cornelius and William K. Vanderbilt—Their Public Trusts and Private Character—A Notable Present—Law-abiding and Self-restraining—Comparison of the Central with other Roads—Reduction of Passenger and Freight Charges.

AFTER the death of the Commodore, William H. Vanderbilt and his two eldest sons planned and built three mansions on Fifth Avenue north of the summit of Murray Hill. The first has been sufficiently described. The two others, rivaling it in elegance and luxuriousness, were located, one at the corner of Fifty-second Street and the other at the corner of Fifty-seventh Street. The pictures of these houses given elsewhere in this volume convey some idea of their spaciousness and sumptuousness.

Cornelius Vanderbilt went into the Treasurer's office when he was twenty-one years of age, and had been there thirteen years when his grandfather died and his functions were enlarged. He was one of the most methodical and industrious of men—the first to get to his desk and the last to leave it. He had a regular and thorough office training, and knew how to work to advantage.

William Kissam was more like his grandfather, finding routine labor irksome, quick and dashing in action, ready to take risks. He was irascible, like the Commodore, too, and intolerant of opposition or correction. But he made himself master of the whole transportation de-

W. K. VANDERBILT'S RESIDENCE.

partment; was quick at calculations; was familiar with freight rates and agreements and the margin of profit, and possessed good judgment on railroad combinations.

When the father retired from the presidency the two sons were made alternately chairmen of the Boards of Directors of the different roads: Cornelius held that position in the Hudson River and New York Central and Michigan Central, and William K. was chairman in the Lake Shore and President of the Nickel Plate.

With the next son, Frederick W., his father adopted a different course. He took naturally to study, and graduated at the Sheffield Scientific School at Yale, and thence was received into the office, doing general railroad work under his father's direction. He was first assigned to one department and then to another till he became somewhat acquainted with the whole complicated machine. He is a director in the different lines.

Besides being chairman of the Boards of Control of the New York Central and Michigan Central, and holding important positions in several other roads, Cornelius Vanderbilt has different trusts to distract his attention. He is an officer in the Young Men's Christian Association, a trustee in the Episcopal Seminary, an active member of St. Bartholomew's Church, the treasurer of the Episcopal Board of Foreign Missions, a trustee of St. Luke's Hospital, and a trustee of St. John's Guild, besides being intimately associated with numerous charitable institutions.

In the spring of 1881 Mr. Vanderbilt gave to the Metropolitan Museum six hundred and thirty-three drawings, where they are arranged, as far as possible, by schools, in chronological order. These are pen-and-ink, sepia, and red-chalk drawings, illustrating the spirit and subject of bygone ages foreign to our own. To the uneducated in art, they are little more than curiosities. Among these are works by Raphael, Del Sarto, Cellini, Rossetti, Baroccios, Salvator Rosa, Tintoretto, Rubens, and many others. Less than a hundred years ago this collection was begun by Count Maggiori, of Bologna, and it has since received many additions from other famous collections, including that of James Jackson Jarvis, our Consul at Florence, from whom Mr. Vanderbilt purchased it in 1880. The schools represented are the Roman, Florentine, Sienese, Parma, Mantuan, Perugian, Bolognese, Neapolitan, Venetian, Dutch, and Flemish, including drawings by Albrecht Dürer, and by Murillo and Velasquez of the Spanish school. These are of great value to American art students.

The Vanderbilts have not abused their trust. They have been obedient to law, and have acquiesced in the conventionalities adopted and observed by their neighbors. They have been friends of social order, and they have never yielded to the temptation which enormous wealth confers to make war upon the institutions about them; to indulge in those coarse vices which are too often assumed to be the privilege of the rich and powerful. They have not preyed upon the poor, for they were all nurtured in the school of self-restraint.

At the celebration by the Commodore of his golden wedding a hundred and forty of his descendants and near relatives assembled at the house, and on that significant and joyful occasion he presented to his wife a beautiful little golden steamboat, with musical works instead of an engine—emblematic at once of his business career and the harmony of his home. If he ever boasted of anything that was his, in the presence of strangers, it was of his mother, his wife, or his long lamented soldier-son. William H. Vanderbilt was equally fond of the home life, and his sons are more domestic than most of their neighbors.

The opulence they possess is not the result of the manipulation of stock. It was not acquired by robbing the frugal and industrious. It was earned by building roads where they were needed and as they were needed; by rolling twenty-six fragmentary lines into one and giving them a single competent and respectable head.

For taxes these roads pay $151 an hour the year round, aggregating about three times what it costs to maintain the canal as a free competitor. The company pays $1 to the State to every $2.70 paid to stockholders.

This system of roads within New York State supports 200,000 people directly and indirectly from the wages paid for service. At the same time it responds to the public need for transit and traffic at a cost less than any other railroad in the world. This is illustrated by the statement which follows:

PASSENGER RATES.

	Cents per mile.		Cents per mile.
New York Central Railroad.	2	Illinois railroads........	4
Connecticut railroads.....	4½	Minnesota "	5
Maine "	5	Colorado "	10
Pennsylvania "	3½	English "	4½
Michigan "	3½	Other European railroads	5½

FREIGHT RATES.

	Cents per ton each mile.		Cents per ton each mile.
Connecticut railroads	6½	Pennsylvania railroads....	5
Maine "	4½	Ohio "	6¾
Massachusetts "	5	New York Central Railroad........ $\frac{9}{10}$ of one cent

The following table shows the increase of tonnage and the reduction of freight charges during thirteen years:

Year.	Number of tons moved.	Cents per ton per mile.
1869	3,190,840	2⅓
1870	4,122,000	2
1871	4,532,056	2½
1872	4,393,905	2
1873	5,522,524	1¾
1874	6,114,678	1½
1875	6,001,984	1¼
1876	6,803,680	1
1877	6,357,356	1
1878	8,175,535	1
1879	9,441,213	0¾
1880	10,533,038	0¾
1881	11,591,376	0¾
1882	11,330,392	0¾
1883	10,892,440	0⅔
1884	10,212,418	0⅔
1885	10,802,957	0⅔

In 1869 the cost of carrying freight was more than two hundred per cent. greater than it now is. When the Erie Canal was the sole dependence for the transportation of grain the cost of carrying wheat from Buffalo to New York City was thirty cents a bushel: now it is two and a half cents a bushel!

Freight can now be brought from Buffalo cheaper than it cost to bring it from Poughkeepsie when Commodore Vanderbilt laid his hand on the track along the Hudson; a bushel of wheat can now be moved from the fields of far Dakota to the poor consumer on the seaboard for less than it cost to bring it from the Genesee Valley when William H. Vanderbilt came from his Staten Island farm and began to study the problem of transportation.

CHAPTER XXX.

SOME REFLECTIONS ABOUT IT.

Commercial Philanthropy—Promiscuous Charity—Do the Vanderbilts Possess their Money ?—The Envious and Malevolent—Can
a Man "Earn a Million Dollars ? "—Brain and Brawn—The
Genealogy of Civilization—Reproductive Wealth.

SOME of the thinkers, or, at any rate, the talkers, of
these days, assume in their discussion of economics that
such men as the Vanderbilts are to be ranked with the
despoilers instead of the benefactors of the race. The
number of such is few, but their opinions may be considered.

William H. Vanderbilt was not a professional philanthropist. Though a man of kindly feelings and benevolent practices, he was a rigid utilitarian, and, like his
father, served others mainly through what seemed mere
service of himself. Avarice moved him, but the net result was the general good. He was probably the best
example that this century has afforded of the great ben-
efits which conspicuous capitalists always confer upon
the community in the studied acquisition and the half-
involuntary distribution of their wealth.

It was once thought that a man's personal virtues
were to be gauged by the amount of his promiscuous
charities, and that it was clearly the duty of every man
who was rich to give to every man who was penniless ;
but we have learned in recent days that charity can

wisely be dispensed only through intelligent organization, and that street alms-giving is a mischievous evil,
multiplying supplicants instead of diminishing their
number. Even organic charity is merely a negative
good, stirring the sympathetic impulses of the race to
support those who through profligacy or misfortune continue to impoverish the world. He who builds a factory
confers ten times more good than he who builds an
almshouse ; and he who launches a steamship or equips
a railroad does far more for the comfort and happiness
of mankind than he who endows an asylum. The
dominant benefactors of the world are those unerring
pilots of finance—those untitled princes of industry—
who ceaselessly strive to aggrandize themselves and so
most richly benefit others ; who renew with vitality the
commercial arteries of the world's life, and who hoard
up great aggregations of capital and keep it busy in the
employment of multitudes of workers. These considerations are to be taken heed of when men are being classified in the broad valhalla of the dead.

Moreover, it is a serious mistake to suppose that a
man as rich as the Vanderbilts can ever get what is
called "the worth of his money." Mr. William H.
Vanderbilt was of an equable and buoyant temper, but
he sometimes spoke bitterly of this limitation. Refer-
ring to a neighbor, he would say : " He isn't worth a
hundredth part as much as I am, but he has more of the
real pleasures of life than I have. His house is as comfortable as mine, even if it didn't cost so much ; his
team is about as good as mine ; his opera-box is next to
mine ; his health is better than mine, and he will probably outlive me. And he can trust his friends."

It is one of the curious compensations of nature that a
man cannot employ for his own comfort and benefit
more than a small sum of money, and that all that he
acquires and invests above that sum must go to the
benefit and comfort of others. Mr. Vanderbilt was
probably worth five hundred tons of solid gold when he
died—more than would have accumulated if his male
ancestors in a direct line had had salaries of $30,000 a
year since the coming of Adam and had saved it all—so
much money that he could not have counted it in ten
years at the rate of a dollar a second if he had counted
night and day, Sundays and all. He never handled his
money. He never saw it. He was never in its presence. In fact, he never had it. It was in the hands of
strangers, and was used by them for their own benefit,
they paying him five or six million dollars a year for
the privilege. But even of this five or six millions he
never saw a tithe. Ninety-nine cents out of every dollar
he " owned " were in the hands and coffers of others,
employed mainly for their exclusive advantage.

In ministering to his own real and imaginary wants,
he could not use more than a small fraction of his income. He constantly overworked, and violated many of
the laws of health, in order to get and keep his fortune ;
and for wages, he received, as Stephen Girard grimly put
it, only his " board and clothes," unless we count among
his imponderable assets the reputation of being an avaricious and dangerous man. The laborer who wheels
gravel on a railroad and who can eat three solid meals
every day and sleep soundly every night gets higher
wages than a dyspeptic king.

To enjoy his wealth relatively, Mr. Vanderbilt ought

to have been able to eat and drink a thousand times as effectively, and sleep a thousand times as refreshingly, and appreciate the beauties of nature and the marvels of art a thousand times as much as a poor man.

But, as a matter of fact, this "magnate" dressed no better than his clerk, and ate less than his coachman. He drank chiefly milk. He could sleep in only one room, like others. He had little taste for books, and not time enough to read the newspapers. Envy and ignorance had raised up an army of enemies about him. The public press stormed at him like a harridan and covered the dead walls with infamous caricatures, representing him as a vampire, a dragon, a Gorgon, a Silenus, a Moloch, a malevolent Hurlothrumbo. He was a victim of insomnia and indigestion. The jockey, Anxiety, rode him with whip and spur. He was in constant peril of apoplexy. He could not take needful exercise by walking in the Park for fear of being accosted by tramps or insulted by socialistic philosophers. Every week his life was threatened by anonymous letters. He kept a magnificent servants' boarding-house on Fifth Avenue, where he made his home, and superbly equipped a stable, whose advantages inured chiefly to the benefit of his employés. He organized the finest picture-gallery in America for the enjoyment of lovers of art, but was compelled to limit his hospitality by the fact that some of the guests rifled the conservatory of its choicest flowers, scratched the Meissoniers with the ends of their parasols, invaded the private apartments of the mansion, and carried away portable things as souvenirs of the visit. An enormous fortune is a heavy burden to bear. To be very rich invites attacks, cares, responsibilities, intrusions and annoyances for which there is no adequate offset.

A man like Commodore Vanderbilt, indeed, has the large satisfaction of feeling that he has given the human race a magnificent endowment in adding to the wealth of the world. He was not a juggler, who managed by a cunning trick to transfer to himself the wealth of others; he created property that did not before have an existence. When he stepped from the deck upon land, the best railroads in the United States had been paralyzed and driven to bankruptcy by blunderers and plunderers. They were largely in the hands of men who cared nothing for them except as they could be made serviceable in the reckless games of Wall Street. Whether they could meet the demands of traffic was regarded by these desperate gamblers as of no consequence. Thieves had pillaged the Erie road till its stock was sold for three cents on a dollar. Michigan Southern was at 5, and Erie at 6.

The Commodore introduced a new policy. Instead of taking money out of the roads, he put millions into them. Instead of breaking them down he built them up. Instead of robbing them, he renovated them and raised them from the grave. He equipped them anew, trusting that the public would respond and give him his money back. He dragged together worthless fragments and made them one; he consolidated parallel roads that were apart and belonged together; he cut down every possible expense, and subjected them to the economic supervision of one despotic will. He fearlessly staked all upon the venture, and upon the belief that the war for the Union would end in the defeat of Secession.

12*

In both he was right. The South was beaten. The public responded. The stock mounted to par and beyond. His roads had all they could do, and he made millions a year from the investment of his marvelous brain. And he made these millions as legitimately as an artisan fashions a hat from wool, or a chair from wood. He received better pay than the artisan, not only because he risked his money where the mechanic risks nothing, but because he invested his consummate brain.

One of the commonest and most pernicious errors is the assumption that the human hand is the chief factor in the creation of wealth, and from this error springs much of the noisy remonstrance of our time. It is not the hand, but the brain, that is the real creator. It was Michael Angelo that built St. Peter's, not the forgotten workmen who, executing the will of the great master, borne to them through a dozen skilled architects and master-artisans, hewed the stone to lines that had been accurately drawn for them. The unit of service underlying all is the faithful workman ; but a brigade of workmen cannot do as much effective good as is done by one strong and intelligent capitalist, whose money employs and whose sagacity directs and renders fruitful the sterile hand. The chief productiveness of the world is due mainly to the skill that plans, the audacity that risks, and the prescience that sees through the heart of the future. So to those captains of industry who succeed in their financial ventures should go that premium called profit which society offers to superior foresight.

It used to be thought by all that as wealth accumulated men decayed ; that the love of money was the root of all evil; that avarice was a vice; that the world would be better off if the division of property could be more nearly equal; that great riches were a curse to society; that the millionaire capitalist was a sort of bandit-king who plundered the people by methods which were sometimes legal but always highly immoral, and under whose tyrannical exactions industry was paralyzed and laboring men were impoverished.

But it is now known that the desire to own property is the chief difference between the savage and the enlightened man; that aggregations of money in the hands of individuals are an inestimable blessing to Society, for without them there could be no public improvements or private enterprises, no railroads or steamships, or telegraphs; no cities, no leisure class, no schools, colleges, literature, art—in short, no civilization. The one man to whom the community owes most is the capitalist, not the man who gives, but the man who saves and invests, so that his property reproduces and multiplies itself instead of being consumed.

It is now known that civilization is the result of labor put in motion by wealth; that wealth springs from self-denial; that self-denial springs from avarice; and that avarice is the child of an aspiring discontent.

It used to be thought that consolidation was a menace to the people, and that great "Monopolies," as they were called, ought to be forbidden by law. It is now known that such consolidation is a public benefit; that the man who owns a thousand houses rents them cheaper than he who owns but one or two; that the greatest oil company in the world furnishes oil cheaper than it was ever furnished before, or could be by any other means of distribution; that the Western Union Telegraph Company sends dispatches far cheaper than they were sent by any of the score of companies from which it sprung, and cheaper than they are sent by any of the telegraphs in the world which are owned and operated by governments; that A. T. Stewart greatly reduced the profits and losses of merchandising and the cost of goods to the consumer, and that, therefore, while he crushed out small dealers, his career was a tremendous public benefit; that the New York Central Railroad, the net result of the combination of many roads, carries passengers at lower fares than any other road in the world —lower even than is required by law—and transports freight so cheaply that it has driven from successful competition a canal that was built by the State and is free to all! The government has reduced the price of postage only one-half in a quarter of a century, and delivers letters at a loss of millions of dollars a year; but frieght from Chicago to New York costs less than a quarter what it did then, and desperate competition keeps the rate at the lowest possible point.

It is to the obvious advantage of society that reproductive wealth shall be concentrated in few hands; for the larger its aggregations the smaller the toll which it will exact from society for the privilege of its use. And before Socialists can rationally demand an abolition of the competitive system and a reconstruction of the industrial methods of society, they must exhibit one railroad somewhere in the world which is owned by a state and managed as wisely and thriftily as are the roads which are allied to the name of Vanderbilt.

APPENDICES.

APPENDIX A.

THE little, snug, and quaint Vanderbilt homestead, where the father and mother of "Commodore" Vanderbilt raised their family and spent the greater portion of their lives, and whence they were finally buried, still stands in the village of Edgewater, a half mile or so from the village which has been known, during the past quarter of a century, as "Tompkinsville," "Vanderbilt's Landing," and "Quarantine." At the present time the whole shore of Staten Island, from New Brighton to Clifton, is one continuous street, well-built up, with only here and there a landmark, or old building, to remind one of the days long since gone by. The Vanderbilt cottage stands on the old "Shore Road," which once ran close to the water's edge, at the corner of Beach Street. There is now a considerable extent of made land between the shore road and the water, which puts the old homestead further inland. But the view of New York Bay, and the highlands of Long Island in the northeast, is still unobstructed. Originally the building was very small, one story high, with a peaked roof, the front part of which projects from the house far enough to form a roof for the piazza. Of the massive chimney at one end, the lower portion still forms a part of the end wall of the house. There was one room at the rear. The windows are high, with small panes of glass. In later years the house has been enlarged about one-half, by the addition of a parlor and sleeping-rooms on the western end, so that now it is a double cottage, containing nine or ten rooms, with a chimney at each end, and a front door in the middle, with two front windows on either side of it.

The house stands back some ten or fifteen rods from the street, on a gentle elevation, in the midst of a good sized plot of ground, inclosed with a rough picket fence. There is a well in the garden in front of the house, which, doubtless, in olden times, possessed a well-sweep. Around it are old cherry-trees, pear trees, and a cluster of Normandy poplars. The cottage is now painted white, with green outside blinds. Entering, we find the rooms low between joints, but very comfortable and cosey in appearance. It is over a hundred years old, yet the mud ceiling of the sitting-room at the left of the hall, is without a crack, and in as perfect a condition to-day, as when it was put on. This room contains a large open fireplace, with a mantel-piece in the Colonial, or George Washington style. Beyond the sitting-room there is a smaller apartment, now used as a dining-room, with a fireplace in one corner, a snug arrangement, suggestive of many a comfortable after-dinner chat. In the rear of this room is the little addition, or kitchen. In the front hall hangs a quaint lithograph, made in Bridgeport, Conn., in 1838, of one of the Commodore's steamboats, the Augusta, a long, narrow, side-wheel craft, with men in rows, stove-pipe hats, and "Newmarket" coats, standing on the uninclosed upper deck. A huge smoke-stack rises from the forward part of the boat, which, judging from its appearance, lacked all the comforts of modern steam vessels.

APPENDIX B.

THE name of Cornelius Vanderbilt first appears in the New York directory for 1815–16, as follows : "Cornelius Vanderbilt, mariner, 93 Broad St."

In 1816, he lived at 13 Stone Street; in 1817, he did business at 17 Stone Street ; in 1818, at 56 Beaver Street ; in 1819, at 18 Stone Street, and all this time he is rated a "mariner." In 1820 he is called a "steamboat master," and seems to have headquarters of some sort at 58 Stone Street. In 1822, his name disappears from the Directory during several years of his New Brunswick residence ; it re-appears in 1827, when he is again classified as a "mariner," and has an office at 457 Washington Street.

In 1833–34–35, the directory describes Cornelius Vanderbilt as a "mariner," living at 134 Madison Street. The next year he moved to 173 East Broadway.

This was a little over half a century ago. The post-office was then in the basement of the Exchange, fronting on Exchange Place and Hanover Street. There were two mails a day to Brooklyn, and mails were made up for as far west as the "frontier counties of Ohio," and the "Territory of Michigan." About one dozen letter-carriers were employed by the post-office. William H. Aspinwall then lived at 3 College Place, opposite City Hall Park ; John Jacob Astor did business at 8 Vesey Street, and lived in Hoboken ; William B. Astor lived at 376 Broadway ; Jacob Lorillard lived at 144 Hudson Street, and Peter Lorillard Jr., at 521 Broadway. Peter Cooper had a glue factory out in the country at the corner of Fourth Avenue and Twenty-eighth Street. Alexander T. Stewart kept a dry-goods store at 257 Broadway, and lived at 5 Warren Street. Prosper M. Wetmore lived at 79 Franklin Street. William E. Dodge lived on Fifth Street, near Second Avenue, and "Delmonico & Brother" were known as confectioners, and kept a "Restaurant Français" at 23 and 25 William Street. Fifth Avenue then extended as far north as Eighth Street, and cross streets, as high as Twenty-eighth Street, had been graded on the eastern side of the city.

APPENDIX C.

ON May 20, 1853, Commodore Vanderbilt, with his his family, started for a tour of the coast of Europe in the steam-yacht North Star. The sole object of the excursion was to gratify his family, and take a complete holiday for himself, he having known no rest from labor during more than forty years. Captain Asa Eldridge, who had been engaged in the India, Liverpool, and California trade, was made sailing-master. Mr. John Keefe, a well-known caterer in New York, was the purser. Several of the hands who shipped for the cruise were young men of the best families in the country. The party on board consisted of Mr. and Mrs. Cornelius Vanderbilt, Mrs. James Cross, Miss Kate Vanderbilt, Master George W. Vanderbilt, Mr. and Mrs. W. H. Vanderbilt, Mr. and Mrs. D. B. Allen, Mr. and Mrs. George Osgood, Mr. and Mrs. W. K. Thorn, Miss Louisa Thorn, Mr. and Mrs. Daniel Torrance, Mr. and Mrs. H. F. Clark, Mr. and Mrs. N. B. La Bau, Dr. and Mrs. Jared Linsly, Rev. Dr. and Mrs. J. O. Choules, of Newport, R. I., and Mrs. Asa Eldridge. As the North Star passed by Staten Island, opposite to the residence of Commodore Vanderbilt's mother, rockets were let off and complimentary guns fired. The night was a beautiful one, with the moon shining in a cloudless sky.

Soon after leaving Sandy Hook, Commodore Vanderbilt requested the clergyman on board to conduct family worship throughout the voyage. It was arranged that prayers should be attended every evening at nine o'clock, and that grace should be said at all meals on board ship. On Sundays a sermon was preached at eleven o'clock.

A little incident occurred, just before the ship left New York, which is worth noting. An hour before the time for sailing the firemen struck for higher wages. Mr. Vanderbilt refused to be coerced by the seeming necessity of the case : he would not listen for a moment to demands so urged, and in one hour selected such firemen as could be collected, and started ! The ship ran as high as three hundred and thirty-seven miles in one day, and the trip across was made in a little over ten days.

The first port made was Southampton, and after a look at Winchester and its cathedral, the party went to London. The first place visited was the Thames Tunnel. After that the sights of the town were seen, with excursions to Windsor Castle, Bristol, Clifton, Bath and other places. One of the first persons to call on Mr. Vanderbilt, in London, was George Peabody. He offered the use of his boxes that evening for the opera at Covent Garden, and the party went. The Queen and Prince Albert were also present, and "Les Huguenots" was sung by Grisi, Mario, Castellan, Formes and Belletti. Among the entertainments attended by the Vanderbilts was a dinner given by Mr. Peabody at Richmond, to meet Senator Douglas ; a levee by the American Minister, Mr. Ingersoll ; a soirée at the Mansion House, by the Lord Mayor, Mr. Carlyle being of the party. While in London a deputation from Southampton waited on Mr. Vanderbilt, proffering a public entertainment. The invitation was accepted. Meanwhile Mr. Vanderbilt and the gentlemen of the party went to Ascot to attend the races. While in London Mr. D. B. Allen made a hasty run to Leipsic, where his son, Mr. William V. Allen, was being educated. The two joined the party.

On June 13th a public banquet was given to Mr. Vanderbilt and his party by the Mayor and merchants of Southampton. Dinner was served at 3 P.M. in the Royal Victoria Assembly Rooms. The Mayor led Mrs. Vanderbilt to the dining-room, while the Commodore took out the Lady Mayoress. Two hundred people sat down to dinner, surrounded by music, flowers, flags, and much popular enthusiasm. Many speeches were made, and the Mayor, in proposing the toast to Mr. Vanderbilt said, among other things, that "he owed his position entirely to his own industry, perseverance, and extensive knowledge of mankind. He had ever been an enemy to all monopoly, and that was the foundation of his great success. And then, look at his family! He was not like many of our anchorites, contented with amassing a large sum of money, but he had brought up a large and interesting family." Commodore Vanderbilt, in replying said:

"Ladies and gentlemen, I am glad to see you. It affords me sincere pleasure to make your acquaintance. It shows that we are all one people, and I hope that, by the power of steam, our common countries will be so bound together that no earthly power can separate us. Since we landed in your beautiful town, we have made a hasty race over part of her Majesty's dominions; and, were I able to express the gratification we have experienced in passing through the country and your town, and the interest we feel in all your citizens that we have had the happiness to meet, I am fearful you would construe it into an attempt to make a speech. But I must refer that task to my friend Mr. Clark, who will address you much better than I can possibly do."

Mr. Clark and Mr. La Bau made speeches, and Mr. William H. Vanderbilt offered his thanks for the reception they had given to the toast, and kept the room in good humor by expressing a hope that, as the bump of cautiousness had always distinguished his father, they would allow the son to exhibit it also, by saying nothing more, especially as this was his maiden speech. He proposed the health of "The Ladies of England."

The next day after the banquet, Commodore Vanderbilt entertained some five hundred of the people of Southampton on his yacht, and gave them an excursion around the Isle of Wight. Refreshments were furnished to the whole party, and there was music and dancing on deck.

After leaving Southampton the Vanderbilt party visited Copenhagen and Peterhoff. At the later place the Grand Duke Constantine, second son of the Emperor, and High Admiral of the Russian navy, visited Mr. Vanderbilt in the royal yacht, and sent round one of the Emperor's carriages, with the royal livery, to take him and Mrs. Vanderbilt round the place. The city of St. Petersburg was visited, and the party received much attention.

After revisiting Copenhagen, a stay of nineteen days was made in Paris. While there several gentlemen and noblemen called on Mr. Vanderbilt, urging him to identify him-self with a new steamship line which the Government pro-posed to open with North, South, and Central America. Mr. Vanderbilt gave no encouragement to these overtures. His aims and objects were strictly private, and personal enjoyment and the happiness of his circle was all he at-tempted.

While the North Star was at Havre she was visited by thousands of persons, the Minister of War among others. The only accident which occurred during the trip was the loss of a young man in the Bay of Biscay, Robert Ogden Flint, one of the crew, who got knocked overboard by the mainsheet, as he stood at the extreme edge of the stern. He was unable to swim and went down at once. Other places visited by the Vanderbilt party were Gibraltar, Malaga, Leghorn, and Florence. At the latter city Mr. Vanderbilt sat to Mr. Powers for his bust, and, at the re-quest of her sons-in-law, Mrs. Vanderbilt had her portrait painted by Mr. Hart. The journey was continued, inclu-ding Pisa, Ischia, Naples, Malta, Pera, Constantinople, Tan-giers, Madeira, and then home, the number of miles ac-complished being 15,024. Fifty-eight days were occupied in sailing, and the coal consumed amounted to 2,200 tons. The party reached home on September 23, 1853.

The London *Daily News*, for June 4, 1853, had "A Word about Mr. Vanderbilt's Yacht," saying, among other things:

"An American merchant has just arrived in London on a pleasure trip. He has come by train from Southampton, and left his private yacht behind him in dock at that port. This yacht is a monster steamer. Her saloon is described as larger and more magnificent than that of any ocean steamer afloat, and is said to surpass in splendor the Queen's yacht. Listening to the details of the grandeur of this new floating palace, it seems natural to think upon the riches of her owner, and to associate him with the Cosmo de Medicis, the Andrea Fuggers, Jaques Coeurs, the Rich-ard Whittingtons, of the past, but this is wrong. Mr. Van-derbilt is a sign of the times. The mediæval merchants just named stood out in bold relief from the great society of their day. Mr. Vanderbilt is a legitimate product of his country—the Medicis, Fuggers, and others were exceptional cases in theirs. They were fortunate monopolists who, by means of capital and crushing privileges, sucked up the wealth of the community. They were not a healthy growth, but a kind of enormous wen on the body-politic. It took Florence nearly fifteen centuries to produce one Cosmo, and she never brought forth another. America was not known four centuries ago, yet she turns out her Vanderbilts, small and large, every year. America, which was only discovered by a countryman of Cosmo running against it by mistake on his way to the Indies, is the great arena in which the individual energies of man, uncramped by oppressive social institutions or absurd social traditions, have full play, and arrive at gigantic development. It is the tendency of American institutions to foster the general welfare, and to permit the unchecked powers of the highly-gifted to occupy a place in the general frame-work of society which they can obtain nowhere else.

"The great feature to be noticed in America is that all its citizens have full permission to run the race in which Mr. Vanderbilt has gained such immense prizes. In other countries, on the contrary, they are trammeled by a thousand restrictions. Look at Liverpool. Look at Manchester. Are not men of colossal fortunes to be found there? Is there anything in the air or the institutions of these towns to prevent men becoming possessors of incomes that are reckoned by tens of thousands? Possibly not : but there is something in the air or the institutions of the country of which these towns are a fraction that prevents these men living as becomes the creators of stupendous fortunes by their own industry. Your men of wealth here—your makers of millions for themselves, and tens of millions for the country—too often spend their time, their intellect, their labor, in order that they may be able to take rank among a class of men who occupy their present position in virtue of what was done for them by some broad-shouldered adventurer, who, fortunately for them, lived eight hundred years ago in Normandy. Those who ought to be the Vanderbilts of England would shrink from employing their wealth in the magnificent manner adopted by their American friend. They would dread the effect of making any unusual display, which would surely subject them to the reproach of being millionaires and parvenus. Here is the great difference between the two countries. In England a man is apt to be ashamed of having made his own fortune, unless he has done so in one of the few roads which the aristocracy condescend to travel by—the Bar, the Church, or the Army, and, if he is vulgar enough not to be ashamed of himself, his wife and children make amends, by sedulously avoiding everything which can put other people in mind of their origin. We wish to point out, as we have pointed out before, the essential weakness, the vicious condition of English society. In precisely the same manner (although in an infinitely greater degree) as the English army is damaged by the cold shade of aristocracy, so are English society and the English nation vitiated by the aristocratic prejudices that run through it. Between the cobbler who patches a shoe and the merchant who imports the leather to make it, there are some three or four grades, the members of each of which would scorn to associate with those of the grade below. It is time that the *millionaire* should cease to be ashamed of having made his own fortune. It is time that the middle classes should take the place which is their own in the world which they have made. The work has been taken out of the hands of the mighty in war, and given to those who are strong in council—to the lords of the elements, to the tamers of the great forces of nature. These must take their position. They must assert it, and scorn to put up with the faded distinctions that formed the glory of the ruling classes centuries back. The middle classes of England are the creators of its wealth and the source of its powers. Let them take example from America, and not shrink from acting as if they knew this."

APPENDIX D.

COMMODORE VANDERBILT'S WILL.

I, CORNELIUS VANDERBILT, of the City of New York, do make and publish my last will and testament as follow :

First.—I direct my executors, immediately after my decease, to pay to my beloved wife, Frank A. Vanderbilt, the sum of $500,000, in bonds of the United States of America, of the five per cent. loan, under the Act of Congress approved March 3, 1864, commonly known as ten-forty bonds, at par, in performance of the ante-nuptial contract made by and between me, and the said Frank A., bearing date the 20th day of August, 1869, whereby I agreed that, if she should survive me as my widow, my executor or administrator should immediately after my death pay to her $500,000 in the first mortgage bonds of the New York and Hudson River Railroad Company at par, and she agreed to waive and release all dower in my estate, except such sum of $500,000 of bonds. This direction or bequest is on condition that my said wife do accept the same as performance of my part of said ante-nuptial contract and in lieu of dower in any and all real estate which I may have been seized at any time during my marriage with her and of all claims upon or share in the personal estate of which I may die possessed, except as hereinafter expressly bequeathed to her. I also give, devise, and bequeath to my said wife, Frank A., the house and lot, No. 10 Washington Place, in the City of New York, with the appurtenances and also the stables therein contained for and during her natural life. I also give and bequeath to her, absolutely, all the furniture, pictures, and other household articles, which may be in or appurtenant to said house at the time of my decease, including books, musical instruments, plate and all other

chattels of that kind, but excepting the portraits of my
mother and my deceased wife, which two portraits I give
to my grandson, Cornelius Vanderbilt, Jr., son of my son,
William H., in fee. I also give and bequeath to my said
wife, two carriages, and one pair of carriage horses, and the
harness appurtenant thereto, to be selected by her from
those I may own at the time of my decease.

Second.—I give and bequeath unto my five daughters—
Phebe Jane, wife of James M. Cross; Emily, wife of William K. Thorn; Marie Louise, widow of Horace F. Clark,
deceased; Sophia, wife of Daniel Torrance; and Mary
Alicia, widow of N. Bergasse Le Bau, deceased; for their
own use, $1,250,000 of the registered bonds of the Lake
Shore and Michigan Southern Railroad Company, of $5,000
each, dated December 1, 1875, payable December 1, 1903,
being part of an issue of not exceeding $25,000,000 secured
by a mortgage on the railroad of said company to the Union
Trust Company of New York, dated the 1st of May, in the
year of 1872, making together $1,250,000 of bonds, which
I direct to be divided by my executors among my five
daughters before named, in equal shares, as soon as can
conveniently be done after my decease.

Third.—I give and bequeath unto the trustees hereinafter
appointed $1,400,000 of the ten-forty bonds of the United
States of America, of the five per cent. loan described in the
first clause of this will, in trust for the uses and purposes hereinafter set forth, viz.: In trust to set apart and hold $400,000
of said bonds, and to receive the interest thereon as it ac-
crues, and pay the same over to my daughter Mrs. Ethelinda
Allen, wife of Daniel B. Allen, for and during her natural
life, for her separate use, and upon her separate receipt, it
being my will that she shall not have power to anticipate
such income, not to transfer or dispose of her right to receive the same or any part thereof. And upon the decease
of my said daughter, Ethelinda I give and bequeath the
last-mentioned $400,000 of bonds unto her children who
may survive her, and the lawful issue of any of her children
who may have died before her, such issue to take the share
or shares which their parent or parents would have taken if
living, and in default of her leaving any lawful issue, her
surviving, I give and bequeath the last mentioned bonds,

after her decease, to my residuary legatee, hereinafter named.

[The will also directed that the sum of $300,000 be set apart, as in the manner of Mrs. Allen, for Mrs. Eliza Osgood, wife of George A. Osgood, the bonds upon her decease to go unto the "residuary legatee." The sum of $500,000 was also set apart for the use of Mrs. Catharine Lafitte, wife of Gustave Lafitte, the sum to be divided among her children after her decease. Should she leave no children, "said bonds shall go to her next of kin as if she had died intestate owning said bonds." The will also set apart $200,000, the interest thereof to be applied "to the maintenance and support of my son, Cornelius J. Vanderbilt, during his natural life." "And I authorize," said the will, "said trustees, in their discretion, instead of themselves making the application of said interest money to his support, to pay over from time to time, to my said son, for his support, such portions as they may deem advisable, or the whole of the interest of said bonds. But no part of such interest is to be paid to any assignee of my said son, or to any creditor who may seek by legal proceedings to obtain the same; and in case my said son should make any transfer or assignment of his beneficial interest in said bonds or the interest thereof or encumber the same, or attempt so to do, the said interest of said bonds shall thereupon cease to be applicable to his use, and shall thenceforth, during the residue of his natural life, belong to my residuary legatee. Upon the decease of my said son, Cornelius J., I give and bequeath the last mentioned $200,000 of bonds to my residuary legatee."

Fourth.—I give and bequeath unto my sister, Phebe Vanderbilt, $1,200 per annum during her natural life. To my niece, Phebe Ann Blake, $300 per annum during her natural life; and Rebecca Little and her daughter Cornelia, during their joint lives, and to the survival of them, during her natural life, the sum of $200 per annum. And I direct that the annuities in this fourth clause provided for, do commence from the time of my decease, and the first payment thereof be made in six months thereafter, and the said annuities be paid half-yearly thereafter.

Fifth.—I give and bequeath unto my brother, Jacob H.

Vanderbilt, $50,000 of the first mortgage bonds of the Staten Island Railway Company, dated the first day of April, 1873, and payable the 1st day of April, 1893, with interest at seven per cent. per annum, payable semi-annually; to my niece, Annie Root, daughter of my sister Ellen, $20,000 of like bonds of the Staten Island Railway Company; to my nephew, Cornelius V. De Forest, two registered bonds, of $5,000 each, of the Lake Shore and Michigan Southern Railway Company, of the issue described in the second clause of this will; to my niece, Phebe Ann Dustan, $5,000 of the consolidated seven per cent. mortgage bonds of the New York and Harlem Railway Company of the issue described in the second clause of this will; to Mrs. Sophia White, daughter of Andrew Hinslie, $5,000 of like bonds; to Charlotte Haskell, daughter of my sister Charlotte, $5,000 of such bonds; to each of the three daughters of my niece, Mrs. Phebe Ann Dustan, $5,000 of such bonds; to Charles Simonson, son of my nephew Charles M. Simonson, deceased, $10,000 of like bonds; to my family physician, Dr. Jared Linsly, $10,000 of like bonds; to Captain James Braisted, formally in my employ, $4,000 of such bonds; and to Lambert Wardell, an old and faithful clerk, $20,000 of such bonds, provided he is in my service at the time of my decease. I further give and bequeath unto my grandson, William K. Thorn, Jr., son of my daughter Emily, $25,000 of registered bonds of the Lake Shore and Michigan Southern Railway Company, of $5,000 each, of the issue hereinbefore mentioned; to Samuel Patten Hand, son of Obediah Hand, a brother of my mother, one of such registered bonds of said company of $5,000; to the Rev. Dr. Charles F. Deems, pastor of the Church of the Strangers, in the City of New York, $20,000 of such registered bonds of said company of $5,000 each; to Mrs. Maria Lecher, wife of General Gordon Granger, $10,000 of such registered bonds of said company of $5,000 each; and to the wife of my nephew, Samuel Barton, $25,000 of first mortgage bonds of the Staten Island Railway Company of the issue in this clause of my will before described."

[The sixth clause of the will provides for the purchase of bonds to make the above legacies good, in case he should not have those described on hand at the time of his death.]

13

[The seventh clause of the will relates to the payment of taxes in respect to the bequests.]

Eighth.—All the rest, residue, and remainder of the property and estate, real and personal, of every description, and wheresoever situated, of which I may be seized or possessed, and to which I may be entitled at the time of my decease, I give, devise, and bequeath unto my son, William H. Vanderbilt, his heirs, executors, administrators and assigns, to his and their own use forever.

Ninth.—I constitute and appoint my son, William H. Vanderbilt, and my grandson, Cornelius, son of the said William H., and also, when he shall become of age, my grandson William, and the son of the said William H., and also my before-named nephew, Samuel Barton, executors of this, my will, and trustees of the several trust estates hereinbefore created. And should any of the said trustees refuse or be unable to act as such, or resign their trusteeship, the said trusts, together with the estates and powers hereinbefore granted to the trustees, shall rest in those of the said trustees who shall act. And should any of the said trustees die, the said trust estates, trusts and powers shall rest in the survivors and the survivor of them. But it is my will that no commissions or compensation shall be charged to my estate, or to any of the said trust estates, or to any of the persons for whose benefit the said trusts are created, by said executors or trustees, for their services as such executors or trustees ; it being my intention that they shall serve as such executors and trustees without any compensation whatever, and they are severally appointed on that condition. And should either of them refuse to qualify and act, or to continue to serve as such executor and trustee without compensation, his appointment herein contained shall be void and of no effect. And should my nephew, Samuel Barton, refuse to act as such executor and trustee without compensation, the bequest to his wife hereinbefore contained shall become void, and the bonds bequeathed to her shall revert to my residuary estate.

Tenth—It is my will that in case any direction or provision of this my will should be held illegal or void, or fail to take effect for any reason, no other part of this my will shall be thereby invalidated, impaired or affected, but this my will shall be continued and take effect in the same manner as if the invalid direction or permission had not been contained therein. And should any of the legacies herein lapse, the same shall go to my residuary legatee before named.

Lastly.—I hereby revoke all wills and codicils by me at any time heretofore made.

In witness whereof I have set my hand and seal to this my last will, written on twenty-four pages of paper, at the city of New York, the 9th day of January, in the year 1875.

C. VANDERBILT.

Signed, sealed, published and declared by Cornelius Vanderbilt, the testator, as and for his last will and testament, in the presence of us, who, at his request, and in his presence, and in the presence of each other, have hereunto subscribed our names as witnesses.

FRANCIS P. FREEMAN,
140 West Forty-third St., New York.
SIDNEY A. COREY,
122 East Thirty-seventh St., New York.
JOSEPH HARKER,
Everett House, New York,
CHARLES A. RAPALLO,
17 West Thirty-first St., New York,

CODICIL.

I, Cornelius Vanderbilt, do make a codicil to my last will and testament, which bears date the 9th day of January, 1875, and is hereto annexed, as follows, viz. :

First.—I give and bequeath unto my grandson, Cornelius Vanderbilt, Jr., son of William H. Vanderbilt, all the shares of capital stock of the New York and Harlem Railroad Company which now stand in the name of my said grandson on the books of said company, and of which I hold the certificates in my possession, being 22,396 shares ; also all the shares of the capital stock of the New York Central and Hudson River Railroad company now standing in the name of my said grandson on the books of the last-named company, and of which I hold the certificates in any possession, being 31,650 shares."

[In the second clause of the codicil, he gave to his grandson, William K. Vanderbilt, 20,000 shares of New York Central and Hudson River Railroad Company.]

[In the third clause he gave to Frederick W. Vanderbilt the same number of shares in the same company. In the fourth clause he gave the same amount to George Vanderbilt. In the fifth clause he gave 2,000 shares of the capital stock of the New York Central and Hudson River Railroad Company to his wife, in addition to the bequests to her in his will. The codicil was dated June 30, 1875.]

APPENDIX E.

THE following letter was written, explanatory of the large charity :

NEW YORK, October 17, 1884.

DR. JOHN C. DALTON,
President of the College of Physicians
and Surgeons.

MY DEAR SIR : I have been for some time examining the question of the facilities for medical education which New York possesses. The doctors have claimed that with proper encouragement, this city might become one of the most important centres of medical instruction in the world.

The health, comfort, and lives of the whole community are so dependent upon skilled physicians, that no profession requires more care in the preparation of its practitioners. Medicine needs a permanent home where the largest opportunities can be afforded for both theory and practice. In making up my mind to give substantial aid to the effort to create in New York City one of the first medical schools in the world, I have been somewhat embarrassed as to the manner in which the object could be most quickly and effectively reached. It seems wiser and more practical to enlarge an existing institution, which already has great facilities, experience, and reputation, than to form a new one. I have, therefore, selected the College of Physicians and Surgeons, because it is the oldest medical school in the State, and of equal rank with any in the United States.

I have decided to give to the College $500,000, of which I have expended $200,000 in the purchase of twenty-nine lots, situated at Tenth Avenue and Fifty-ninth and Sixtieth Streets, the deed of which please find herewith ; and in selecting this location, I have consulted with your treasurer, Dr. McLean. The other $300,000 please find inclosed my check for. The latter sum is to form a building-fund for the erection thereon from time to time of suitable buildings for the college.

Very truly yours,
W. H. VANDERBILT.

Letters of thanks were sent to Mr. Vanderbilt, by Dr. Dalton, by the Faculty of the College, by the Trustees, the Alumni Association, and the students.

APPENDIX F.

THE New York papers on the morning of January 12, 1885, published the letters which passed between William H. Vanderbilt and General and Mrs. U. S. Grant. They are thoroughly characteristic of the writers, and call for no comment. The correspondence began with the following letter :

640 FIFTH AVENUE, January 10, 1885.

MRS. ULYSSES S. GRANT.

DEAR MADAM : So many misrepresentations have appeared in regard to the loan made by me to General Grant, and reflecting unjustly upon him and myself, that it seems proper to briefly recite the facts.

On Sunday, May 4th last, General Grant called at my residence and asked me to loan him $150,000 for one day. I gave him my check without question, not because the transaction was business-like, but simply because the request came from General Grant. The misfortune which overwhelmed him in the next twenty-four hours aroused the sympathy and regret of the whole country. You and he sent me, within a few days of the time, the deeds of your joint properties to cover this obligation, and urged my acceptance on the ground that this was the only debt of honor which the General had personally incurred, and these deeds I returned.

During my absence in Europe the General delivered to my attorney mortgages upon all his own real estate, household effects, and the swords, medals, and works of art which were the memorials of his victories, and the presents from governments all over the world. These securities were, in his judgment, worth the $150,000. At his solicitation the necessary steps were taken by judgment, etc., to reduce these properties to possession, and the articles mentioned have been this day bought in by me, and the amount bid applied to the reduction of the debt. Now that I am at liberty to treat these things as my own, the disposition of the whole matter most in accord with my feelings is this : I present to you, as your separate estate, the debt and judgment I hold against General Grant, also the mortgages upon his real estate, and all the household furniture and ornaments, coupled only with the condition that the swords, commissions, medals, gifts from the United States, States, cities, and foreign governments, and all articles of historical value and interest shall, at the General's death, or, if you desire it sooner, be presented to the Government at Washington, where they will remain as perpetual memorials of his fame and of the history of his time.

I inclose herewith assignments to you of the mortgages and judgments, a bill of sale of the personal property, and a deed of trust in which the articles of historical interest are enumerated. A copy of this trust-deed will, with your approval, be forwarded to the President of the United States for deposit in the proper department.

Trusting that this action will meet with your acceptance and approval, and with kind regards to your husband,

I am, yours respectfully,

W. H. VANDERBILT.

NEW YORK CITY, January 10, 1885.

DEAR SIR : Mrs. Grant wishes me to answer your letter of this evening to say that while she appreciates your great generosity in transferring to her the mortgage given to secure my debt of $150,000, she cannot accept it in whole. She accepts with pleasure the trust which applies to articles enumerated in your letter to go to the Government of the United States, at my death or sooner, at her option. In this matter you have anticipated the disposition which I had contemplated making of the articles. They will be delivered to the Government as soon as arrangements can be made for their reception.

Papers relating to all other property will be returned, with the request that you have it sold and the proceeds applied to the liquidation of the debt which I so justly owe you. You have stated in your letter, with the minutest accuracy, the history of the transaction which brought me in your debt. I have only to add that I regard your giving me your check for the amount without inquiry as an act of marked and unusual friendship. The loan was to me personally. I got the money, as I believed, to carry the Marine National Bank over a day, being assured that the bank was solvent, but owing to unusual calls needed assistance until it could call in its loans. I was assured by Ferdinand Ward that the firm of Grant & Ward had over $660,000 to their credit, at that time in the Marine Bank, besides $1,300,000 of unpledged securities in their own vaults.

I cannot conclude without assuring you that Mrs. Grant's inability to avail herself of your great kindness in no way lessens either her sense of obligation or my own.

Yours truly,

U. S. GRANT.

W. H. VANDERBILT, ESQ.

640 FIFTH AVENUE, January 11, 1885.

GENERAL U. S. GRANT.

MY DEAR SIR · On my return home last night I found your letter in answer to mine to Mrs. Grant. I appreciate fully the sentiments which actuate both Mrs. Grant and yourself in declining the part of my proposition relating to the real estate. I greatly regret that she feels it her duty to make this decision, as I earnestly hoped that the spirit in which the offer was made would overcome any scruples in accepting it. But I must insist that I shall not be defeated in a purpose to which I have given so much thought, and which I have so much at heart. I will, therefore, as fast as the money is received from the sales of the real estate, deposit it in the Union Trust Company. With the money thus realized I will at once create with that company a trust, with proper provisions for the income to be paid to Mrs. Grant during her life, and giving the power to her to make such disposition of the principal by will as she may elect.

Very truly yours,

W. H. VANDERBILT.

NEW YORK CITY, January 11, 1885.

DEAR SIR: Your letter of this date is received. Mrs. Grant and I regret that you cannot accept our proposition to retain the property which was mortgaged in good faith to secure a debt of honor. But your generous determination compels us to no longer resist.

Yours truly,

U. S. GRANT.

W. H. VANDERBILT.

NEW YORK, Sunday, January 11.

MR. W. H. VANDERBILT:

Upon reading your letter of this afternoon General Grant and myself felt that it would be ungracious to refuse your princely and generous offer. Hence his note to you. But upon reflection, I find that I cannot, I will not, accept your munificence in any form.

I beg that you will pardon this apparent vacillation, and consider this answer definite and final.

With great regard and a sense of obligation that will always remain.　　　　I am, yours very gratefully,

JULIA D. GRANT.

To MR. W. H. VANDERBILT.

This action was not taken without serious consideration by both parties, and Messrs. Chauncey M. Depew and Whitelaw Reid were consulted by the principals several times between the incurring of the obligation and the writing of these letters.

The final declination of Mrs. Grant's was afterward modified so far as to accept for the Government the trophies and souvenirs turned over to Mr. Vanderbilt, and these were sent to Washington ; the rest of the mortgaged property was sold and went toward the liquidation of the debt. The loan having been effected by an exchange of checks, and General Grant's check proving not to be good, it was felt by the family that to pay the debt was the only honorable thing to do.

13*

APPENDIX G.

Following is the full text of Mr. Vanderbilt's will, with the exception of the formal description of the real estate embraced in his late residence and the stables belonging thereto, and in the houses which the testator bequeaths to his four daughters:

I, William H. Vanderbilt, of the City of New York, do make and publish my last will and testament as follows, viz.:

First.—I devise unto my beloved wife, Maria Louisa, for and during her natural life, the dwelling-house in which I now reside and the lot on which it stands. . . . I also give and devise to my said wife, for and during her natural life, the three lots of land on the northeasterly corner of Madison Avenue and Fifty-second Street, in the city of New York, . . . together with the stables and improvements thereon erected. I also give and bequeath to her, for and during her natural life, all the paintings, pictures, statuary and works of art which I may own at the time of my decease, except the portrait and the marble bust of my father, which I have bequeathed to my son Cornelius. I also give and bequeath to her, for and during her natural life, all the furniture of every description—including plate, silver, library, ornaments, musical instruments and other articles of household use—which may at the time of my decease be in or appurtenant to my present residence, corner Fifth Avenue and Fifty-first Street, and also all the horses, carriages, vehicles, harness, stable furniture and implements which I may have on hand at the time of my decease and usually kept in my said stables, on Madison Avenue and

Fifty-second Street ; and I empower my wife during her life to exchange or dispose of any of my said household furniture and other chattels, except pictures, statuary, and works of art, and of any of said horses, carriages, and stable furniture to such extent as she shall deem necessary from time to time, to renew or replace the same.

I also give and bequeath to my said wife an annuity of $200,000 per annum during her natural life, to be computed from the date of my decease, and paid to her in equal quarter-yearly payments thereafter. And I direct that a sum sufficient to produce such annuity be set apart and at all times safely invested by my executors for that purpose during the life of my wife ; and I empower her to dispose by will of $500,000 of the principal of the sum so directed to be set apart in any manner she may desire and which shall be legal.

All taxes, assessments, and charges which may be imposed on the real estate devised to my wife for life shall be payable by her during the same period. And I declare that the foregoing devises and bequests to her are to be in lieu of dower.

Second.—I devise unto my daughter, Margaret Louisa, wife of Elliott F. Shepard, Esq., her heirs and assigns forever, the house in which she now resides and the lot on which it stands . . . at Fifty-second Street and Fifth Avenue, southwest corner, together with all my rights in Fifth Avenue and Fifty-second Street in front of said premises, excepting, however, out of the lot of land hereby devised and described an irregular strip of land, part of the rear thereof, which strip extends from the southerly line of Fifty-second Street to a line parallel therewith, and distant 44 feet southerly therefrom, and is 7 feet and 11 inches wide at Fifty-second Street, narrowing by jogs and curves to 4 feet 4⅗ inches in the rear, as now inclosed by the iron fence which separates said strip from the residue of the lot in this clause described.

Third.—I devise to my daughter Emily Thorn, wife of William Sloane, her heirs and assigns, the middle one of the three houses erected by me on the westerly side of Fifth Avenue, between Fifty-first and Fifty-second Streets, and the lot on which it stands, which lot is bounded and described

as follows : Easterly in front by Fifth Avenue, westerly in
the rear by a line parallel with Fifth Avenue and distant
149 feet and 11½ inches westerly from the westerly line
thereof, northerly by the lot of land herein before devised
to my daughter Margaret Louisa and by said strip expected
therefrom, and southerly by the lot of land hereinbefore
devised to my wife for life, containing 53 feet 5 inches in
width in front on Fifth Avenue and 39 feet and 7 inches in
width in the rear, and embracing all the land lying between
the lots described in the first and second clauses of this
will.   I also devise to my said daughter Emily, her heirs
and assigns, for the purpose of being kept open as a rear
entrance to the premises devised to her, the before described
irregular strip of land excepted from the rear part of the
lot in the second clause of this will described and extending to Fifty-second Street.

Fourth.—I devise unto my daughter Florence Adele, wife
of Hamilton McK. Twombly, her heirs and assigns forever,
the lot of land on the southwest corner of Fifth Avenue and
Fifty-fourth Street, in said city, and part of the lot in the
rear thereof fronting on Fifty-fourth Street, . . . together with the dwelling-house erected on said premises,
and all my right, title, and interest in and to the street and
avenue bounding said premises.

Fifth.—I devise unto my daughter Eliza O., wife of William S. Webb, her heirs and assigns forever, the lot of land
on the westerly side of Fifth Avenue, next adjoining on the
south the corner lot described in the next preceding fourth
clause of this will, and also the remaining part of said rear
lot fronting on Fifty-fourth Street, said premises beginning
at a point on the westerly side of Fifth Avenue, distant 48
feet 3½ inches southerly from the southerly line of Fifty-
fourth Street.   The strip of land on the westerly side of
said lot fronting on Fifty-fourth Street is given to my said
daughter Eliza O., for the purpose of affording her a rear
entrance from Fifty-fourth Street to her house, and the
easterly line of said entrance may be shaped in such manner as shall be or have been devised by the architect in
charge of the erection of said two houses, but keeping as
nearly as possible within the dimensions herein before prescribed.

Sixth.—Should the dwelling-houses now being erected for my daughters—Florence Adele and Eliza O.—upon the two lots of land devised to them not be finished at the time of my decease I direct that they be completed as soon as practicable thereafter at the expense of my estate.

Seventh.—I give and bequeath to the trustees hereinafter appointed $25,000,000 of bonds of the United States of America bearing interest at the rate of four per cent. per annum, the principal falling due in the year 1907; $5,000,000 of second mortgage bonds of the Lake Shore and Michigan Southern Railway Company, due in the year 1903, bearing interest at the rate of seven per cent. per annum; $800,000 of the first mortgage bonds of the last named company, due in the year 1900, bearing interest at the rate of seven per cent. per annum; $2,000,000 of the sinking fund bonds of the Chicago and Northwestern Railway Company, due in the year 1929, bearing interest at the rate of six per cent. per annum; $2,000,000 of the sinking fund bonds of the last named company, due in the year 1929, bearing interest at the rate of five per cent. per annum; $200,000 of the general consolidated sinking fund bonds of the last named company, due in the year 1915, bearing interest at the rate of seven per cent. per annum; $4,000,000 of the mortgage bonds of the New York Central Railroad Company, due in the year 1903, bearing interest at the rate of seven per cent. per annum, and $1,000,000 of the mortgage bonds of the New York and Harlem Railroad Company, due in the year 1900, bearing interest at the rate of seven per cent. per annum, making in the aggregate $40,000,000 (forty million dollars) of the above-named securities at par in trust, to divide the same into eight (8) equal parcels of five (5) million dollars each, and each of said parcels to contain an equal amount of each of the above specified kinds of bonds; to set apart and hold one of said parcels in trust for each of my four sons, Cornelius, William K., Frederick W. and George W. Vanderbilt, and one of said parcels in trust for each of my four daughters hereinbefore named, and to collect and receive the income of each of said eight trust-funds, and pay the same over as it accrues and is collected to the beneficiary for whom it is set apart during the natural life of such beneficiary, and I direct that no payment be made in anticipation of such income, and that no part of the principal of either of said trust funds be paid over or alienated or transferred during the lifetime of the child entitled to the income thereof, and upon the death of each of my said children I direct that the principal of the fund so set apart and held in trust for him or her be paid to his or her lawful issue in such shares or proportions as he or she may by last will have directed or appointed, and in default of such testamentary direction I direct that such fund be divided among his or her lawful issue in the proportions in which they would be by law entitled thereto had my child, so dying, died possessed thereof his or her absolute ownership.

In case either of my sons should leave no lawful issue him surviving I direct that the fund so held in trust for him be divided among his brothers him surviving, and the issue of any of his brothers who may have died before him, such issue to take the share which the brother so dying would have taken if living. And should either of my said daughters leave no lawful issue her surviving I direct that the fund so held in trust for her be divided among her sisters living at the time of her death, or should any of her sisters have died before her leaving issue, such issue shall take the share which such deceased sister would have taken if living.

Eighth.—I authorize the trustees of the said several trust-funds to receive and reinvest the proceeds of the bonds so given to them in trust as they mature, and also in their discretion to change from time to time the investments of said trust funds, but I direct that they do at all times keep the said principal of the said several trust-funds securely invested during the continuance of said trusts respectively in bonds of the United States of America or of the State or City of New York, or in mortgage bonds of the New York Central and Hudson River Railroad Company, the New York and Harlem Railroad Company, the Lake Shore and Michigan Southern Railway Company, or the Chicago and Northwestern Railway Company, or bonds guaranteed by it or some one or more of said specified securities. They may change such investments from time to time and may also invest on bond and mortgage on unencumbered real estate in the State of New York, and they may apply to the reinvestments of the principal of said trust-funds, or either of them, any of the securities of the classes above specified which I may have on hand at the time of my decease at their market value at the time of such application.

And I direct that all securities in which such trust-funds shall from time to time be invested be taken and held by said trustees in their names as trustees for the parties respectively for whose benefit the funds are separately set apart and held, so that each of said eight trust-funds shall be kept separate and distinct from the others, and the accounts thereof shall be separately kept.

Should I not have on hand at the date of my decease a sufficient amount of each of the descriptions of bonds hereinbefore specified to make up the amounts in the seventh clause bequeathed in trust, I direct that the deficiency be supplied with bonds of the New York and Harlem Railroad Company at par or any other bonds I may leave.

Ninth.—I give and bequeath unto my four sons and my four daughters hereinbefore named, to be equally divided between them, $10,000,000 of bonds of the United States of America bearing interest at the rate of four per cent. per annum, the principal falling due in 1907 ; $920,000 of the bonds of the New York Central Railroad Company, payable in the year 1903, and bearing interest at the rate of seven per cent. per annum ; $80,000 of the mortgage bonds of the New York and Harlem Railroad Company, payable in the year 1900, and bearing interest at the rate of seven per cent. per annum ; $1,000,000 of the bonds of the Detroit and Bay City Railroad Company, payable in the year 1931, and bearing interest at the rate of five per cent. per annum ; $3,000,000 of the second mortgage bonds of the Lake Shore and Michigan Southern Railroad Company, payable in the year 1903, and bearing interest at the rate of seven per cent. per annum ; $3,000,000 of the mortgage bonds of the Pine Creek Railroad Company, payable in the year 1932, and bearing interest at the rate of six per cent. per annum ; $2,000,000 of the mortgage bonds of the Pittsburg, McKeesport and Youghiogheny Railroad Company, payable in the year 1932, and bearing interest at the rate of seven per cent. per annum ; $2,000,000 of the guaranteed stock of the last named company, bearing interest at the rate of six per cent. per annum ; $2,000,000 of the debenture bonds of the Chicago and Northwestern Railway Company, payable in the year 1933, and bearing interest at the rate of five per cent. per annum ; $2,000,000 of the bonds of the Dakota Central Railroad Company, payable in the year 1907, bearing interest at the rate of six per cent. per annum, and guaranteed by the Chicago and Northwestern Railway Company ; 40,000 shares of the capital stock of the New York Central and Hudson River Railroad Company, 30,000 shares of the capital preferred stock of the Chicago and Northwestern Railway Company, 50,000 shares of the capital stock of the Lake Shore and Michigan Southern Railway Company, and 20,000 shares of the capital stock of the Michigan Central Railroad Company, making in the aggregate $40,000,000 of securities at par, to be divided among my before-named eight children in such manner that an equal amount, as nearly as may be, of each kind of security shall be allotted to each child.

Should I not have on hand at the time of my decease a sufficient amount of bonds and stocks of all the descriptions above named, after providing the trust-funds created in the seventh clause of this will, to make up the amounts in this ninth clause bequeathed, I direct that the deficiency be made up with cash to the amount of the bonds or stock which may be deficient at par.

Tenth.—I having transferred on the books of the Chicago and Northwestern Railway Company to each of my three daughters, Margaret Louisa, Emily Thorn and Florence Adele, 4,000 shares of the preferred stock of said company, but I holding the certificates of said shares with powers to transfer the same executed by my said daughters respectively, I hereby declare that the foregoing bequests to my said daughters are to be in place of said shares, and that said shares are to be part of my residuary estate.

Eleventh.—I direct that the bonds and the stocks in the ninth clause of this will bequeathed to my daughter Eliza O. be not delivered to her or placed under her control until she attains the age of thirty years, but that they be set apart and held for her by my executors in the meantime ; that the interest accruing thereon be collected by them and paid over to her as it is received until said bonds and stocks

APPENDIX G. 305

are delivered to her; but it is my will that if my said
daughter Eliza O. should die before attaining the age of
thirty years, leaving children her surviving, the said bonds
and stocks shall be divided among such children in such
proportion as she may by will direct, or if she should leave
no will, then in equal shares. Should she leave but one
child, that child is to take the whole. And in case she
should die before attaining the age of thirty years and
should leave no child her surviving, the property bequeathed to her in said ninth clause shall revert to my estate.

Twelfth.—I direct that the interest and dividends on the
several bonds and stocks bequeathed in the seventh and
ninth clauses of this will be apportioned up to the date of
my decease, and that so much thereof as shall have accrued
after that date shall belong to the legatees.

Thirteenth.—I bequeath unto my son, Cornelius Vanderbilt, the sum of $2,000,000 in addition to all other bequests
to him in this will contained.

Fourteenth.—Upon the decease of my wife I devise to my
son, George W. Vanderbilt, for and during his natural life,
the hereinbefore described lot of land and house on the
northwesterly corner of Fifth Avenue and Fifty-first Street,
where I now reside, and the lots and stables on Madison
Avenue and Fifty-second Street, being the same properties
in the first clause of this my will devised to my wife for
life. I also bequeath to my said son, George W., for and
during his natural life, all my pictures, statuary, and works
of art, except the portrait and marble bust of my father,
which I bequeath to my son Cornelius. I also bequeath to
my son George W. all the furniture, carriages, and other
chattels mentioned in the first clause of this my will for
and during his natural life; and after the decease of my wife
and of my son George W., if he shall leave any son or sons
him surviving, I give, devise, and bequeath absolutely and
in fee the said house and lot on Fifth Avenue and Fifty-first
Street, and said lots and stables on Madison Avenue and
Fifty-second Street, and all the pictures, statuary, furniture,
and all the property of every description which is in the
first clause of this my will devised and bequeathed to my
wife for life, unto such one of the sons of said George W.

as he shall by his last will direct and appoint to take the same. And in default of such testamentary direction, then the eldest son of said George W. who shall survive him.

And in case the said George W. shall leave no son him surviving, then on his decease and after the death of my wife, I give, devise, and bequeath all and singular the said real and personal property so given to George W. for life, unto my grandson William H. Vanderbilt, son of my son Cornelius, his heirs and assigns forever, and in the event last mentioned I also give and bequeath to my said grandson, William H., $2,000,000. But, without regard to the event of my son George W. dying as aforesaid, I bequeath to my said grandson, William H., $1,000,000, to be paid on his attaining the age of thirty years: in the meantime the income thereof shall be applied to his use by my executors during his minority, and thereafter shall be paid to him at such times and in such amounts as his father, if living, shall approve, until he becomes entitled to the principal. And in case the said William H. becomes entitled to the said legacy of $2,000,000, the $1,000,000 last given shall be deemed part thereof.

In case my son George W. shall die without leaving any son him surviving, if said William H. is not then living, the real and personal estate so given to said George W. for life shall after his death and that of my wife go, and I devise and bequeath the same, to my grandson Cornelius, in fee, and in that event I give to my last-named grandson $1,000,000, my object being that my present residence and my collection of works of art be retained and maintained by a male descendant bearing the name of Vanderbilt.

Fifteenth.—I direct that no deductions shall be made from any of the legacies to my children by reason of any sums which I have heretofore given, or advanced to, or for account of either of them.

Sixteenth.—I give and bequeath to William Vanderbilt Kissam, son of Peter R. Kissam, of the City of Brooklyn, and nephew of my wife, the sum of $30,000, to be paid to him when he attains the age of twenty-five years, provided his father and my son Cornelius, or the survivor of them, shall in their or his discretion approve in writing of such payment at that time; otherwise at such later period as they or the survivor of them shall approve, and I direct that interest on said legacy be paid to said William V. Kissam from the time of my decease until he shall receive the principal.

Seventeenth.—I give and bequeath unto my uncle, Jacob H. Vanderbilt, the dividends which shall accrue during his life on 1,000 shares of the capital stock of the New York Central and Hudson River Railroad Company, now standing in his name on the books of said company but owned by me, I holding the certificates with power. I also give to each of the children of my said uncle—viz., Mrs. Ellen Cæsar, Jacob H. Vanderbilt, Jr., and Mrs. James McNamee—the sum of $2,000 per annum to each during their respective natural lives.

Eighteenth.—I give and bequeath to Mrs. Annie Reid, wife of J. E. Reid ; to Mrs. Emma De Forest, wife of Frank A. Howland and daughter of the late Daniel C. Van Duzer, of Staten Island ; to my aunt, Miss Phœbe Vanderbilt ; to Sophia White, daughter of Andrew Ainslie ; to Jeremiah Simonson ; to Anna Root, wife of George M. Root ; to Miss Emma Simonson, daughter of Cornelius Simonson, deceased, and to Miss Charlotte Dustan, an annuity of $2,000 per annum to each. To Mrs. Edith Dustan, wife of Charles Dustan, who resides at Demopolis, in the State of Alabama, an annuity of $2,500 per annum ; to Mrs. Georgiana Hitchcock ; Mrs. Emily V. Snedeker, wife of Livingston Snedeker, and to Mrs. Catharine McGregor, of the City of New York, an annuity of $1,200 per annum to each ; all the said annuities to be computed from the day of my decease, and to be paid quarterly thereafter to the several annuitants during their respective natural lives.

Nineteenth.—I give and bequeath to Mr. E. V. W. Rossiter the sum of $10,000, and to Lambert Wardell the sum of $10,000.

Twentieth.—I give and bequeath to the Board of Trust of the Vanderbilt University, of Nashville, Tenn., incorporated under the laws of the State of Tennessee, $200,000 of the second mortgage bonds of the Lake Shore and Michigan Southern Railway Company, to be applied to the uses and purposes of said University.

Twenty-first.—I give and bequeath to the following named

societies and incorporated bodies, organized under the laws of the State of New York, the sums hereinafter specified, viz :

To the Domestic and Foreign Missionary Society of the Protestant Episcopal Church in the United States of America, $100,000 for domestic purposes.

To St. Luke's Hospital, incorporated in the year 1850, $100,000.

To the Young Men's Christian Association of the City of New York, $100,000.

To the General Theological Seminary of the Protestant Episcopal Church in the City of New York, $50,000.

To the New York Bible and Common Prayer-Book Society, whereof the Bishop is president, $50,000.

To the Home for Incurables, incorporated in 1845, $50,000.

To the Protestant Episcopal Church Missionary Society for Seamen in the City and Port of New York, $50,000.

To the New York Christian Home for Intemperate Men, $50,000.

To the New York Protestant Episcopal Mission Society of the City of New York, $100,000.

To the Metropolitan Museum of Art, incorporated April 13, 1870, $100,000.

To the American Museum of Natural History in the City of New York, $50,000.

To the Moravian Church in New Dorp Lane, Staten Island, organized under the name of the "United Brethren's Church," $100,000.

Twenty-second.—All the rest, residue and remainder of all the property and estate, real, personal, and mixed, of every description and wheresoever situated, of which I may be seized or possessed, or to which I may be entitled at the time of my decease, I give, devise, and bequeath unto my two sons, Cornelius Vanderbilt and William K. Vanderbilt, in equal shares, and to their heirs and assigns to their use forever.

Twenty-third.—I constitute and appoint my wife, Maria Louisa, and my sons, Cornelius, William K., Frederick W., and George W., and the survivors and survivor of them, executrix and executors of this my will, and trustees of the several trust-funds hereinbefore mentioned and created ; provided, however—and this appointment is subject to this exception—that neither of my said sons shall be trustee of the fund hereinbefore directed to be set apart and held in trust for him or for his benefit ; but as to such fund, in the case of each of my said sons, the trust shall rest in and be executed by the others of the trustees hereinbefore named and the survivors or survivor of them. And provided further, and the said appointments of executrix, executors and trustees are subject to the further condition that no commissions or compensation shall be charged by or allowed to either of them for their services as executrix, executor or trustee, and if either of them shall decline to serve on that condition his or her appointment as such executrix, executor or trustee shall cease and terminate.

And for the purpose of guarding against the contingency of any unsuitable person being appointed trustee of any or either of the trust-funds hereinbefore created, I direct as to each of said trust-funds that, in case of the death, disability, or resignation of any of the trustees hereinbefore appointed, the trust shall rest in and be executed by the others of those whom I have named, and upon the death of the last survivor of the acting trustees during the continuance of the trust the trust shall cease, and the entire trust-fund shall be paid to the beneficiary entitled to the income.

Twenty-fourth.—Should any or either of the provisions or directions of this will fail, or be held ineffectual or invalid for any reason, it is my will that no other portion or provision of this will be invalidated, impaired, or affected thereby, but that this will be construed as if such invalid provision or direction had not been herein contained.

Lastly.—I hereby revoke all former wills and codicils by me at any time made.

In witness whereof I have hereunto set my hand and seal at the City of New York, the twenty-fifth day of September, in the year one thousand eight hundred and eighty-four.

W. H. VANDERBILT.

Signed, sealed, published, and declared by William H. Vanderbilt, the testator, as and for his last will and testament, in the presence of us, who at his request and in his pres-

ence, and in the presence of each other, have hereunto subscribed our names as witnesses.

The words "or bonds guaranteed by it" interlined on
the twenty-first page.

CHARLES A. RAPALLO,
17 West Thirty-first Street, New York.
SAMUEL F. BARGER,
17 West Thirty-third Street, New York City.
C. C. CLARKE, Sing Sing, N. Y.
I. P. CHAMBERS,
26 East Forty-ninth Street, New York City.